Another Sort of Learning

JAMES V. SCHALL

Another Sort of Learning

*Selected Contrary Essays on the Completion of Our Knowing
or How Finally to Acquire an Education While Still in
College, or Anywhere Else: Containing Some Belated
Advice about How to Employ Your Leisure Time
When Ultimate Questions Remain Perplexing in
Spite of Your Highest Earned Academic Degree,
Together with Sundry Book Lists Nowhere
Else in captivity to Be Found*

IGNATIUS PRESS   SAN FRANCISCO

Cover by Victoria Hoke Lane

Contents

Part III
Have You Thought about It This Way?

Preface

Several years ago, almost thirty now, I ran across the following passage in a book called *Self-Made Mad*, which, of course, is nothing less than the famous *Mad Magazine*. Let me cite it here:

> Did you ever stop to wonder about how recent historical events will be reported in elementary school history books 100 years from now? We hate to think so, but in the year 2060, say, elementary school history books will probably be exactly the way they are now. Which means they will be simply written so that children who study them can find easy answers to everything, even things that college professors and historians won't fully understand. For instance, every historical figure will be either good or bad, with nobody a little good and a little bad, the way most people *really* are.[1]

I have always loved this particular citation because it warns us that real education and formal education may not be at all the same things. There are, moreover, many things college professors and historians indeed do not understand. Do not be surprised at this. I am a college professor, and I know.

Eric Voegelin, in his wonderful book of *Conversations*, was not at all hesitant to remind us that it is rather common to go through our higher education without ever having been confronted with the questions that are basic to mankind wherever and whenever man has appeared on this earth. And what are these questions? Voegelin remarked:

[1] *Self-Made Mad*, ed. William Gaines (New York: New American Library, 1960), p. 65.

7

> The quest for the ground . . . is a constant in all civilizations. . . .
> The quest for the ground has been formulated in two principal
> questions of metaphysics. The first question is, "Why is there
> something; why not nothing?" and the second is, "Why is that
> something as it is, and not different?"[2]

Such are questions behind which we cannot go, of course.
That is to say, they constitute the ultimate questions concerning *what is,* about which we must ask. Yet, we are not regularly allowed to ask ourselves such questions. And often, as
E. F. Schumacher, in a book I shall recommend again and
again, remarked, even when we are allowed to ask such
questions, we do not know how to pose them properly, freely.[3]
So there is room for some kind of guidebook, as it were, some
help to find our way out of a system that is designed, consciously
or unconsciously, to prevent us from confronting in our own
lives the ultimate questions of existence and essence, the two
questions that Voegelin posed as fundamental.

As the passage from *Self-Made Mad* implied, we are fallible
beings, a combination of a little bad and a little good. Our age,
in a strange way, is an age of perfectionism. We are no longer
aware of the classical and Christian tradition that would free us
from the utopian premises by the reminder of "the way most
people *really* are". The classics were often nothing more than
books on education. They sought to teach us how pass from
esse to *bene esse,* from "being" to "being well", to use Aristotle's
famous phrase for the task of politics. But politics, as Aristotle
knew, led us to contemplation, to the consideration of the
right order of things.

The premises of "modernity", a phrase I take from Leo

---

[2] Eric Voegelin, *Conversations with Eric Voegelin,* ed. R. Eric O'Connor
(Montreal: Thomas More Institute, 1980), p. 2.

[3] E. F. Schumacher, *A Guide for the Perplexed* (New York: Harper
Colophon, 1977).

Strauss and Eric Voegelin, however, do not allow us to think there is such a thing as a right order in anything, particularly in ourselves. Philosophic "pluralism" or skepticism typical of modernity constantly reminds us that nothing is true, that it is in fact dangerous even to propose that there might be truth, for this would imply that some kind of decisions about reality can be made. And for many, this would jeopardize the foundations of the modern republic, which is said to be based, at best, on the pursuit of truth, never on the possibility of its being found.[4]

The signs of human fallibility, it seems to me, are at least four. The first is the passing of time as fixed in our minds by recurring days that serve to define where we are in our past and our present, days like Thanksgiving and birthdays and New Year's. Second, there is a certain humor that forbids us from claiming personal perfection. Then come our travels, which reveal to us how different the ways of other men are, yet how we are all precisely men, human beings, in all time and in all places. Finally, we have our broodings, which cause us to realize somewhere within ourselves how different we ourselves might be, how different perhaps we really ought to be, how stubborn in fact we actually are.

And so this is what we actually are—brooding creatures who while away the hours and the days reflecting and laughing. This will be a book then about time and learning, about humor and wonder. And we shall soon discover, I think, that such things are not so separate, nor even are they always different things. We can brood or chuckle in our voyages as in our readings. And the great feasts that mark our passing—the New Year, Ash Wednesday, Christmas, our birthdays—these are at once delightful, prayerful, and poignant.

[4] See James V. Schall, "Truth and the Open Society", in *Order, Freedom, and the Open Society: Critical Essays on the Open Society,* ed. George Carey (Lanham, Md.: University Press of America, 1986), pp. 71–90.

We are thus fallible creatures, and we should recognize it. And yet, and this is what I want to pursue in these various wonderments and ponderings of mine, we do search, we do seek. I believe that we are in a world today where most of this searching must take place outside the normal educational process and outside the myriads of media images and opinions with which we are constantly confronted.

Thus, this will be a kind of reflective effort to tell us what ought to attract us. Plato was eternally right when he realized that we are attracted in fact by the Good, however it might appear. We are constantly being drawn from outside of ourselves by what we had not accounted for. We are not already complete beings, but beings seeking completion. And Christianity was right to suspect that not only are we attracted by the Good, which brings us outside of ourselves, but that God also comes in search of us.

In his marvelous book the *Intellectual Life,* the French Dominican, A. G. Sertillanges, wrote:

> "Why hast thou come?" St. Bernard asked himself about the cloister: *Ad quid venisti?* And you, thinker, why have you come to this life outside the ordinary life, to this life of consecration, concentration, and therefore of solitude? Was it not because of a choice? Did you not prefer truth to the daily lie of a scattered life, or even to the noble but secondary preoccupations of action?[5]

The "scattered life"—this is either a description of a life that is founded on the premise of no theoretic order in the soul or the description of a life based on no disciplined virtue that would enable us to follow the important things, even if we should want to do so.

[5] A. G. Sertillanges, *The Intellectual Life,* trans. Mary Ryan (Westminster, Md.: Christian Classics, 1980), p. 49.

And so I have given this book a rather long and bemused secondary title: to wit, "Selected Contrary Essays on the Completion of Our Knowing, or How to Acquire an Education While Still in College: Containing Some Belated Advice about How to Employ Your Leisure Time When Ultimate Questions Remain Perplexing in Spite of Your Highest Earned Degree, Together with Sundry Book Lists Nowhere Else in Captivity to Be Found." These essays will be precisely "contrary" because I believe it is possible to be open to and confronted by the highest things. And I believe that this is what education, ultimately, is about. In this, I am a follower of Plato and Aristotle, of the two Testaments, of the Fathers and Doctors of the Church, of the tradition that singles out this civilization as one in which the highest things ought to be confronted by us.

I have suggested, then, that the education of many students and many who were once students—in the end, there is no distinction—is devoid of a proper consideration of the ultimate things. Moreover, I think that honest men and women know this someplace in their hearts. And no, I do not believe everyone is always honest, not necessarily excluding myself. I am essentially an Augustinian. And I am an Augustinian because, on the whole, the evidence favors Augustine in this matter of the diverse directions our hearts and minds take us when left to themselves.

But there comes a time when we know that something is missing. And when this time comes, we need to know where to turn. Often, I will suggest, we should turn to Augustine himself. Without too much exaggeration it might be said that the first step in the intellectual life after we are in our thirties is surely to read or reread Augustine's *Confessions*. We will find there that, so often, our hearts are led astray because our minds were first deflected from the good and we chose to let them be so deflected. When we know this, we can again take another look at *what is* and realize that we did not make it, but it made us.

Scattered throughout this text are various book lists. (The publishing information for these books appears in the bibliography at the end of this book.) Generally these lists are short, but they are aimed at our escape from the prevailing fads and moods, particularly intellectual ones, that we have learned in our lives and in our formal instruction. I have been brash enough to suggest that we may have a problem in acquiring an education even while we are in the university or college. Indeed, I would hold this is a very serious problem. As a result, I also must presume that many who have completed their education—with their highest earned degree—will begin to suspect that they are still not completely educated. I do not mean not "educated" in their so-called "major", which they may have mastered quite well, but in the highest things, about which they never seriously reflected.

Needless to say, I do not intend to suggest specifically that we read Shakespeare, or even Aristotle, or Faulkner, because I will presume that most people somehow already suspect that they should read these classic authors, even if they have not. The problem with most people is that they need a guide just to begin, when they once realize that they should in fact begin. And if they did not have such a guide in college or in school or in life itself someplace, it is normally doubly difficult to know where to commence. What I am mostly concerned with here are books that I think take us to the heart of *what is.* I intend these reflections to challenge what is most fundamental about us.

I am interested not only in books, of course. I do say something about sports, and probably I should say more about music and art. Yet these latter are often seen most clearly only when we already have some grasp of the higher things in our lives. But this book is directed *both* to those who have somehow neglected serious thought either in school or in life *and* to those who, even though they may have read much, even of the finest works, have not seen how everything fits together. This consideration leads us to questions of what it is about our public life that might cause us problems here, what it is in our religious or personal lives, even, that might prevent us from wondering more directly about the highest things.

Consequently, this book can be looked on as a kind of odd guidebook through unknown intellectual territory. I talk about being a student, about reading, about the fact that each of us is called to understand, as a friend of mine recently told me, "the truth about our lives". And this is a serious enterprise, not without humor, of course. Since this seriousness itself directly leads us to questions of faith, doubt, truth, evil, and good, I have not hesitated to talk about such realities, not hesitated to recommend something further to read, something that the reader might not otherwise have heard about. How available these books might be is anybody's guess. Some books are new, some are old but still in print, and some will have to be sought in a good library. But the discovery of a good book is a precious experience that I recommend to anyone. Clearly I intend many such experiences here.

Again, I am not mainly interested in merely giving book lists. Rather I am interested in the pursuit of the highest things, and I have found certain books or authors to be of especial help, at least to me. I have realized that it is most difficult to find a guide for this, a guide that might really enable us to come to grips with the highest issues. I talk about this difficulty of finding a proper guide, often in words of Leo Strauss, himself one of the best guides here. This is why in the beginning, I have tried to direct my thoughts to the topic of the highest things, to the questions and authors that most directly confront the deepest things about us—the deepest and the highest, the beginning and the end. These are worthy themes, I think.

And yet I write this with a certain amount of amusement, as the subtitle of this endeavor hints, because I know how pretentious our public and academic life can be, even how pretentious it is for me to suggest that I myself know something of the highest things. Most folks will think this book on "another sort of learning" to be an odd sort of thing. And it is, but its oddness, I believe, arises from its uniqueness, from its endeavor to suggest that we ought, as Aristotle told us, to spend our best time on those higher, divine things that define what we are about in our lives.

Two Books about Books to Read

1. James J. Thompson, Jr., *Christian Classics Revisited.*
2. Dinesh D'Souza, *The Catholic Classics.*

Part One

So You Are Still Perplexed Even in College?

Introduction

In this section, I intend in particular to address college and university students. But I have something broader in mind. For many years, I have been struck with the fact that many students and friends, often quite well educated, have not really learned much about the most fundamental issues in their formal educational career. I can argue that this is not too surprising. In many ways, we meet the more ultimate things in our churches, in our families, in our living, in our friendships. As I do not in the least doubt this latter truth, neither do I wish to imply that I think that the university or academia either can or should take on tasks for which it is not really equipped. There is a kind of academic totalitarian mind that would claim a sort of total comprehension of reality, but only in its own terms.

Nevertheless, I do think that the relatively leisured time we have or ought to have in institutions of higher learning can lead us to some basic truths and that we are indeed cheated if they do not. Likewise, I have little patience with the intellectual who refuses to consider religious or metaphysical claims and who has little of the tools or humility that it takes to discover them.

The following rather short essays in this first section are designed to give us something of the incentive and something of the direction in which we can, as it were, transcend the actual education we might have been given, even in supposedly good schools. I believe that universities can help us learn ultimate things, but I also know that often they do not help us learn what is really important. Thus, I have tried to suggest some ways both to learn while we are in school and to find the more central elements if we somehow are not introduced to them.

Obviously, I think that Plato and Aristotle are still fundamental. Likewise, I think that Scripture is the central experience of our civilization and that in it, we are confronted with realities that respond directly to what we are most perplexed by in the philosophers, poets, artists, and scientists. Beyond that, however, I have a certain enthusiasm about the learning process, both the process and the end of the process: truth itself. I also think that we must confront the central issues that are found in the tradition, because they are found also in our lives. In a way, we should, with many things, learn about them in the schools before we learn about them in life.

Thus, if I am concerned about teaching or lecturing or grading, it is because I am most concerned about the highest things to which we are called, called by being attracted to them in our souls, which are themselves somehow open to what is beyond us. Yet we want truth and love and wisdom to end in us, so that the kind of learning I am interested in always comes back, in these reflections, to that which calls us outside of ourselves, but only because there are things or truths about our lives which we should know and want to know.

Chapter One

Another Sort of Learning

One day a student of mine, Mr. Thomas Smith, came up to me after class to show me a present he had just bought for his brother's birthday. At the time, his brother was a graduate student at Catholic University. On seeing the book Mr. Smith had bought, I could hardly believe my eyes, for Mr. Smith had somehow found, in a used book store in Washington, a well-preserved first volume of an 1850 edition of Boswell's *Life of Johnson,* the cover of which I damaged in my enthusiasm over it. There is just nothing better than Boswell's *Life of Johnson,* so I could participate in Mr. Smith's pleasure at finding such a gem to give to his own brother on his birthday.

By chance, that very morning I had been reading my own two-volume-in-one set of Boswell, which in 1979 a kindly graduate student, Mr. Gary Springer, had given to me after I had read something of Johnson in class one day. Mr. Springer had found it for a few dollars in a used book store in Miami, evidently a throwaway by the markings on it, from St. Paul's High School in Saint Petersburg. This very fact makes one wonder about parochial education, I must say. My volume was a 1931 Oxford University reprint of the 1794 edition – "London, Printed by H. Baldwin & Son, for Charles Dilly, in the Poultry". I wish I knew enough of 1794 London to know where this "Poultry" was; presumably it was where chickens had once been sold. Today, no doubt, we would say, "Next to Kentucky Fried", or something like that.

The full title of this magnificent book is not to be neglected: "The Life of Samuel Johnson, LL. D., Comprehending an Account of His Studies and Numerous Works, in Chronological Order; a Series of Epistolary Correspondence and Conversations with Many Eminent Persons; and Various Original Pieces of His Composition, Never Before Published; the Whole Exhibiting a View of Literature and Literary Men in Great Britain, for Near Half a Century, During Which He Flourished, by James Boswell, Esq." Needless to say, except perhaps in the case of the present volume, they do not make titles like that any more.

I was telling Mr. Smith, Mr. Walter Thompson, and a nice young lady by the name of Ruth (whom I did not then know but who happened to be there also) that I was curious to see what Johnson had to say about Cicero, but that Cicero, with whom Johnson is sometimes compared, was not mentioned in the index. This seemed strange to me, so I also looked under *Tully* and *Marcus,* to no avail. Finally, I looked under *Rome,* a place in which I had lived for so long. In the beginning of the book, Boswell had noted that Johnson, as a young man, reviewed several books for *The Literary Magazine,* one of which concerned a volume entitled *Memoirs of the Court of Augustus,* in which Boswell tells us that Johnson spoke his own mind, "regardless of the cant transmitted from age to age, on the praise of the ancient Romans". As it turned out, Johnson had little truck with the good Romans, "a people, who, while they were poor, robbed mankind; and as soon as they became rich, robbed one another". Even though, as my students who read with me Tacitus' *Annals* or Cicero's speech "Against Verres" will recognize, this is a largely true, if biting, description of many a Roman, still the Romans were perhaps, as Chesterton said, the best of the ancient rulers, if only again to revert to Cicero, because they condemned their own corruption in most eloquent terms.

But this is not an essay on Johnson or the Romans, but rather an exhortation to young students about the importance of used book stores in their intellectual lives. I know some have heard the advertisement for Crown Books that tells us (rightly) that "books cost too much in Washington". To prove this obvious point, I had assigned Frederick Wilhelmsen's fine book, *Christianity and Political Philosophy,* from the University of Georgia Press, in one of my classes. The price, I thought, was $10.95, the price listed on the book cover. It was from this book, in fact, that my curiosity about Johnson on Cicero had arisen in the first place. However, I discovered from some disconcerted students that this same book was actually being sold in the book store for some $22, a price probably due to laws of scarcity and taxation on inventory. (This book is, in fact, worth $22, but shop around.)

My basic advice to students is to begin building their own libraries—how the computer will affect this library building, I am not certain. Still, anyone with a taste for wonder—not all, apparently, have it—should learn to haunt used book stores, even more than stores that sell new books. Washington, as far as I can tell, is not as well supplied with used book stores as other cities, such as San Francisco, which I know better. But there are some good outlets in Washington and especially good annual sales sponsored by the churches and by the Salvation Army. Each person should take pains to scout his own city on this score.

Russell Kirk wrote in 1969:

> The dwindling of second-hand bookshops is at once a symptom and consequence of this decline in literacy. Once upon a time I was a second-hand-book dealer myself, and I could cite perhaps a hundred instances of the extinction, over fifteen years, of long established old-book shops that had endured for decades or generations.... One pities the rising generation, which may know only the ordered rows of paperbacks, deprived of all the Gothic enchantments and infinite variety

that emanated from the dust of the chaotic book-and-curio emporium.[1]

The used book store, unlike the catalogue or even the library, puts us in a place where we can come across and buy some un-suspected title that turns out to get at the essence of *what is.*

One summer in San Francisco, for example, a friend of mine told me that she wanted a "perfect" book to give to a friend's mother, who, I believe, had just lost her husband. I suggested a particular used book store. My friend, Denise Bartlett, told me she did not know exactly what she wanted, but she would know "when she saw it". So she wandered through the poetry section, finding a Phyllis McGinley book, *The Love Letters of Phyllis McGinley* — a good choice, I believe — which she bought for herself.

Then Denise looked at several lives of saints and other devotional books. Finally she disappeared somewhere in the depths of the store to reappear a quarter of an hour later telling me enthusiastically that she had indeed found the perfect book. I took a look at it. It was Thomas à Kempis' *The Imitation of Christ.* I said, "Denise, do you know what this book is?" She replied, "It is a book on prayer, just the right thing for my friend's mother at this time." I continued, "You know, you have found only the most important and widely read book of devotional meditations in the history of Christianity." She was unimpressed: "All I know is that it is the right book for what I wanted." And of course, she was right.

To acquire an "education" it is often necessary not to do what the "course" of studies in high school or college requires. If I might be so bold, there are two types of education that must be pursued at the same time. In the first, we have to look

[1] Russell Kirk, *Enemies of the Permanent Things: Observations of Abnormity in Literature and Politics* (La Salle, Ill.: Sherwood Sugden, 1984), p. 142.

to making a living. This is not an ignoble task, and it usually requires some such relatively dull enterprise as going to law school or figuring out the stock market or passing the foreign service examination. The second is of quite a different nature. For this we need what Aristotle called leisure—space and time for questions that have little directly to do with business or keeping alive.

Nothing is wrong with either of the latter, of course, but this is not what life is finally about. For this latter, we want friends, and we want to know what others, mostly before our era, have held. This does not simply mean having a lot of books to cart about, but it means having some good ones, ones we have read, marked, and read again, and ones we intend to keep. And if we intend to keep books, we must plan our houses and dwellings so that we can keep them—shelves, rooms, ways to organize them.

Not too long ago, I heard a tape of the memorial service held at Stanford University Chapel at the death of Eric Voegelin. On the tape, Professor William Havard, I think, remarked that Voegelin read the *Complete Works of Shakespeare* once a year all his adult life. Well, as I had also seen a wonderful performance of *Hamlet* at Washington University in Saint Louis that August, I realized that I did not possess a copy of these *Complete Works*. So I put a note in to my friend Solomon Sara, our local librarian, hoping an old copy of Shakespeare might be lying about.

I now happily have a Pelican edition of these works. At the end of *The Tempest,* Prospero says, in a famous passage:

> Now I want
> Spirits to enforce, art to enchant;
> And my ending is despair
> Unless I be relieved by prayer,
> Which pierces so that it assaults
> Mercy itself and frees all fault.

How many used, torn books, you ask, might be helpful in understanding such lines? I can think of something in Plato, something else in Aristotle and the Apostle John. Aquinas on the relation of mercy and justice is also essential. I would add also à Kempis—which went through some 1800 editions by 1799, as Father Joe Tylenda tells us in his own new translation of *The Imitation of Christ.*[2] So there must be a few copies lying around somewhere.

Thus, if in some rustic used bookstore, you come across any such books, by chance or design, acquire them, keep them, read them. Until you do, you will not really have begun that second education for which all other education exists, whether we know it or not. This alone can bring us to the other sort of education in which we finally seek and confront the ultimate things.

Three Books that Begin to Open up the World
in Spite of Our Previous and Present
Educational Accomplishments or Lack Thereof

1. E. F. Schumacher, *A Guide for the Perplexed.*
2. J. M. Bochenski, *Philosophy: An Introduction.*
3. G. K. Chesterton, *Orthodoxy,* in *Collected Works of G. K. Chesterton,* vol 1.

---

[2] Thomas à Kempis, *The Imitation of Christ,* ed. and trans. Joseph Tylenda (Wilmington, Del.: Michael Glazier, 1984).

Chapter Two

Why Read?

Leo Strauss, in a memorable remark, noted that we are lucky if more than one or two great minds are alive in the generations during which we are ourselves alive. This meant, in Strauss' view, that we would have to encounter the greatest minds mostly in books. Strauss, himself one of the great teachers of our century, is worth citing here:

> Teachers themselves are pupils and must be pupils. But there cannot be an infinite regress: ultimately there must be teachers who are not in turn pupils. Those teachers who are not in turn pupils are the great minds or, in order to avoid any ambiguity in a matter of such importance, the greatest minds. Such men are extremely rare. We are not likely to meet any of them in any classroom. We are not likely to meet any of them anywhere. It is a piece of good luck if there is a single one alive in one's time. For all practical purposes, pupils, of whatever degree of proficiency, have access to the teachers who are not in turn pupils, to the greatest minds, only through the great books. Liberal education will then consist in studying with the proper care the great books which the greatest minds have left behind. . . . [1]

This consideration about the importance of reading the great books to confront the greatest mind needs, however, to be recalled in the context of the fact that at least two of the most important human beings that ever lived, Socrates and

---

[1] Leo Strauss, "What Is Liberal Education?" in *Liberalism: Ancient and Modern* (New York: Basic Books, 1968), p. 3.

Christ, did not write any book at all.[2] They did, nevertheless, have scribes or students who listened carefully to what they said. The records of these sayings and reflections constitute some of the most precious readings that we possess, on which much of our particular civilization, on which civilization itself, rests. Not to know or possess these books is not to have begun any serious intellectual endeavor.

Yet reading must mean reading very carefully and attentively to discover just what an author meant. And when we do discover to the best of our ability just what an author meant, we will still have to decide whether what he said was true or not. Knowing what is said, no doubt itself a first step, is not necessarily knowing *what is.* There are people who know *what is* without ever having read a book. We should keep our eyes open for these, since they are worth a lifetime of looking and reading. But again, we are fortunate if we find any alive in our lifetime. Sometimes even, we can live with the wise and not even recognize them. As Augustine would have said, we often choose what it is we will know.

But what to read? Surely, anyone who has been in or through a university, graduate school, or professional school has already read a considerable number of works. There are few university programs that do not in some manner at least hint at the notion of general or liberal education. Moreover, there are several definitions of *liberal* that need to be attended to. The word *liberal* itself is a noble one. First, as in Aristotle, it means ruling our possessions with generosity so that we can use them for purposes of life, friendship, and openness. The liberal man is one who does not deny his relation to matter,

[2] See James V. Schall, "The Death of Christ and Political Theory", *The Politics of Heaven and Hell: Christian Themes from Classical, Medieval, and Modern Political Philosophy* (Lanham, Md.: University Press of America, 1984), pp. 21–38.

but enjoys it and uses what he has to provide an atmosphere of superabundance and ease so that the higher things can happen in his world.

Thus, in a higher sense, liberality is freeing ourselves from the "not-knowing" condition so that we come to know *what is.* And all knowledge in some basic sense is interesting. Chesterton's remark that there are no uninteresting subjects, only uninterested people, has its profound point. To be liberal, in this sense, means to be free — not free to create a world that does not exist or one that does not relate to us, but free to be able to take within ourselves, into our knowledge, what is there, *what is.*

Yet, we wonder, is it everything in just any order that is the point of learning, or is there some order to learning? Are there some things that are more important to know than others? Is there, as Scripture says, "one thing" that is necessary for us to know? And if some things more important than others, how do we go about deciding which things are more worthy of knowledge? The order of knowledge and the order of experience are not necessarily the same. Nevertheless, if we are fundamentally realists, that is, people who believe that there is a reality found outside the mind and not merely one imposed on a kind of chaos out there by this same mind according to our own wishes or desires, we must expect that learning can take place in any time, place, or situation. This is really something very wondrous, since it suggests that no *thing* is cut off from everything. We always have a direct contact with *what is.*

On the other hand, there is no need to reinvent the wheel just because we did not invent it ourselves. That is, it is perfectly all right to learn something from others, from books. We cannot doubt that *what is* to be known is practically infinite, so that beginning from where someone else left off is in no way a denial of reality itself. We ought not to be overly surprised, then, if someone who lived two centuries before us, or ten, or twenty-five, can still teach us much. This means that the effort to know includes the effort to know from others: hence, the value of learning both how and what to read. Reading is not the only way to learn, of course, but merely one way. We need to test reading against other forms of learning, such as film or theater or various forms of art. Such is the importance of learning that we ought to pursue it wherever we encounter it: in reading, living, seeing, or reflecting.

Yet we wonder if there are not particular things to read, such as *The Republic* of Plato or *The Metaphysics* of Aristotle. And is it possible just to sit down and read these works, or is it necessary to be a student? Must we sit at the feet of the great masters who do not live in our time, or if they do, who are not in our personal or academic environment? And must we do this with the help of others who are not so great? Of course, we must choose to read the important tracts of our heritage; we are fortunate if someone aids us. It is not a defect in the universe that not everyone is the greatest thinker or artist or saint; the universe allows for the less than the perfect. The Sailor in Belloc's *The Four Men,* on sitting down near the fire and pouring out a glass of ale, remarked, "Beware of perfection. It is a will-o-the-wisp. It has been the ruin of many."[3]

However romantic the perpetual student might be then, the fact is that there comes a time when it is necessary not to be a student. The whole purpose of learning is to be in a situation wherein we are not always learners, but those who have learned, those capable of standing on their own, be it in prudence or in wisdom, so that we are, in a sense, independent. This is what we look for and what we need to be in a position to find out how to be. Yet, however adult or mature or learned we might become, we will remain receivers of *what is.* Reading, to go

[3] Hilaire Belloc, *The Four Men* (New York: Oxford, 1984), p. 68.

back to our topic, will, for most, be the guide to *what is.* Why read? Because we are given more than we are.

Five Books Addressed to the Heart of Things

1. Josef Pieper, *In Tune with the World: A Theory of Festivity.*
2. C. S. Lewis, *George MacDonald: An Anthology.*
3. Dorothy Sayers, *The Whimsical Christian;* also called, in the English edition, *Christian Letters to a Post-Christian World.*
4. Eric Mascall, *The Christian Universe.*
5. Flannery O'Connor, *The Habit of Being: The Letters of Flannery O'Connor.*

Chapter Three

What a Student Owes His Teacher

Let me begin with the following passage from Augustine's treatise "On the Teacher":

> For do teachers profess that it is their thoughts which are perceived and grasped by the students, and not the sciences themselves which they convey through thinking? For who is so stupidly curious as to send his son to school that he may learn what the teacher thinks? ... Those who are pupils consider within themselves whether what has been explained has been said truly; looking of course to that interior truth, according to the measure of which each of us is able. Thus they learn, and when the interior truth makes known to them that true things have been said, they applaud. ... [1]

Notice the seriousness with which Augustine stated the fact that students must consider "within themselves" whether what has been said has been said "truly". The truth does not leave us indifferent, and when it does, it is not the truth that is at fault.

Students have obligations to teachers. I know this sounds like strange doctrine, but let it stand. No doubt someone will object that teachers also have an even greater obligation to students. Teachers who do not consider this same "interior truth" of which Augustine spoke, woe to them. But the former doctrine, if less popular, especially among students, is probably still more important. For students are in some sense spiritual beings and have, therefore, precisely "obligations". The order

---

[1] St. Augustine, *De Magistro,* chap. XIV, 389 A.D., in *The Basic Works of St. Augustine,* vol. I, ed. Whitney J. Oates (New York: Random House, 1948), p. 394.

of soul ought to correspond to the order of reality, the reality in which soul itself came to be in the first place.

For his part, the teacher probably knows his basic obligation, even if he does not practice it. The student may not yet know. The teacher-student relationship is, in fact, primarily a spiritual relationship—both, teacher and student, participate in what is not properly theirs. Something can be known in the spiritual order without becoming less. This is what teaching and learning are about.

Some writers, indeed, like Mortimer Adler, will say that there are *no* teachers, only different degrees of learners.[2] There is considerable truth here, if the statement is understood properly. I do not think I have ever assigned anything to students that I did not want to learn myself—even if I already knew it. Something worth learning is worth learning again. Indeed, most things you cannot learn at all if you do not attempt to learn them again. A teacher is someone distinguished only by the fact that he has more time than most to learn again, someone who has hopefully tried to learn again more often. Society desperately needs enclaves like monasteries and universities wherein men and women have such leisure. But we should never forget that the primary place of leisure and of the knowledge of the higher order of things begins and ends almost always in our homes.

At a modern university, where the student or his good parents have to pay a heavy, nondeductible penny to keep him in class, the issue of a student's responsibility to the teacher may be also an economic one, even a mutual contractual obligation of the kind that lawyers are trying to define in the courts in order to attack tenure and the vagaries of rambling

[2] See Mortimer Adler, *How to Read a Book* (New York: Simon and Schuster, 1940); *The Difference of Man and the Difference It Makes* (New York: Holt, 1967).

professors. Such legal efforts to make the student-teacher relationship contractual and legal are probably already signs of civilizational decay. The attempt to bring "justice" into the classroom is at best a failure to understand things beyond politics—the most important things, really.

At a university, students and teachers are formally related to each other because each is related to something else outside of each. The essential "activity" of teaching and learning is mostly independent of the personal relationship of student and teacher, if there even be such. Too much is made, I think, of the idea of the small, intimate atmosphere of a classroom, where everyone can really "get to know each other". Much of my most important learning took place in huge classrooms. I remember especially Professor Rudolf Allers at Georgetown during my graduate school days. He never actually looked at the class, but his wisdom did.[3] I do not want to deny that sometimes—rarely, probably, especially in the Aristotelian sense—students and teachers become friends. But at universities, students are usually too busy becoming friends with each other—and changing friends, as Aristotle also said—ever to worry much about crotchety old Professor Jones, or Schall, as the case may be.

But I have had too many students in class over the years, in San Francisco, in Rome, and now in Washington, D.C., to think that normally a professor is going to know many students in more than a formal fashion during a brief semester or two in Government 117 or whatever the course may be. Knowing students too well can in fact be something of an impediment to learning, especially for the other students in the class—*acceptio personarum,* as Aquinas called it. The activity of learning goes on, perhaps even better, when student and teacher

[3] See Rudolf Allers, *The Psychology of Character* (New York: Sheed and Ward, 1930); *The Philosophic Work of Rudolf Allers: A Selection,* ed. Jesse A. Mann (Washington, D.C.: Georgetown University Press, 1965).

are addressing themselves to the matter at hand, to the reason why they are in the same place, at the same time, with a kind of mutual awe before something they neither created nor made.

But here, it is the functioning of the student I am concerned about. From my experience, I would say that the students I have had have been good students; so I do not write about the problems of lack of intelligence, but what to do with superior intelligence. Furthermore, I am one of those who think we learn in order to learn the truth, so that the prestige of a university is not necessarily a good criterion of education itself. I know a lot of famous places where one can learn a lot of things that are not true.

Moreover, one can be a good student and still not be very bright, just as someone can be very bright in native ability but quite a poor specimen of a student. Some wag once said that college education is when the notes of the professor pass into the notebooks of the students without passing through the minds of either. The purest learning probably takes place in direct speech with those who know or when we are alone, when, as my classes recall with Cicero, we are never less alone.[4] With our memories, with our books, we can also be taught by teachers like Plato and St. Augustine, who are not actually living in our time.

Most universities, like the one at which I teach, have a system by which students grade their teachers, an evaluation that can be helpful or vindictive or worthless, depending on how it is designed, filled out, and used. So students have some obligation to judge teachers both fairly and frankly. But like-

---

[4] Cicero thus began the third part of his *De Officiis* (On Duties) with these famous lines: "Publius Cornelius Scipio, the first of that family to be called Africanus, used to remark that he was never less idle than when he was by himself." *Selected Works*, trans. Michael Grant (Baltimore: Penguin, 1960), p. 157.

wise the teacher must judge the students not merely against each other, but against the standard of the discipline, against the performance of the best. The teacher always stands, as it were, for the higher law of the best before the student, even though teaching is also the effort to pass on what can be learned, even if it be a minimum.

This inner tension we feel within ourselves, too, is why Aristotle had said of God that even if we cannot learn much about him, still we ought to spend as much time as we can learning what we can. Indeed, since I will often refer to these powerful lines of Aristotle, let me cite them:

> And we ought not to listen to those who counsel us "O man, think as man should" and "O mortal, remember your mortality." Rather ought we, so far as in us lies, to put on immortality and to leave nothing unattempted in the effort to live in conformity with the highest thing within us. Small in bulk it may be, yet in power and preciousness it transcends all the rest (1177b31-78a2).[5]

Classrooms, then, are in a sense like golf courses, where the standard of par looms over our performances, good or bad, no matter by how much we have beaten the others in the foursome with whom we are actually playing. The highest things require our attentive efforts no matter how satisfied we be with what is less than the highest. The imperfect is not the perfect and ought not to be confused with it. None the less, the highest things do call us out of ourselves, even in our happiest moments.

This being said, let me state the obligations of students. The first obligation, particularly operative during the first weeks of a new semester, is a moderately good will toward the teacher, a

---

[5] Aristotle, *The Ethics,* trans. J. A. K. Thompson (Baltimore: Penguin, 1969), bk. X, chap. 7, p. 305.

trust, a confidence that is willing to admit to oneself that the teacher has probably been through the matter, and, unlike the student, knows where it all leads. I do not want here to neglect the dangers of the ideological professor, of course, the one who imposes his mind on *what is*. But to be a student requires a certain modicum of humility.

Yet to be a student also requires a certain amount of faith in oneself, a certain self-insight that makes a person realize that he *can* learn something that seems unlearnable in the beginning. This trust in the teacher also implies that the student, if he has trouble understanding, makes this known to the teacher. Teachers just assume that everything they say or illustrate is luminously clear. A student does a teacher a favor by saying, "I do not understand this". But the student should first really try to understand before speaking. To quote Augustine again, students should "consider within themselves whether what has been explained has been said truly".

The student ought to have the virtue of docility. He *owes* the teacher *his* capacity of being taught. We must allow ourselves to be taught. We can actually refuse this openness of our own free wills. This refusal is mostly a spiritual thing with roots of the profoundest sort in metaphysics and ethics. In the beginning, we only have a "blank tablet", as Aristotle said of our minds, but it is a brain we have and not just nothing. We can only discover something, even ourselves, by being first given something.

Students do not, as St. Augustine said, go to schools to learn what professors happen to think. Rather, they go that they might, along with their professors, hear together the "inner truth" of things, a grace that engages all alike in one enterprise that takes them beyond the confusions and confines of the classroom to the heart of reality, that to which our own intellects ought to "conform", as Aquinas said, when we possess the truth.[6] When a teacher, crusty as he may be, sees his students leave his classroom for the last time at the end of some fall or spring semester, he wants them to carry with them not so much the memories of his jokes—though he hopes they laughed—or his tests, but the internal possession of the subject matter itself. The student ought to become independent of the teacher to the point of even forgetting his name, but not the truth he learned. This latter is what education is about—not about class lists and rank and the tenure of professors.

So the student owes to his teacher the effort of study. A good teacher ought to exercise a mild coercion on his students, a kind of pressure that takes into account their lethargy and fallenness and distractions, a pressure that indicates that the professor wants the students to learn, lets them know it is important, a pressure that has the purpose of guiding the students through the actual thought process, the actual exercise of the mind on the matter at hand. Few students, on being given *The Republic* of Plato or *The Confessions* of St. Augustine to read, will bounce right up to their room, shut off the stereo, cancel a date, and proceed to ponder the eternal verities in these books. The teacher who assigns such books—and a university in which they are *not* assigned has little claim to that noble name—always must wonder if the intrinsic fascination, the thinking through of such works will somehow reach into his students' minds. He hopes that the next time they read Plato or Augustine, they will do so because they want to,

[6] See Etienne Gilson, *Thomist Realism and the Critique of Knowledge* (San Francisco: Ignatius Press, 1986); Frederick D. Wilhelmsen, *Man's Knowledge of Reality* (Englewood Cliffs, N.J.: Prentice-Hall, 1960); Mieczylaw A. Krapiec, *I–Man: An Outline of Philosophical Anthropology,* trans. M. Lescoe et al. (New Britain, Conn.: Mariel, 1983), pp. 120–85; Schumacher, *A Guide for the Perplexed,* pp. 40–120.

because they are challenged by them, and not because they might receive a C– grade if they do not.

Thus, the student owes the teacher trust, docility, effort, thinking. And what is it the teacher can expect of his students? Augustine said it well. The students actually learn, when they actively think the thoughts of mankind, when the "inner truths" of things themselves actually make themselves known to them, in their own minds. Thus, they learn as a result of their own going through what the teacher hopefully advises, guides them through, what the teacher has said. Only then, Augustine said, in the marvelous passage we cited in the beginning of these reflections, do "they applaud. . . . " They applaud not so much the teacher who was once like them a pupil, the teacher whom they will soon forget, but the "inner truth" itself, which, as Aristotle also said, is a part of the "all things" of reality that we are given, that we actually "become", that we are blessed to know even by ourselves in this vale of tears. Ultimately, teaching is an act of humility, as is learning. It is the realization that the highest things, of which we possess but the beginnings, are to be known, can be known by each of us in our own selves, and none of us is the less in the learning.

Six Books on Learning and Teaching

1. Jean Guitton, *Student's Guide to the Intellectual Life.*
2. A. G. Sertillanges, *The Intellectual Life.*
3. Mortimer Adler, *How to Read a Book.*
4. Eric Voegelin, *Conversations with Eric Voegelin.*
5. Jacques Barzun, *The House of Intellect.*
6. Gilbert Highet, *The Art of Teaching.*

Chapter Four

Grades

Walking across the Georgetown campus to St. Mary's hall a couple of years ago with Kristin Lund and Ghida Salaam, on the way to a final examination, in fact, I asked them, "What do you think a grade is?" Kristin replied without hesitation, "A grade is the measure of the student's insecurity." We laughed at that quite unexpected but valuable observation, though I myself had always thought that a grade was rather a measure of accomplishment of sorts, even more perhaps of potential accomplishment.

Yet I am also open to the thesis that a grade is a measure of a teacher's ability, even of a teacher's enthusiasm. Yves Simon once suggested that a university, to exist, needs in it masses of professors who think and act as if their subjects were the most important things in the world, whether the subject be Latin grammar or the Fathers of the Church or zoology.[1] On this basis, Simon made a case for the validity of university administrations, the only case that can be made for that rather odd part of the university, I think. Probably, the worst element a university can have is an administration that thinks it, the administration, knows the content of the courses taught, for if an administration took the time to know the separate disciplines, it could do nothing else, which was Simon's point.

Aristotle, as we know, suggested that we ought not to expect more certitude of a science than it is capable of yielding. In Aristotle's sober words, "In studying this subject [ethics], we

[1] Yves Simon, *The Philosophy of Democratic Government* (Chicago: University of Chicago Press, 1977), pp. 45–47.

must be content if we attain as high a degree of certainty as the matter of it admits" (1094b12–13).[2] Recently I came across a syllabus for a course, a very good syllabus, incidentally, of a colleague of mine, who announced in his prospectus that 10 percent of a student's grade would be based on class discussion, 40 percent on the tests, and 50 percent on the term paper.

I envy such clarity, but I have always been reluctant to give such statistics to students who ask me how I arrive at a grade. I read Aristotle every semester, after all, and know about expecting too much certitude. Rarely do we have mathematical certitude in university courses, though, as a friend once told me, it is always good to have a few absolutely clear right or wrong questions on every test: names and dates and quotations that are either one way or another. Moreover, we live in an era of "recommendations" and LSAT scores and grade-point averages, in a world where some computer wants to know objectively how we did.

Probably the great majority of students in good schools think a B is a *very* low grade, as it prevents them from getting into the medical or law school of their dreams—and every such school, alas, is somebody's dream. *Grade inflation* means that schools tend to adjust to meet the demand. I have seen many a pained look on the faces of students to whom I gave a B. They seemed not consoled when I told them that a B was quite a good grade, that the question really was not "what grade you got, but whether you learned anything, even if you got a D". Someday we all, even aging professors, meet people smarter than we are, often sitting in our own very classes. Knowledge is humbling as well as exalting.

Thus, when students get as ancient as certain unnamed professors, of course, as they inevitably will, something Cicero

2 Aristotle, *The Ethics,* bk. I, chap. 3, p. 27.

taught in his marvelous essay "On Old Age", just what grade they got back in Government 117 will tend to be obscured by their inability to recall whether they actually ever took Government 117 in the first place. The only thing we need to recall is what we read, what we spoke about, and if we are lucky, what we wrote about.

I was talking to a friend of mine who is in the university drama department. He was talking of the advantage of having several small theaters on a campus, where many of us could, when we are as old as, again, certain unnamed professors, recall when we performed as Julius Caesar or Portia or in Dolly's *Hello,* when we could also recall seeing our own very professors act, so we could contemplate in our own very midst the dramas of our kind.

One semester, I read with one of my classes the Theban plays of Sophocles. It would be nice if some of those students could say they acted in, for example, *Oedipus Rex,* while they were in college. That would be worth a lifetime of A's even if the play itself was not a very good production. Some things worth doing, Chesterton said in *What's Wrong with the World?,* are worth doing badly.

Anyhow, a grade, it seems to me, is a judgment, an informed judgment that a professor *must* give. It is what Aristotle called precisely an act of discrimination, something whose very function is to acknowledge that no things are exactly alike among us humans, however much we may be alike in our natures. A practical judgment is, unavoidably, fallible. It is one of those things that might be otherwise. Yet it is what we have to do, what we must do in academia; and it can be quite adequate within its limits.

For myself, I think a professor needs to know how a student writes, how he reads, how he speaks, how he responds on his feet, as it were. The professor needs to know about the student's diligence and thoroughness. This takes some time; it is a human thing. As I mentioned in the previous essay, students also grade teachers in most universities, something most administrations take relatively seriously. But it also takes students time as well as trust to know their teachers.

Grades, to be worth something—imagine a university where all students get A's no matter what—need to be measured against the "competition" of other students: those in an actual class, those myriads of students a professor has had in previous years, and those in other universities.

Theoretically, by this standard of comparison to other standards than the class at hand, everyone in a given class could legitimately be given A's or F's, though the laws of probability militate against it. But grades also need to be measured against the discipline itself, no matter what the competition does. Something ought to be there to be learned, beyond learning just how you did in comparison with the cute co-ed in the seat next to you in Chemistry 1A.

Thus, a professor needs, in grading, input from his student's output, as it were. I was at a conference on sports journalism once at the University of Nevada at Reno (see Chapter 18), where Mr. Win Elliott, long-time announcer for CBS radio, told me to tell my students to remember that they should learn, for God's sake, "how to speak". They would spend 95 percent of their lives talking (some, more). Be sure they know how to get up and talk well.

Ironically, the old Jesuit *Ratio Studiorum,* which early Jesuits formed to define what they wanted to get across and which has not been really followed for decades, was of the same mind. Its goal was called *eloquentia.* And no doubt the electronic world once again stresses speaking—tapes and televisions and radios and computers that translate onto discs what we say. Thus, *The Rhetoric* of Aristotle may well be the most important book to read at college these days, though it is well worth reading in any college, on any day.

So what is a grade? A measure of knowing and not knowing, to be sure. Grades are intended also to encourage, challenge. There is a certain special, sweet pleasure in getting a D– in Freshman Composition and an A– in Advanced Writing three years later. At the Reno conference, I ran into a young man who majored in political science at the University of Georgia, where, he told me, he took his first and only writing course by accident as a senior. He liked the course, so he wrote his very first story about an elderly lady in Atlanta who had been to every baseball game played in that city for the last half-century. He sent the story to *Sports Illustrated.* A couple of weeks later, he received a check for $750. That is a good grade, I think; and there is no pleasure quite like having one's first article accepted by someone for publication and not merely read by some obscure college professor, who has no choice, since he assigned it.

Grades are things not to worry about. Says who? Well, I do, in a way. No one is in a university to "get good grades", even though your grades may be the main concern of the good tuition payers back home. Your dear mother could probably care less what you actually "do" or "learn" in Schall's rambling class, to be sure, but she probably does care about whether you got a good grade. You see, such are the fates, she probably trusts Schall's report more than yours! (What one actually "does" in Schall's class is a mystery understood only by God!) If to get a good grade a student reads St. Augustine—well, terrific. But I am also impressed by someone who reads St. Augustine and gets a D–, but who five or twenty-five years later is still reading him. It takes all one's life to read St. Augustine, so the first dozen times through probably deserve a D– anyhow.

What's a grade? A grade can also be the measure of a university's insecurity. If the course content or methods are not exactly like the "big name" schools, therefore, some think, there is something wrong. I suspect there is something more wrong if the course contents always are just like those of the well-known schools.[3] Allan Bloom's essay "Our Listless Universities" is well worth reading in this context.[4] Bloom maintained that if we are learning in any university just what students are learning at Yale or Ohio State or Chicago or Berkeley, it probably is not worth the effort or money.[5] This is not to deny, of course, the classic tradition of things that ought to be learned everywhere, in all times, as Newman wrote.[6]

Previously I talked about "what a student owes to his teacher". Well, I suppose, in a way, a grade is what a teacher in justice owes to his student. This grade will require a judgment that includes a certain amount of Aristotelian uncertainty and practicality, but also the student's efforts and accomplishments, how the student writes, how he speaks, how he compares, whether he desires simply "to know", as Aristotle said.

[3] See William J. Bennett, *To Reclaim a Legacy: A Report on the Humanities in Higher Education* (Washington, D.C.: National Endowment for the Humanities, 1984).

[4] Allan Bloom, "Our Listless Universities", *National Review,* December 10, 1982, pp. 1537–48. See especially, Allan Bloom, *The Closing of the American Mind* (New York: Simon and Schuster, 1987).

[5] See also David Ricci, *The Tragedy of Political Science* (New Haven, Conn.: Yale University Press, 1984).

[6] See John Henry Newman, *The Idea of a University* (Garden City, N.Y.: Doubleday Image, 1959); Russell Kirk, *Decadence and Renewal in the Higher Learning* (South Bend, Ind.: Gateway, 1978); J. M. Cameron, *On the Idea of a University* (Toronto; University of Toronto Press, 1978); John P. Leary, *Don't Tell Me You're Not Confused (A Critical Look at College)* (San Francisco: New College Press, 1979).

We can, I Suppose, give A's, B's, C's D's, and F's to these judgments, or 93.7 percent or 78.4 percent, or as we did in Rome when I taught there, 10 for the highest grade or 5 for the lowest. But eventually, all comes back to the same thing: a teacher's judgment of a student's objective accomplishment compared to what the said student "ought" to accomplish.

The purpose of a grade, I suppose, to get back to Kristin Lund's remark, is to enable the student to pass from uncertainty to certainty, from insecurity to security about himself, to feel confident, on an objective basis, that he knows more or less what he is expected to know. By ourselves, we do not know this. Kristin was right.

Aristotle said that we have a mind capable of knowing all things. This means metaphysically, no doubt, that we are all insecure until we confront a final grade, a final grader, as it were, when we will indeed "know all things", and yet remain, as Aristotle hoped, just ourselves, rather finite human beings: professors, students, administrators, all. Aristotle would like that. So would Augustine.

Books You'll Never Be Graded on Except by Reality

1. Isaiah, Jeremiah, Ezekiel, Genesis, the Psalms.
2. The Gospel according to St. John.
3. St. Augustine, *The Confessions*
4. Plato, *The Apology; The Crito; The Phaedo*
5. Thomas à Kempis, *The Imitation of Christ.*
6. The Epistles of St. Paul.
7. Cicero, *De Officiis* (On Duties).

Chapter Five

On Teaching the Important Things

Not long ago, I was sent a review copy of the Bodley Head–Ignatius Press collection, *A Chesterton Anthology*.[1] The first thing I read in the wonderful book was a 1910 Chesterton essay entitled "What Is Right with the World?" some of which I read aloud in a medieval theory class I was teaching at the time. The passage I read began, "It is at the *beginning* that things are good, and not (as the more pallid progressives say) only at the end."

But there was a passage in that same remarkable essay that I did not somehow read to that class. Let me cite it here:

> Sincerely speaking, there are no uneducated men. They may escape the trivial examinations, but not the tremendous examination of existence. The dependency of infancy, the enjoyment of animals, the love of woman, and the fear of death—these are more frightful and more fixed than all conceivable forms of the cultivation of the mind. It is idle to complain of schools and colleges being trivial. Schools and colleges must always be trivial. In no case will a college ever teach the important things. For before a man is twenty, he has always learned the important things. He has learned them right or wrong, and he has learned them all alone.[2]

---

[1] G. K. Chesterton, *A Chesterton Anthology*, ed. P. J. Kavanaugh (San Francisco: Ignatius Press, 1985). Another new collection of Chesterton is *As I Was Saying: A Chesterton Anthology*, ed. Robert Knille (Grand Rapids, Mich.: Eerdmans, 1985). Another useful collection of G.K.C. quotations is *The Quotable Chesterton*, ed. George Marlin, Richard P. Rabatin, and John L. Swan (San Francisco: Ignatius Press, 1986).

[2] Chesterton, *A Chesterton Anthology*, p. 344.

This is not, of course, common doctrine in our academia, where we like to think the highest things are our private preserves.

And yet it is a sober testimony to the fact that what is of ultimate importance is most often disclosed to us through our parents, our localities, our churches, and our rooted openness to the being, to the *what is* that stands before us wherever we are. Perhaps the most satisfying doctrine in Aquinas, in this sense, is his bold affirmation that each of us has his own intellect, complete in itself, looking out on a world none of us made, so that each of us first begins to know what is not himself. Only having thus begun can we reflect on the famous Socratic admonition to "know thyself".

Leo Strauss often talked about the care with which we must talk earnestly about the highest things—because there are so few who seem willing to listen. Sooner or later we must come to realize that most of the important things we do *not* in fact learn are not learned because we choose not to learn them. At some point we must recognize that our own natural capacities are not the real causes of our personal status before the highest things. And we cannot, at times, but be conscious of the fact that we do not, often dare not, talk about the important things.

In 1770, Boswell recorded this passage from Samuel Johnson on the occasion of the death of Johnson's mother:

> He [Johnson] lamented that all serious and religious conversation was banished from the society of men, and yet great advantage might be derived from it. All acknowledged, he said, what hardly anybody practiced, the obligation we were under of making the concerns of eternity the governing principles of our lives. Every man, he observed, at least wishes for retreat: he sees his expectations frustrated in the world, and

begins to wean himself from it, and to prepare for everlasting separation.[3]

Such are solemn words, fit for pubs and walks and other places where we engage in serious conversation.

Universities, to be sure, are places where we can hear some questions formalized, refined in a way we could never encounter otherwise. Yet modern universities seem more like Socrates' "democracy", where every possible opinion can be heard and no one, in principle, is able to tell the outlandish from the commonplace, the odd from the sane. Such universities where all opinion is created equal and departmentalized have begotten the "think tank", as it is called, a newer institution where more and more of the real thought in our societies seems to be taking place. When we are unable to take a stand because, in theory, no stand can be taken, it is logical and inevitable that vital thought surfaces elsewhere. Some, like Alasdair MacIntyre at the end of his famous *After Virtue,* even seem to hint that we need to refound the monasteries.[4]

In a touching essay, Professor Ralph McInerny recalled listening as a young man to the last lecture the French Thomist philosopher Jacques Maritain gave one autumn night in 1958 at the Moreau Seminary on the South Bend campus. Here is what McInerny—whose book *St. Thomas Aquinas* is a must (see Chapter 7), and whose novel *The Noonday Devil* a delight— said, reflecting on the event:

---

[3] James Boswell, *The Life of Samuel Johnson,* vol. 1 (London: Oxford, 1931), p. 418.

[4] Alasdair MacIntyre, *After Virtue* (Notre Dame, Ind.: University of Notre Dame Press, 1981), p. 245.

> He [Maritain] was a saintly man. That is what I sensed as I
> scuffled through the leaves on my way back from Maritain's last
> lecture at Moreau (later published as *The Uses of Philosophy*).
> He loved the truth, but his purpose in life was not to win
> arguments. He wanted to be wise. Such an odd ambition for a
> philosopher! He succeeded because he prayed as well as he
> studied.[5]

This sort of experience is why we go to a university as young
men and women: the chance that we might find there, once or
twice if we are lucky, a wise man to teach us, or at least to
teach us about the wise men and women who lived before our
own lifetimes.

Many people, no doubt, will talk to us, and the sum total of
a year's worth of courses at the average university campus may
come closer to the Tower of Babel than to the Seat of Wisdom.
This is why we must somehow be rightly oriented to reality
even before we arrive at ivy-covered colleges and mega-
universities, as Chesterton told us. Plato, in *The Republic*, said
much the same thing before him: " . . . when it comes to good
things, no one is satisfied with what is opined to be so but each
seeks the things that *are* . . . "(505d).

In 1985, the philosopher Eric Voegelin died at Stanford
University in California. Voegelin was one of the most important thinkers of our time. In 1980, in Montreal, a book of his
conversations was published, as I have previously mentioned.
In one of the lectures in this book, he told his audience at the
Thomas More Institute, speaking of his own students and
following Aristotle:

> One should be aware that we always act as if we had an
> ultimate purpose in fact, as if our life made some sort of sense. I
> find students frequently flabbergasted, especially those who are
> agnostics, when I tell them that they all act, whether agnostics

[5] Ralph McInerny, *Notre Dame Magazine*, summer 1985.

or not, as if they were immortal! Only under the assumption of immortality, of fulfillment beyond life, is the seriousness of action intelligible, which they actually put in their work and which has a fulfillment nowhere in this life however long they may live.[6]

Rarely, I think, are we spoken to so seriously. Often we do not want to be so addressed because we sense where such conversation might lead us. And that brings us back to the original discussion of "beginnings" found in the early chapters of the Book of Genesis.

As I shall mention often, I think that the most remarkable scenes in pure philosophy, those in Plato, have to do with young students instinctively gathering around Socrates, the philosopher, hardly knowing why, to listen to penetrating philosophical doctrines spoken and lived. Most young philosophers began in the curiosity and delight caused by hearing their old professors and parents made fun of, little suspecting that each himself must confront the issue of which Socrates and Voegelin spoke.

And this brings me back to Chesterton—to the idea that before we are twenty we have learned the important things. We have learned them right or wrong, and we have learned them alone. "The tremendous examination of existence", as Chesterton called it, will not be based on whether we have been to college, but on whether we seriously, yet in good humor, confronted in our lives the highest things. St. Paul intimated, in a famous passage, that learning could easily deflect us into "foolishness", even if we be, perhaps especially if we be, professional philosophers (1 Cor 1:18–24).

Our purpose in life is indeed "not to win arguments", but to be wise. For this latter, we cannot neglect study or prayer, or especially that openness to existence about which we must

---

[6] Voegelin, *Conversations,* p. 6.

learn even if we learn nothing else, or even if we learn all else. We must seek out where the important things are taught if the "seriousness of action" is to be intelligible, however long we may live.

My last words here are again those of Chesterton: "The ordinary modern progressive position is that this is a bad universe, but it will certainly get better. I say it is certainly a good universe, even if it gets worse.... We are to regard existence as a raid or great adventure.... The most dangerous thing in the world is to be alive."

Living is "dangerous", I might add, not because we have been given the chance to fail, but because we have been given the chance to see that in the beginning, all things were good and we did not notice.

Three Books on Education

1. John Henry Newman, *The Idea of a University.*
2. Christopher Dawson, *The Crisis of Western Education.*
3. Jacques Maritain, *The Education of Man: The Educational Philosophy of Jacques Maritain.*

Four Books on Philosophy and Literature by Marion Montgomery

1. *Reflective Journey toward Order: Essays on Dante, Wordsworth, Eliot, and Others.*
2. *Why Flannery O'Connor Stayed Home.*
3. *Why Poe Drank Liquor.*
4. *Why Hawthorne Was Melancholy.*

Eight Books on Christianity and Political Thought

1. Jacques Maritain, *Man and the State.*
2. Charles N. R. McCoy, *The Structure of Political Thought.*

3. Heinrich Rommen, *The State in Catholic Thought.*
4. Rodger Charles, *The Social Teaching of Vatican II.*
5. John Courtney Murray, *We Hold These Truths.*
6. Thomas Molnar, *Politics and the State.*
7. Yves Simon, *The Philosophy of Democratic Government.*
8. Glenn Tinder, *Political Thinking: The Perennial Questions*

Chapter Six

On Teaching the
Political Thought of Plato

In such a state of society, the master fears and flatters his
scholars, and the scholars despise their masters and tutors; young
and old are all alike; and the young man is on the level with the
old, and is ready to compete with him in word and deed; and
old men condescend to the young and are full of pleasantry and
gaiety; they are loathe to be thought morose and authoritative,
and therefore they adopt the manners of the young.

Plato, *The Republic*, 563a

For youngsters . . . argue for amusement, and are always contra-
dicting and refuting others in imitation of those who refute
them. . . . And when they have made many conquests and
received many defeats at the hands of many, they violently and
speedily get into a way of not believing anything which they
believed before, and hence, not only they, but philosophy and
all that relates to it is apt to have a bad name with the rest of the
world.

Plato, *The Republic*, 539b–c

Political science departments, I think, are generally ready to
admit that their student products should graduate with at least
an acquaintance with Plato, surely the intellectual founder of
the discipline of political science and, indeed, of most other
disciplines. Good departments may even wonder over the
years if their students need to study much else. A political
science faculty not requiring Plato could hardly be worthy of
the noble name of *politics* in its title. Indeed, I would argue for

a minimum much more stringent than mere "acquaintance"
with Plato, since political theory deals with substantially more
than justice, even as *The Republic* itself, with its astonishing
end, affirms.

Thus, I would begin "Fundamentals in", or "Elements of",
or "Great Ideas about", whatever be the rubric for classes in
political thought, with this sincere, friendly oration:

> My dear young friends: We are going to begin our considera-
> tions of political philosophy by reading together during the
> next few weeks *The Republic,* the main work of Plato. Then we
> shall read his three dialogues on the death of Socrates, then his
> last dialogue, *The Laws.* I have read each of these books many,
> many times, as I hope you eventually will. Be patient with me
> if I even tell you that many actually think it better to read them
> in Greek.

> Each time I have read *The Republic* or *The Laws,* more-
> over, it has been a new book, yet a familiar one. Why
> this is so is something of a mystery. Perhaps it is because
> Plato was right: our very capacity to understand politics
> presupposes our lifetime experiences, our control of our own
> conflicting desires (498). Perhaps too, it is because I am a
> slow learner, though in this case, there is something nice about
> learning slowly.

> The function of a professor is to aid, encourage, require,
> even mildly coerce the student to read *The Republic* and *The
> Laws* once at least, or even twice. He can do no more. If these
> books do not perchance grip the student in spite of anything
> the professor can do to make them attractive and intelligible—
> many professors have, to be sure, some very odd ideas about
> Plato, the very founder of the university in our culture—if the
> professor does not incite you to wonder and to argue, not with
> the professor but with Plato and Glaucon and thought itself,
> you cannot even begin the enterprise of political philosophy
> properly. In fact, you cannot begin it at all.

> And contrariwise, once you do begin political philosophy,

once you begin to walk with Socrates, Polemarchus, Adeimantos, and Thrasymachus from the Piraeus, political philosophy will not let you go. And from here, you will eventually pass to philosophy itself, and finally to the wonder of whether anything more has been addressed to the questions that philosophy has asked.

So, with such hopefully noble sentiments of professorial wisdom, the first two books of *The Republic* are bravely assigned.

A few days later, the class reassembles. Looks of confusion abound. One brave young man on the way in tells you, earnestly, that he could make nothing of the book. The adventure begins.

"Why was Socrates at the Piraeus?" Indeed, "What was the Piraeus anyhow?" "When did Socrates live? — say, within 500 years, either way?" Few will know. But that is all right. The students will learn quickly. 399 B.C. is easy to remember somehow. "And what was the conversation with Cephalus about?"

In the beginning, not all of the students will be sufficiently liberally educated to commence with the actual text, the text you want them to own, hold, and mark. They are not yet free to begin where Socrates began, with the raw argument, with the common opinion itself, with *what is* before them.

"How come Plato sets up all those straw men so easy to knock down?" a skeptical student inquires. A mild look of pain comes to the professor's face, to the not so humble man who is himself still trying to knock down in his own mind such enigmatic straw men.

"Wasn't Plato the cause of Hitler?"

"At least they have heard of Hitler", you mutter to yourself, somewhat relieved.

"Wasn't Plato an elitist? a racist?" The clear implication snakes out: we ought not to read Plato. He is dangerous.

So you leap to Plato's defense: "So you think we ought not to read him? We ought to censor him perhaps?" Then you are carried away. "Do you not know that the idea that books we read affect us comes from Plato? That the theory of censorship you advocate is also from Plato? That to refute Plato you need Plato?" Of course, they do not know such things; how could they?

Yet suddenly in your very class, any class on Plato, all the problems and prejudices described in *The Republic* itself are alive and well in a typical lecture hall in the late twentieth century. The class as yet is unprepared to live the examined life, unaccustomed to allow a problem to arise, to be stated before a definitive answer to it be given.

Fortunately, you have read your Plato, about the vanities of old tutors, about the arguing amusements of the young just beginning to wonder about wondering, about wisdom and philosophy amidst their passions and even amidst their own incipient injustices, the ones they are not yet old enough to believe they themselves could commit.

So, patiently, "Be slow. You do not yet know where Plato is going, what his method is, what his certainties. He is the father of philosophy. For now, trust a little in the judgment of mankind. It is not always wrong."

You repeat, helplessly: "All thought is a commentary on Plato." The students do not know you are quoting somebody.

The students before you are skeptical, as they should be, as Plato said they would be. "How could anything written 2500 years ago be relevant?" The pain again comes into your eyes. How you hate the word "relevant"! But you know you once thought the same way. You recall in *The Apology* how the potential philosophers, the young men, delighted in imitating Socrates to the annoyance of their fathers, the ones who persecuted Socrates for daring even to be a philosopher.

Yet at this moment, you know, hopefully—for you have by now taught, led many classes through Plato—that when they have reached the Myth of Er and the Night Guardians, when Plato tells them that if they do not choose to be just and good in this life, they will never be able to choose anything else but the paltry things they choose in fact, then they will begin to wonder if anything more significant has been said in the meantime, in the 2500 years.

When you answer, answer your own question, about why Plato is relevant, you find yourself admitting, "Well, yes, perhaps Plato's pupil Aristotle would qualify. He could well have been wiser." You catch the eyes of the students again in doubt. For it is difficult to let go of Plato. And you know that no one writes like Plato. The first experience of reading Plato will never come again. No other voice will sound as his does. And yet, the voice of Plato will come again, for rereading Plato, every time you read him again, you insist once more, is to read him for the first time.

Nonetheless, you, aging professor that you are, have been listening to the raucous music these dear young scholars blare at you from their campus windows. You ask them again the perennial question, the one you ask every class—"Was Plato right after all about music and politics: What you like reveals what you become? That change in music portends the first sign of political change?" You speculate about these things out loud to your class. "Can Plato even be read with a stereo?" You suspect perhaps he can. The class wonders, by this time, if it is still possible to change classes.

So after the fourth book, a confused, harried student admits: "This is the hardest thing I have ever read." You answer: "It is the hardest thing I have ever read too." The student does not believe you, of course. But you are telling the truth.

And so class continues, dialogue fashion, as Plato taught.

"What is it that Socrates hoped to learn from Cephalus?" Someone responds correctly "that the old have almost finished a journey we all must follow". You are pleased at the answer, though, as ever, worried somewhat by it, for you, dear Professor, are already along the way, a considerable way down the same journey and by no means as rich as Cephalus was, nor indeed as poor as Socrates seemed to have preferred the philosopher to be. Nor do you have as much to say about the journey as you once thought you would. "And what was the definition of justice that the old man left, the one that began the argument?" "And what was the second definition?" "And what was the third?"

Then the student who asked about Plato and Hitler puts up his hand again. He still thinks the professor a fascist for teaching Plato with some sympathy, this before even coming to the eighth and ninth books where Socrates rejects such tyranny in what still must be its most graphic condemnation in political thought. Half the students have been told in high school or in philosophy or history class, or even, alas, in the government department, that Plato was a fascist. Karl Popper's annoyingly selective misinterpretation still persists.

So, learnedly, you recall Professor Morrow's address at Ohio State back in 1940, not too far from when this generation of students' parents was born. Morrow analyzed how both the German and Russian professors claimed Plato for themselves.[1] So Plato is now not just a fascist but also a communist, the father of all those who believe we can cure human ills by rearranging our property laws.

Then you recount, as you often do, the story of the young Hungarian student in your class in Rome some time ago. He told the class of potential Latin European and Latin American

---

[1] Glenn R. Morrow, "Plato and the Rule of Law", *Plato II*, ed. G. Vlastos (New York: Doubleday Anchor, 1971), pp. 144–65.

revolutionary clerical sympathizers that in Hungary no one was allowed to study *The Republic.*

"Why didn't the Hungarian government want Plato studied?" you question. Finally, someone answers, "Because it asks about the best possible state?" "Yes, that is it, because a government that insists to its citizens that they already live in the best possible state does not want anyone wondering about a better society. No subversive Plato allowed."

Next, you wonder out loud if the Christian religious orders did not also have something to do with the fifth book of *The Republic,* the chapter on women, children, and property. You gently suggest that no one is a more radical female liberationist than Plato. No one is yet ready to go as far as he did. You wonder if there is not some relation between Plato's eugenics program and the birth of the test-tube baby in England several years ago.

But back to religious orders. The Christians seemed to have solved Plato's problem by simply vowing no property and no wives to their "guardians".[2] "Could the Platonic purpose be achieved in another way?" Again quizzical looks.

"And who was the greatest Christian commentator on Plato?" you ask. "Machiavelli?" someone tries. You try not to notice. "Augustine?" You are pleased.

The suspicion begins to arise that everyone took something from Plato. With this suspicion, you are satisfied, for that is the truth. You offer a pedantic conclusion. "First, be loyal to Plato, not to part of him, or to what others wrongly or even rightly deduced from him."

---

[2] See James V. Schall, "The Christian Guardians", *The Politics of Heaven and Hell: Christian Themes from Classical, Medieval, and Modern Political Philosophy* (Lanham, Md.: University Press of America, 1984), pp. 67–82.

"But did not Plato teach the state to lie?" You again suppress the temptation to wonder if the students of today really believe lying to be wrong theoretically, morally. If not, of course, Plato would be doing just what they think right. A colleague, perhaps wiser, also teaching this same Plato suggests that the students are pure nominalists, looking on academic political philosophy as a kind of intellectual supermarket in which they can fill the baskets of their minds with this and that in a kind of mental impulse buying. Anyhow, they seem to be appalled that the state can lie, even if they do not think lying wrong, even if they live in a republic in which the public order of recent times has been torn apart, most vividly, by apparent lying.

And you are not so sure your colleague is wrong either. So you congratulate the class in thinking it wrong for the government to lie. After all, if they did not, how could they be angry at Nixon, and everyone is still angry at Nixon!

But then, loyal again to Plato: "Did not Plato love Homer?" They nod.

"And what was the reason he wanted to censor Homer?"

"Because he thought Homer lied about the gods" (383).

"So a government ought to be concerned in the name of truth about the truths its poets and novelists teach?"

They are silent. And so are you.

Then you tell them about all the government-controlled radio networks you have heard in the various countries in the world you have visited. We all want our nominalism. We all want to condemn lying. We all want to live in the best state and in our own too.

To conclude: the first principle in teaching Plato is that Plato is his own best teacher. You are sad on finishing *The Republic* and *The Apology* because you know that such literary power will not be found again in any required product of subsequent political philosophers—except perhaps Augustine. Then you belatedly notice that a current book of readings you have selected to illustrate great political thinking contains nothing of Augustine, or of Aquinas either.[3] Plato was right to talk about censorship. Often today, intellectuals themselves perform this operation better than governments.

The first task of the professor in the already late twentieth century, or in any other time, for that matter, is not to stand in the way, not to be an obstacle to this crucial function of political science departments: that of insisting, encouraging, wanting Plato to be read, carefully, slowly, completely, by each student, preferably each year.

"If you read Plato only once, you have failed Plato. And if you have failed Plato, you have failed yourself."

Salvador de Madariaga once said that our culture should give to each man and woman, when each reaches the age of voting, a sturdy, elegant book containing an account of the death of Socrates and the death of Christ, the two men in the ancient world who never wrote a book, the two who were killed by the state.[4]

And so once again in class you point out that Plato already asked the questions of what would happen to the good man if he appeared in any existing state (361). Glaucon spoke for us all: "They will tell you that the just man who is thought unjust will be scourged, racked, bound—will have his eyes burnt out, and, at last, after suffering every kind of evil, he will be impaled. . . . "

The class is again silent. By this second reading all are aware

[3] John Somerville and Ronald E. Santoni, eds., *Social and Political Philosophy* (Garden City, N.Y.: Doubleday Anchor, 1963).

[4] Salvador de Madariaga, "Europe of the Four Karls", *The Tablet*, London, June 23, 1973.

that Socrates was talking not just about the ancient Athenians, not about someone else, but about ourselves, the readers, about our own principles, our own control, our own blindness.

Plato wrote *The Republic,* the lecture concludes, because the best state killed the best man. This is what began political theory.

When you leave class, you do not know if these same students will ever read Plato again. You know you will — partly because a new class will be in with much the same questions next semester. You solemnly believe of yourself no doubt, that you would reread Plato for himself, for the sake of praising truth and justice, not for reward or punishment, not to seem to be learned rather than to be so.

What you do not know is what you would do if you met the just man in the just state, or more especially in the unjust one, the one in which you are relatively sure you now live. You want, in any case, to think Plato to have been wrong, at least in your case.

So you return to your study. Somehow you feel you should read one last time to the class the end of book VIII, or was it book IX? Yes, book IX (592):

> Glaucon: I understand; you mean that he will be the ruler in that city of which we are the founders, and which exists in idea only; for I do not believe that there is such a one any place on earth?
>
> Socrates: In heaven, I replied, there is laid up a pattern of it, methinks, which he who desires may behold, and beholding may set his house in order. But whether such a one exists, or even will exist in fact, is no matter; for he will live after the manner of that city, having nothing to do with any other.

You again realize it is risky to be a teacher of Plato, to reread such passages each year to students who never heard them before. If you were sure Plato were wrong, it would be easier. And as you get older, you wonder, you begin to suspect he was wrong on fewer and fewer things.

Perhaps we should not read Plato after all. What was the old Latin saying? *Amicus Socrates, Amicus Plato, magis Amicus Veritas.* What you discovered this year, in rereading Plato, was that this is mostly what Plato himself said (391).

In the end, it is true: we cannot refute Plato without Plato.

Four Books and Two Essays to Help You Begin Wondering about Plato

1. Josef Pieper, *Enthusiasm and the Divine Madness: On the Platonic Dialogue "Phaedrus".*
2. Eric Voegelin, *Order and History.* Vol. 3, *Plato and Aristotle.*
3. John Wild, *Plato's Modern Enemies and the Theory of Natural Law.*
4. Leo Strauss, *Studies in Platonic Political Philosophy.*
5. Allan Bloom, "Interpretative Essay," in the Basic Books edition of Plato, *The Republic.*
6. Thomas Pangle, "Interpretative Essay," in the Basic Books edition of Plato, *The Laws.*

Part Two

Books You Will Never Be Assigned

Introduction

In this section, what I want to do essentially is to provide reviews of certain books that I think help us gain some insight into the heart of reality. This section is, if you will, a continued discussion of Chapter 2, "Why Read?" These are not reviews of Shakespeare's *Hamlet* or of Machiavelli's *The Prince* or of the truths of faith. Yet, I think, they are books that enable us to see that we should know about certain things and that such knowledge is possible.

All of the reviews in this section take us to the highest things in one way or another. In the previous section of this book, I mentioned a collection of essays on education by Jacques Maritain. One of these essays was entitled "The Education of Women".[1] I had observed over the years the very different reaction young men and young women have with regard to the classical discussions of the highest things. This had always perplexed me, though Chesterton's book *What's Wrong with the World?* and Gertrude von le Fort's *Eternal Woman* went a long way toward explaining how man and woman could react in his or her own individual person to the same higher things to which each is called.

I had discussed this with my perceptive friend from Cincinnati, Anne Burleigh. And though this section does not discuss this difference, I feel it is important to report what Anne Burleigh had to say on this topic, since the spirit of these reviews is the confrontation of the highest things:

[1] Jacques Maritain, "The Education of Women", *The Education of Man: The Educational Philosophy of Jacques Maritain*, ed. Donald and Idella Gallagher (Garden City, N.Y.: Doubleday, 1963), pp. 154–58.

That was a very interesting piece by Maritain on "The Education of Women", which you sent to me. It gives me much pause. I wish I could re-cast what he is saying in my own words, but somehow I cannot get a good enough handle on what he means. I have just a general idea of how young men and women absorb things differently. How would you describe what he is talking about?

I do think he is correct when he says that girls want ideas to come right into their lives. But then so do boys, don't they? I wonder if you might try something, a little experiment, next time you are teaching Leo Strauss or Eric Voegelin to some girls. And let me know what happens.

Could you try to let them know ahead of time that the ideas of these men will be something that the girls can take into the core of their lives? I wonder if you might try giving your students some brief lectures on some practical considerations, moral questions, that they face every day and how these questions apply to Strauss and Voegelin. You will need to touch on the whole problem of pluralism, that is, on the problem of whether truth exists. You will need to tell them to look at what is real, the real nature of men and women.

Too, it would seem so important to get across to the students that how they *act* is intimately related to their intellectual life. They cannot think straight if they do not act right. And acting right is something that does not come entirely naturally. Somebody has to help them think through things. Ideas and beliefs are so exciting. They call for great passion, for stout hearts and disciplined minds. They call for great movements of the will, in the sense of deciding to stake one's life on them, on dying for them if necessary. It seems to me that girls ought to understand that. Girls are naturally so willing to give everything they have. And that is just where they are vulnerable. It has to be giving to the right thing, the right person, in the right circumstances.

These words are, of course, very powerful ones, words that

end with intimations of Aristotle's discussions of how to act in his *Ethics.*

I will not try the experiment Anne Burleigh suggested to me here, except to remark that, as Plato recalled, men and women are called to the same higher truths and goods and realities and that their right relationship to one another depends on their understanding and loving the higher things in their own being. Each person sees this understanding and love in the being of another whom they choose. This is but a variant, perhaps the profoundest variant, of Aristotle's moving discussion on friendship in the same *Ethics,* particularly where he discusses (in bk. VIII, chap. 12) whether husbands and wives can be friends in the highest sense.

What I am interested here in emphasizing is the seriousness with which our lives are endowed, a seriousness that does not at all exclude humor, but rather is based in an ultimate joy, as Chesterton related at the end of *Orthodoxy.* And I wish to point out that the seriousness of our lives, the tragedies, the loves, the sacrifice, that we are called on to confront in the reality given to us, in the real difference between men and women, will itself be a path by which we can be "educated" in the highest things, even though prevailing cultural and academic philosophies allow no final meaning and seriousness to our actions.

The problems of whether truth exists, how to take it into the core of our being, how to see the reality even though we are constantly deflected from it by our culture—for our environment is a moral one—these issues need to be seen, in spite of our "education". I have found the books in this section, often obscure ones, to provide a path to this seriousness in which men and women exist. They are initial reminders that reality is that from which we begin to know. We do not create it, but we can will against it. Anne Burleigh was correct; there is a relation between our thinking and our acting in reality.

Four Beginning, Though Difficult, Books
by Leo Strauss and Eric Voegelin

1. Leo Strauss, *City and Man.*
2. Eric Voegelin, *Science, Politics, and Gnosticism.*
3. Leo Strauss, *What Is Political Philosophy?*
4. Eric Voegelin, *The New Science of Politics.*

Two Essays by Anne Burleigh

1. "Twenty Years After Damascus", *Crisis,* March 1986, pp. 6–13.
2. "Ancient Cathedrals, Modern Pilgrims", *Crisis,* November 1986, pp. 26–31.
3. "Pluralism, Religious Belief, and Civic Virtue", *Crisis,* October 1987, pp. 24–29.

Seven Books of Christopher Dawson on Religion and Culture

1. *The Judgment of the Nations.*
2. *The Making of Europe.*
3. *Religion and the Rise of Western Culture.*
4. *The Movement of World Revolution.*
5. *Beyond Politics.*
6. *Christianity and the New Age.*
7. *The Dynamics of World History.*

Chapter Seven

Straining for the Highest Things

(*This chapter is a consideration of*
Ralph McInerny's book St. Thomas Aquinas.)

The recruitment of alert young scholars to a consideration of
the highest things, no doubt, has had its dangers. We should
have all read, at least sometime, Plato's *The Apology of Socrates,*
in which we learn that one of the causes of Socrates' death
concerned this very attraction of potential young philosophers
to the higher things. Further, this consideration has been
hampered by the young scholar's own lack of experience and
virtue, as well as his difficulty in ascertaining how he might go
about the endeavor.

Few universities, it seems, need worry about killing Socrates
a second time, something Aristotle worried about. Of course,
the young scholar is told, and rightly so, to read the greatest
books, to read them very carefully, like a rabbi with Scripture
or a William of Moerbeke with the text of the same Aristotle.
The student is to be alert to learn what these precious texts say
openly and, more ominously, what they hint in secret and in
circumspection, a topic Leo Strauss returned to again and
again.[1]

Often, let us acknowledge, such a student cannot turn to
his teachers, even if he goes to them; they do not know.
Often, too, he cannot go by himself to the greatest teachers not
alive in his lifetime, because he does not know *how* to read

[1] Leo Strauss, *Persecution and the Art of Writing* (New York: Free Press,
1952).

69

them in books or, even, *whether* to read them, so much else is "going on" and he does not want to miss out. He finds himself imprisoned in a flood of facts, now aided by computers in every dormitory room, along with the music, with little or no sense of their meaning or whether they could bear on anything outside his own desires or those of his fellows.

What was it *The Times* of London wrote recently?

> It is hardly surprising ... that so many people in Europe are being tempted to reject the rigours of ... mental self-discipline when in schools, churches and universities they have been encouraged for so long to regard all forms of discipline as unwelcome.[2]

The grain thus falls on barren ground, while an infinite multiplicity of explanations vie in the academic marketplace, itself largely isolated from life. Philosophers generate myriad speculations. Professors go off on endless tangents. All departmental faculties are of equal import.

Here, briefly, I will suggest what will surely look like an unlikely way to begin, at least, to inquire rightly about the ultimate issues on which we should spend, as much as we can, what little time we have, as Aristotle told us in the last book of *The Ethics.* These issues are most often neglected in political science, among other places, even though, for the most part, a right ordering of political things is necessary before the ultimate things appear to most men. The daemon of Socrates was, then, not wholly unnecessary in the normal city to call us out of our immersion in passing things.

I will here suggest to the student, then, to the one who begins to wonder and to think—and he may be a very old

[2] Editorial, *The Times,* London, December 18, 1982.

man, as Cicero recounted in a famous essay, "On Old Age"—
that he should quietly read a few books, small ones, to be
sure.[3] If these books do not "speak" to the student about that
which he is wondering, he should put them down and go
away, perhaps sad, perhaps not, to recall the fate of the rich
young man in the Gospel of Luke (18:18–23). One book will
be about Plato, one about Aristotle, one about Augustine.
One will be named after a famous medieval book, yet another
will be called, simply, *philosophy;* one, curiously, will be about
reason and revelation. Two final books about Thomas Aquinas
should be read when the earlier ones are completed, probably
not before. One is by Josef Pieper, and one is by Ralph
McInerny, whose remarks originally occasioned these reflections on the place of political philosophy in the range of
things.

The books, some of which I have already mentioned, are
these—books, as you will see, that constitute another list:

1. Allan Bloom's translation of Plato, *The Republic,* with his
   interpretative essay.
2. Henry Veatch, *Aristotle: A Contemporary Appreciation.*
3. Herbert Deane, *Political and Social Ideas of St. Augustine.*
4. E. F. Schumacher, *A Guide for the Perplexed.*
5. J. M. Bochenski, *Philosophy: An Introduction.*
6. Etienne Gilson, *Reason and Revelation in the Middle Ages.*
7. Josef Pieper, *The Silence of St. Thomas.*
8. Ralph McInerny, *St. Thomas Aquinas.*

These books reinforce each other in the pursuit of the highest
things. And there are others to be noted, such as Ernest Fortin's
Political Idealism and Christianity in the Thought of St. Augustine,

---

[3] Marcus Tullius Cicero, "On Old Age", in *Selected Works,* ed. Michael
Grant (Baltimore: Penguin, 1962), pp. 211–50.

Charles N. R. McCoy's *The Structure of Political Thought,* and
G. K. Chesterton's *St. Thomas Aquinas* (in *Collected Works of
G. K. Chesterton*).

But let me explain what I am doing. I am "recruiting", to
use Leo Strauss' phrase from Machiavelli. For what? I would
say, no doubt, "for the truth", but we have all read the words
of Pontius Pilate, the Roman governor in Judea, addressed to
Christ: "What is truth?" (Jn 18:38) I am recruiting those who
have passed through the family, the schools, and business,
through politics to political philosophy, but who now begin to
suspect something more needs to be confronted, philosophy
itself, perhaps even more. Perhaps we are also listeners as well
as thinkers.

For the students I am concerned about are the ones who
have worried about the unanswered questions in books VIII and
IX of *The Ethics* of Aristotle, those about friendship and
justice, the cruelty of the latter and the warmth of the former.
So I am recruiting for those interested in the whole but who
insist that nothing be compromised on the ascent, the inheri-
tors of Adeimantos and Glaucon, who wanted to listen to the
highest things praised for their own sakes.

But, secretly, I am also recruiting the cleric, now usually so
hopelessly lost in politics that he confuses justice with goodness.
I want to see if I can interest the cleric again in what is *not*
political. Machiavelli was right in a way: the last thing politics
needs is the cleric who has lost his faith but not his zeal, the one
who ends up benightedly destroying actual political life by
praising politics as such. He sees now a Mao and then a Stalin,
and even a Nicaragua, and calls them the Kingdom of God.

Malcolm Muggeridge had been long perplexed by this
phenomenon of apparently intelligent men and women not
seeing where evidently good ideas might lead. This incapacity
seems to be particularly serious in many religious and aca-

demic minds of our era. Muggeridge, after he had been disillu-
sioned by Stalin's regime in the Moscow of the late 1920s,
wrote in his wonderful autobiography, *The Chronicles of Wasted
Time*, of his assignment to the International Labor Organization in Geneva:

> As a place of pilgrimage, Geneva lacked the melodrama of
> Moscow; its cult more fatuous than sinister. Yet, just as, pounding
> round the Red Square, I endlessly asked myself how it came
> about that the choicest spirits of the age—all the gurus and
> dancing dervishes of enlightenment—prostrated themselves
> before a brutish tyrant like Stalin, so, pounding along the Quai
> Woodrow Wilson, I kept wondering what Pied Piper had been
> able to lead them to the shores of this sullen Lake, endlessly
> expecting to find there Tennyson's Parliament of Man and
> Federation of the World. In both cases, as it seemed to me, the
> significant thing was the ready acceptance of fantasy as reality;
> even a predilection in favour of fantasy, and a corresponding
> abhorrence of reality. Why?[4]

Those who follow this latter path, the reason for which
Muggeridge so poignantly queried "why?" are perhaps already
recruited to the sound of another ideological trumpet, though
we have read *Darkness at Noon*, and we know about the
gulags, thanks to Solzhenitsyn. But we are looking for the
eminently teachable, for those who know that they know not
and that there is much yet to know, who begin to suspect that
evil can somehow also be attractive to bright minds, as Plato
already taught, and Augustine too.

Political philosophy, clearly, is not related to philosophy
merely as part to whole. Nor was Strauss' question at the end
of *City and Man*, "*Quid sit Deus?*"—What is God?—improperly

[4] Malcolm Muggeridge, *Chronicles of Wasted Time: The Infernal Grove*,
vol. 2 (New York: Morrow, 1974), p. 16.

placed at the end of a discussion of classical political philosophers. And the *City and Man* was a book that began with a consideration of what we could know about the "queen of the social sciences", that is, political philosophy, by our own unaided powers. Only when we knew what we could know by our own powers, it was suggested, could we then begin to confront the Divine City of Righteousness.

The city, in some sense, as Socrates' life suggested to the young Plato, must be constructed in a way to allow questions of the highest import to be asked. The common good of the city itself requires that some of us, perhaps all of us, wonder about what transcends the city at its highest perfection. Moreover, if, as Harry Jaffa noted in his beautiful eulogy of Leo Strauss, questions of reason and revelation are of great moment, the city should not be fashioned so that, in principle, truths of revelation and metaphysics are excluded from its environment, however much political philosophy is not revelation, however much the statesman as such does not rise above questions that only law can deal with.[5] Law itself is limited by that in man and reality which surpasses it. That is, there are fundamental questions that politics cannot properly deal with.

The law of the city, then, leads to law of nature, and nature leads to origins and causes, ends and means. Yet we also know from Solzhenitsyn that time spent in the gulags of the worst state is marvelously purifying as a teacher of what is not merely politics.[6] The highest end of man can be reached in the worst state. But perhaps it takes Augustine as well as Aquinas for us to see this clearly.

[5] Harry V. Jaffa, "Leo Strauss, 1899–1973", *The Conditions of Freedom: Essays in Political Philosophy* (Baltimore: Johns Hopkins University Press, 1975), pp. 3–8.

[6] See Aleksandr Solzhenitsyn "The World Split Apart: The Harvard Address," in *Solzhenitsyn at Harvard,* ed. Ronald Berman (Washington, D.C.: Ethics and Public Policy Center, 1980), pp. 3–20.

Revelation appears in the modern city more and more as politics, almost as if it intends to teach that politics is what revelation is about. *The City of God,* to be sure, was written to suggest that revelation was *not* primarily about politics. The City of God in revelation limited the ambition of the city of man. This allowed it to be merely the city of man with no pretensions of becoming itself the City of God. Augustine read Plato well. The modern attempt to define revelation as politics, therefore, appears to political philosophers who read the classics as a confirmation of an ancient suspicion— the one that suggested that the highest practical science, politics for Aristotle, is itself the highest science there is, as such.

Politics, thus, has come to be seen as ontology. Consequently, presupposed to no given or created being, the modern political task is said to be the construction of a polis out of the minds of the best thinkers. This was called gnosticism in the ancient world. Some, such as Eric Voegelin, still call it that in the modern world. Contemplation and action become interchangeable. Revelation now merely seems to confirm ideology, so that the context of the latter is given cohesive moral strength from the reserves of enthusiasm in the former.

But nothing so radically new as original being itself is permitted in the ideological city, where *what is* is only what is thought and what is enforced by men. Many mystics run about, not illogically, trying to put the project of the fifth book of *The Republic* into existence, rather than, as Allan Bloom would have it, allowing Plato to teach us that such mystical projects finally destroy our real cities. Because it is not the highest science, politics is limited. Yet, we must search for the highest things. We must seek to erect cities where the search is not forbidden, even though in those cities where it is not forbidden, it is not often pursued. Still, the recruitment goes on.

This brings me finally to McInerny's *St. Thomas Aquinas.*
At first sight, political philosophers will list this book, as do its
publishers, only under the category of philosophy. Since it is
about Aquinas, it might also be listed under theology. Indeed,
since it is about Aquinas, it is properly listed under theology,
philosophy, and political theory, for it belongs to all three
disciplines as a reminder of their orderly relationship to each
other. Henry Veatch, in his book *Aristotle: A Contemporary
Appreciation,* surely an apt companion volume to McInerny's
book, suggested that we treat Aristotle as if he were a modern
philosopher, since the modern experiment that built itself on
rejecting him has itself now largely failed, a position similar to
that also argued brilliantly by Leon Kass in his book *Toward a
More Natural Science.*[7]

Likewise, we can argue on the same basis for a renewed
consideration of Aquinas in theology, philosophy, and political philosophy. Aquinas, the medieval writer who stands at the
very fountainhead of wisdom itself, is ever at the threshold
of renewing our thought. In this sense, I can agree with
McInerny's principal observation that Aquinas read Aristotle
correctly, contrary to several contentions in, say, Strauss, Jaeger,
and Jaffa.[8] On this basis, of course, we can focus on that
key passage in Leo Strauss' *Natural Right and History,* where
Strauss rejected some of Aquinas' observations because they
were arrived at with the aid of Christian revelation.[9]

---

[7] Leon Kass, *Toward a More Natural Science: Biology and Human Affairs*
(New York: Free Press, 1985).

[8] See Leo Strauss, *Natural Right and History* (Chicago: University of
Chicago Press, 1953); Werner W. Jaeger, *Aristotle: Fundamentals of the Hist-
ory of His Development,* trans. R. Robinson (London: Oxford, 1948); Harry
V. Jaffa, *Thomism and Aristotelianism* (Westport, Conn.: Greenwood, 1979).

[9] Strauss, *Natural Right and History,* p. 164.

What McInerny does, and this is why his book also fits properly into political philosophy, is to show how it is "reasonable" to allow revelation to be directed at natural intellect for its instruction precisely as natural intellect.

In suggesting the centrality of those truths that are both revealed and reasoned, then, McInerny showed how it is that revelation does not contradict nature, however much it may be beyond it in some areas of this life. This is not because the truths ascribed only to revelation are intrinsically "unintelligible", but because we are finite beings exposed to a higher intelligence than that natural to ourselves. That is, there is more intelligibility of being than is due to the sort of substance we possess ourselves.

The great problem of both politics and revelation, however, is that men remain only men in thinking about the perfect polis, in thinking about the good, in thinking about God. This means in logic, then, that the truths found in revelation that are also found in reason will be found to be rational in experience and in thought. And those truths that are purely revealed truths will be found noncontradictory to reason as we possess it in such a way that they "ironically", to use a favorite word of Strauss, shed light on real problems and difficulties that the philosophers and political philosophers have, in perplexity, encountered. Incarnation, creation, resurrection, grace, in other words, are not merely irrational surds from unintelligible revelation, but prods to our intellects already wrestling with enigmas that seem insolvable.

This is why it is a "grace", as it were, to have a Plato, an Aristotle, a Thucydides, and a Cicero, the classical political philosophers, on the scene before the revelational tradition is present intellectually in an Augustine, an Al-Farabi, a

Maimonides, or an Aquinas.[10] Theology is not merely a "mythical" explanation, a "civil religion" designed to keep the nonphilosophic masses satisfied while the philosophers contemplate the higher things by their own powers. Rather, revelation suggests that there can be an affirmative answer to the question of whether ultimately every human person, on that account alone, whatever be his regime, can attain the highest object of intellect and being.

Nevertheless, through Aquinas and Augustine, revelation also suggests that the locus of this attainment of the highest things is not precisely a political regime in this world, not even a pure philosophic power, but a gift addressed to that power of intellect which is appropriate to each individual being who properly possesses it. This is ultimately the reason why politics is free to be politics and not metaphysics or revelation, something Aristotle sensed in book X of *The Ethics,* when he distinguished two kinds of happiness, something Hannah Arendt also suggested with her views on natality, mortality, immortality, and eternity.[11]

The recruitment of young scholars presupposes both that they have original intellects and wills *and* enough curiosity and wonder to sense that the ultimate questions are not adequately broached in the schools, in the great books, or especially in the polis. We have read that rich young men, good young men, can go away sad. The Aristotelian and Platonic discussions of the decline of regimes are, from one point of view, nothing but accounts of what it is we can choose that is less than the best, not denying that less than the best *is* and in itself, as Genesis says, likewise good.

[10] On this point, see C. S. Lewis, "Modern Man and His Categories of Thought", in *Present Concerns: Ethical Essays* (London: Collins, 1986), pp. 61–66.

[11] Hannah Arendt, *The Human Condition* (Garden City, N.Y.: Doubleday Anchor, 1959).

Fortunately, McInerny never lets the reader forget that for all his massive intelligence, Aquinas never failed to teach us about prayer, about the fact that what political philosophy and philosophy itself pointed to also came to us from outside politics and philosophy as a gift. The import of this should not be lost on the young scholar, for it suggests, as Stanley Jaki noted in his powerful *The Road of Science and the Ways to God,* that the issues of creation and finite essence drive us back to a nothing that is not simply nothing.[12] McInerny's book is a perceptive recounting of the meaning of these ideas.

The political philosopher also has a stake in the origins of the finite, stable being *ex nihilo* as well as in the permanence of those kinds of being that Aristotle indicated when he said whoever lives naturally without the city is either a beast or a god. We humans are a certain kind of beings who, through our minds, as Aristotle said, are *capax omnium,* capable of knowing all things. The whole world is given to us, and we remain only ourselves, the mortals. Men would not wish to have everything, as Aristotle remarked, if it meant ceasing to be themselves. Friendship is the highest act among us because it exchanges the highest things without taking anything away.[13] That Aristotle should have wondered on this very basis about friendship with God is, in the light of the discourses in John's Gospel at the Last Supper, precisely *thought* provoking. That is to say, unless our young recruits legitimately know, feel, and love the good of being—something Plato and Aristotle knew would be

[12] Stanley L. Jaki, *The Road of Science and the Ways to God* (Chicago: University of Chicago Press, 1978).

[13] See Gilbert C. Meilaender, *Friendship: A Study in Theological Ethics* (Notre Dame, Ind.: University of Notre Dame Press, 1981). See also the final chapter of James V. Schall, *Redeeming the Time* (New York: Sheed and Ward, 1968).

difficult for them to do, along with their perplexities as long as they are in the human condition — they will not recognize gifts when they are given, even though the giving is not a demand or a right.

Leo Strauss and Eric Voegelin, then, were correct to worry about the ongoing ravages of modern natural right thought because it leaves, logically, only an anthropologically self-centered and self-contained world that cannot even explain man to himself. The reabsorption of the revelational tradition into economics and politics beginning with the Enlightenment has cut off many from the founts of *what is.* The recovery of political philosophy is probably, then, a first and necessary step to the recovery of philosophy itself.

The importance of McInerny's book on Aquinas for our purposes here, then, is this: neither political philosophy nor philosophy can be fully reconsidered without each person arriving at the necessary questions that come from just living in the world. Modern political philosophy, with its ethical and metaphysical presuppositions, has often begun to wonder about the classical questions because its own answers are not working. The confusion within modern revelational religion, however, has often convinced the political philosopher and the philosophers themselves that they were on the right track in the first place, because religion was busy imitating ideology, not confronting being itself.

Ralph McInerny's book on Aquinas sets the intellectual stage for a recalling of religion back from ideology to being. At the same time, it addresses to the political philosopher and to the other philosophers those lines of thought that must arise if both philosophy and political philosophy "think" properly about precisely *human* being. The project of a Strauss or a Voegelin is correct. The modern project is a false turn. What seems yet lacking is the intelligence to admit that revelation does contain intelligence directed to human intelligence, where human intelligence is thinking and living correctly.

Chesterton has argued that the primary difficulty with the central tradition of revelation is that it is too good to be true. We know, however, that goodness and truth are interchangeable. This means, at a minimum, the willingness to consider the limits of the queen of the social sciences within a real openness to being, to thought that confronts our conception of *what is,* of what we are. The prospects for doing this are brighter because of McInerny's valuable *St. Thomas Aquinas.* It is a book I would put on all my lists.

Eight Books on St. Thomas Aquinas

1. G. K. Chesterton, Collected Works. Vol. 2, *St. Thomas Aquinas.*
2. Josef Pieper, *Guide to Thomas Aquinas.*
3. Thomas Aquinas, *St. Thomas Aquinas,* vol. I, *Philosophical Texts,* vol. II, *Theological Texts,* ed. and trans. Thomas Gilby.
4. Jacques Maritain, *The Angelic Doctor: The Life and Thought of St. Thomas Aquinas.*
5. Frederick Copleston, *Aquinas.*
6. *One Hundred Years of Thomism,* edited by Victor Brezik.
7. Thomas A. Weisheipl, *Friar Thomas D'Aquino: His Life, Thought, and Works.*
8. Thomas Gilby, *Between Community and Society.*

Chapter Eight

The Supernatural Destiny of Man

(This chapter is an account of the book
Shakespeare as a Political Thinker,
edited by John Alvis and Thomas G. West.)

For a long time, political philosophy has needed, even to save its own integrity, to rediscover the classical tradition as a basis for understanding the place of politics within the human enterprise. Through the work of Leo Strauss, Hannah Arendt, Jacques Maritain, and Eric Voegelin, this endeavor has largely been accomplished, at least for those with eyes to see. But in re-covering the classics— Plato, Aristotle, Thucydides, Xenophon, Cicero—there has been an embarrassed, unsettling silence about the place of revelation of the Old and New Testaments, es-pecially, and also of Islam.

Political philosophy in the modern era has believed it could be sufficient unto itself so that it was not even open to a hint of any intelligence not reduced to exclusively rationalist confines. The result was—since religion continued to be and even in many ways increased being a major factor in human affairs, in the lives of most men, in most places, and in most eras—an incapacity of political philosophy and those formally trained in it to account for the way men really act and why.

Political philosophy, thus, tried to explain human action in categories drawn exclusively from an understanding of man as abstracted from transcendent realities and considerations. This position ironically resulted in a view of religion that described its motivations and institutions as "political" and thereby prevented any adequate comprehension of why men really act as they do in major areas of their lives. Reality was "reduced" to the methods used to discover it.

The narrowness of such modern political philosophy forced the Straussians and the Voegelinians, as the major proponents of the revival of the classics, to treat revelation with extreme care, if not actually in secret writing. No one wanted to scandalize, as it were, the academic moderns by appearing to take revelation too seriously, even when it was clear that faith must be taken into account if political philosophy itself were to understand even itself and its own intrinsic limits. Athens, Jerusalem, Rome—even Mecca, as Strauss recognized—loomed in the background of a discipline that prided itself on imitating modern natural science. The endeavor of being like unto science, however, did not reckon, as Stanley Jaki has shown, with the relation of this same science to the doctrines of creation and finite essence, doctrines, theological or philosophical, refined within the tradition of revelation.

Modern political philosophy, consequently, has not known how to broach revelation as an element intrinsic to its own integrity, to its own understanding of itself within Western intellectual experience. The "modern project", as Strauss called it, was simply to rid ourselves of revelation, to lower our sights, in order to erect a society according to norms that man could make "for himself", on the grounds that only what man could know of his own power was worthy to exist in the first place. The only trouble with this approach was that the elevated goals of the Christian tradition did not cease to lure the modern political thinker even when the faith that originated and sustained them disappeared. The fruitless effort to find a "natural" substitute for supernatural motivations is, in one sense, what the modern political philosophy of the Left is about; it is both its rationale and its terrible danger.

The merit of *Shakespeare as a Political Thinker,* and it is an

inestimable merit, is its discovery, almost from outside of political theory itself—though the relation of art to politics is, as
Charles N. R. McCoy reminded us, a basic one—of a way to
treat legitimately the question of the relation of classical,
medieval, and modern thought without ignoring or distorting
the Judaeo-Christian revelational factor, which itself, as much
as the classics, made Western civilization unique and gave truth
a further universal, not merely parochial or cultural, claim.
This remarkable book lies squarely within the tradition of Leo
Strauss in particular. That is to say, it lies within the only
academic tradition that is intellectually willing and, more
importantly, able to ask what difference Christianity makes to
the classics and to modern theory.

The Thomist tradition, to be sure, used to be a major factor
here, as Strauss recognized, but with the exception of the
papacy and a few advanced places like the University of Dallas,
where many of these essays originated, this tradition has largely
been voluntarily abandoned or rejected by believers themselves,
who, under the aegis of liberation theology or ecology or
liberalism or feminism or psychology, have embraced the
"modern project" itself, as if the Enlightenment were what
religion is now about. This book also represents one of the few
remaining avenues by which revelation can begin to be understood even by the intellectual representatives of religion, who
no longer seem to understand what they are about in the
world of politics.

These fifteen essays on Shakespeare and on how political life
appears in his tragedies, comedies, histories, and poems are the
most perceptive and brilliant efforts in recent decades to locate
within the Western tradition a way to reintroduce the factor of
revelation as an element with which to understand politics, its
limits, what lies beneath (the family) it, and what lies beyond
it. The only comparable endeavor, I think, was the neo-Thomist
movement of half a century ago, a movement itself intrinsic to

the understanding of the significance of this penetrating book. Shakespeare, however, has the advantage of having lain fallow for so many years, outside the usual ken of political thinkers, so that the abundance of what can grow out of his wisdom is both fresh and almost unlimited. We are not accustomed to reflect upon art as itself a way to comprehend politics, even though we recall that an Aristotle wrote the *Poetics,* and Plato never ceased to worry about Homer while at the same time attracting the young gentlemen with the brilliant poetry of his Dialogues.

Harry Jaffa and Michael Platt's essays on this relationship between politics and poetry are simply remarkable. These essays were in part written for an Intercollegiate Studies Institute conference at the University of Dallas, in part written for the book itself. They treat the major political works of Shakespeare—his tyrants, best kings, common men, bishops, matrons, and villains. The realization that Shakespeare is as profound as Cicero or Aristotle in political things should come as a surprise to no one. Yet it is a surprise, as political thinkers have left Shakespeare largely to the literary scholars, just as they have left the Bible largely to the theologians—that is to say, in both cases, to people themselves largely ignorant of political things.

Political science, the highest of the practical sciences as Aristotle called it in *The Ethics,* has in the modern era acted as if its area of reality were so narrow that it focused only on the "political", whereas it was meant, by its own reality, to expand itself so that it could see and account for all there was, even that which came from no known political source. Politics had to be humble enough to leave metaphysics and theology to their practitioners, provided these latter themselves, as Aquinas knew, understood, as politicians do, how most men really are. This is also why there is no Christian political theory without Augustine.

"In the plays set before the advent of Christianity", John Alvis wrote in the first essay, human lives take shape from individual propensities responding to the laws of cities. In the plays set within Christian times, Shakespeare's characters consult not only their native inclinations and laws of their state, but, concurrently, certain transcendent prescriptions decreed by their Scriptural God. To follow Shakespeare's reflections upon human beings and citizens, one must reflect upon the political consequences of Christian belief. The political subject necessarily embraces the religious subject.[1]

This observation is surprisingly like the metaphysical reflections of a Karol Wojtyla discussing the nature of politics and faith.[2] The shadows of Machiavelli, however, are never far from the Christian characters in Shakespeare. That is to say, we also find in the great English bard modern political theory precisely in its relation to the classics and to revelation.

In the beginning of *City and Man,* as we recalled earlier, Leo Strauss remarked that we ought to study the classics in order to grasp what man can learn by his own powers so that we can learn about the limits of the queen of the social sciences.[3] John Alvis likewise concluded: "To know what extends beyond politics, it helps to know the full scope of the political realm. Shakespeare's poetry assists us in understanding what surpasses

[1] John Alvis, "Shakespearean Poetry and Politics", in *Shakespeare as a Political Thinker,* ed. John Alvis and Thomas G. West (Durham, N.C.: Carolina Academic Press, 1981), p. 11. See also Allan Bloom and Harry Jaffa, *Shakespeare's Politics* (Chicago: University of Chicago Press, 1964); Paul A. Cantor, *Shakespeare's Rome: Republic and Empire* (Ithaca, N.Y.: Cornell University Press, 1976).

[2] See Andrew N. Woznicki, *A Christian Humanism: Karol Wojtyla's Existential Personalism* (New Britain, Conn.: Mariel, 1980); Karol Wojtyla, *The Acting Person* (Boston: D. Reidel, 1979). Collections of the many speeches and documents of John Paul II since he has been Pope have been published by St. Paul Editions in Boston.

[3] Leo Strauss, *City and Man,* (Chicago, University of Chicago Press, 1964), pp. 1–2.

politics by allowing us to grasp how far politics extends in the determination of human lives."[4] That politics ought to be a consummation of human lives, of the mortal while he is mortal, as Hannah Arendt would say, is no more than Aristotle's dictum that we are by nature political beings. We do what we are. But that politics ought to consume *all* of human life is totalitarianism, in whatever form it might appear.

Thus, it is probably no accident that no Shakespearean play depicts the life of a modern totalitarian state since the latter is produced by a process that denies the classic *and* Judaeo-Christian revelational elements in man, the religious and political subject. Yet Shakespeare knew tyranny and corruption, ambition and vanity, at a depth that few, if any, have ever equaled. Jaffa rightly suggested that this Shakespearean art enables us to avoid such a politics of destruction, even though we may still choose in actual deeds not to avoid it.

The central theme of these essays seems to be, in essence, what is and what is not political. Once knowing this, the human mind, as Aristotle already implied, seeks to spend its life in wondering about the narrow light of the divine shining into its world. In this context, no doubt, Jaffa's essay and that of Professor Allan Bloom are of special interest in this book. Jaffa is surely correct in calling attention to the political im-plications of chastity, of what it means for love and for the city to found precisely a family. Nothing is quite so important for politics as the family, which itself is not political. This is why those theories that deny it, beginning with Plato, can be so dangerous. Bloom remarked, in his essay "Richard II", that "the exquisitely refined souls do not belong in the best political men".[5] This conclusion makes us wonder even with

---

[4] Alvis, "Shakespearean Poetry and Politics", p. 26.

[5] Allan Bloom, "Richard II", in *Shakespeare as a Political Thinker*, p. 60.

greater interest about Shakespeare's treatment of Sir Thomas More.

On this point, Bloom continued:

> There are two sins mentioned in *Richard II:* the sin of Adam and the sin of Cain. They seem to be identical, or at least one leads to the other. Knowledge of practical things brings with it awareness that in order for the sacred to become sacred, terrible deeds must be done. Because God does not evidently rule, the founder of justice cannot himself be just.[6]

We have here, I suppose, what Frederick D. Wilhelmsen worried about in his *Christianity and Political Philosophy:* the relation of Jewish to Christian intelligence, both revelational, both related to the classics, to modernity, and to each other.[7]

For the Christian intelligence, as I have suggested elsewhere, the reality of a religious "elite" and of a drive to God and higher excellence is not designed to deny the normalcy of politics nor to turn against the usual expectations of common men.[8] This conclusion is why monasteries are neither homes nor states.[9] It is only when the monastic tradition becomes secularized in movements, parties, think tanks, and specifically antifamily presuppositions that it can destroy politics. Caesar really is legitimate in the Christian tradition. He is just not everything, nor the highest element.

Thus, Augustine's notion that the City of God—alluded to by Strauss at the beginning of the *City and Man*—is not the proper object of worldly politics, prevents us, in our drive for the best, from using politics as the vehicle for its advancement

[6] Ibid.

[7] Frederick D. Wilhelmsen, *Christianity and Political Philosophy* (Athens: University of Georgia Press, 1978).

[8] See James V. Schall, *The Politics of Heaven and Hell* (Lanham, Md.: University Press of America, 1984), pp. 68–82.

[9] See James V. Schall, "Monastery and Home", in *The Distinctiveness of Christianity* (San Francisco: Ignatius Press, 1982), pp. 200–17.

and achievement. The experience of fallen men is included in the political experience, just as is Aristotle's experience of a real, but limited, worldly human perfection. The current infatuation of Christian monks with politics rather than with transcendence is, as Jewish thinkers seem instinctively to sense, extremely dangerous, because it jeopardizes both politics and transcendence. Jaffa's reminder of the family, of the unworldliness of love — Hannah Arendt's point in *The Human Condition* also — of the place of the autonomous family, needs to be set also in the context of the City of God. Otherwise, secular monks will end up destroying both family and state. Louise Cowan put her finger on this issue:

> No man is able to perform his task perfectly; in the Biblical tradition within which Shakespeare's imagination works, all earthly things are flawed and yet all are carriers of something flawless. Shakespeare sees the human enterprise as a series of catastrophes, brought about by the clash of human wills; yet within this turbulent and painful chronicle he testifies to the gradual mysterious growth of the kingdom.
>
> Shakespeare shows us that human communities and political regimes exist in order to further what Allan Tate has called the "one lost truth that must be perpetually recovered — the supernatural destiny of man". It is in the constant rediscovery of shared love — between all sorts and conditions of men — that the true meaning of human history lies concealed.[10]

This recovery of "the supernatural destiny of man", which elites and mystics really seek to understand and to achieve, is alone what prevents these same elites, these choiceful elites, from turning on politics and destroying it by imposing truly transcendent goals among its demands. What is new about our era, as opposed to the Christianity of an Augustine, of an

---

[10] Louise Cowan, "God Will Save the King: Shakespeare's 'Richard II'", in *Shakespeare as a Political Thinker,* pp. 80–81.

Aquinas, or of a Shakespeare, is that now we actually see Christians themselves betraying their own traditions of political limitations. This, too, is why the testimony of both Jews and Christians actually living under Marxist states goes unheeded in the West.[11]

Shakespeare as a Political Thinker not only allows us to reintroduce the transcendent into politics, both in their proper place, but it also enables political theory to instruct theology on how to recover its own reality. "But in our age", to recall Strauss' words again, "it is much less urgent to show that political philosophy is the indispensable handmaid of theology than to show that political philosophy is the rightful queen of the social sciences, the sciences of man and human affairs".[12] Some quarter-century after these remarkable lines were written, this book on Shakespeare suggests, through the supreme dramatic artist of our tradition, that both theology and social sciences are in desperate need of their own handmaiden. This handmaiden is none other than political philosophy now lying within the ken of the religious "subject" who knows that politics produces of itself no everlasting kingdom, even when proposed by "elites", by "the theologizers", clerical or lay. While we can agree with Strauss that "it is not sufficient for everyone to obey and to listen to the Divine message of the City of Righteousness", reflection on the political thinking in Shakespeare will also teach us that it is not sufficient to neglect this same Divine message.

Seven Books on the Limits of Politics

1. Allan Bloom and Harry Jaffa, *Shakespeare's Politics.*
2. Christopher Dawson, *Beyond Politics.*
3. Oscar Cullmann, *The State in the New Testament.*

---

[11] See Igor Shafarevich, *The Socialist Phenomenon,* trans. William Tjalsma (New York: Harper and Row, 1980).

[12] Strauss, *City and Man,* p. 1.

4. Barrington Moore, *Reflections on the Causes of Human Misery and Upon Certain Proposals to Eliminate Them.*
5. Glenn Tinder, *Political Thinking: The Perennial Questions.*
6. Carens Lord, *Education and Culture in the Political Thought of Aristotle.*
7. Dante Germino, *Political Philosophy and the Open Society.*

Eight Helpful Books on Metaphysics

1. Joseph Owens, *An Elementary Christian Metaphysics.*
2. George P. Klubertanz, *An Introduction to the Philosophy of Being.*
3. Raymond Dennehy, *Reason and Dignity.*
4. Frederick D. Wilhelmsen, *Man's Knowledge of Reality.*
5. Jacques Maritain, *A Preface to Metaphysics.*
6. D. J. B. Hawkins, *Being and Becoming.*
7. Ferdinand van Steenberghen, *Ontology.*
8. Etienne Gilson, *The Unity of Philosophical Experience.*

Chapter Nine

On Doctrine and Dignity:
From "Heretics" to "Orthodoxy"

*(This chapter presents a reconsideration of
G. K. Chesterton's two famous books,
Heretics and Orthodoxy.)*

Let me begin by citing two passages, one from Russell Kirk, the other from Chesterton himself. "Yet, behind the arrogance of twentieth-century intellectuality", Kirk wrote, "Chesterton believed, there works a corrupting power that is not merely human".[1] And Chesterton wrote, in an essay entitled "In Defence of Ugly Things", that

> There are some people who state that the external, sex or physique, of another person is indifferent to them, that they care only for the communion of mind with mind; but these people will not detain us. There are some statements that no one ever thinks of believing, however often they are made.[2]

Common sense, thus, forbids us from believing some silly things, just as it makes us suspect that there is more to the disorder in the world than ourselves alone.

We are who we are first because of our existence, itself a gift we did not bestow on ourselves or call into being through our own efforts. We are neither reincarnated simians nor gods, neither an unstable process on the way to becoming something

---

[1] Russell Kirk, "Chesterton, Madness, and Madhouses", *Modern Age,* winter 1971, p. 15.

[2] G. K. Chesterton, "In Defence of Ugly Things", in *The Defendant* (London: Dent, 1914), p. 113.

else, not ourselves, nor anything less than the fittest of the survivors. For as Chesterton remarked, with his accustomed wit, the survival of the fittest merely means the survival of those who have in fact survived. And we know that we have at least done this. We know that we have survived. We know we have rejected the ultimate peril that doubts even whether we are.

"That peril is that human intellect is free to destroy itself", we read in *Orthodoxy.*

> Just as one generation could prevent the very existence of the next generation, by all entering a monastery or jumping into the sea, so one set of thinkers can in some degree prevent further thinking by teaching the next generation that there is no validity in any human thought. It is an act of faith to assert that our thoughts have any relation to reality at all. . . . There is a thought that stops thought. That is the only thought that ought to be stopped. That was the ultimate evil against which all religious authority was aimed.[3]

Thus, we have survived for we are here, so we want to ascertain what it is a human survivor on this planet ought to do on discovering that he does indeed exist.

The "heretic" is substantially someone who says we ought to set about ourselves to create a world that does not contain any of the obvious limits and defects of this world, that we ought to fashion another sort of man, for what we find ourselves to be is surely some sort of gigantic, cosmic mistake. The "orthodox" thinker, on the other hand, no doubt agrees that something is surely wrong. He knows that the doctrine of original sin needs little more proof than a walk in the streets.

[3] G. K. Chesterton, *Orthodoxy,* in *Collected Works,* vol. 1 (San Francisco: Ignatius Press, 1986; first printed 1908), p. 236. See also T. F. Torrance, "Ultimate Beliefs and the Scientific Revolution", *Cross Currents,* summer 1980, pp. 129–49.

"And to the question, 'What is meant by the Fall?' " Chesterton reflected,

> I could answer with complete sincerity, "That whatever I am, I am not myself." This is the prime paradox of our religion; something that we have never in any full sense known, is not only better than ourselves, but even more natural to us than ourselves. And there is really no test of this except the merely experimental one with which these pages began, the test of the padded cell and the open door. It is only since I have known orthodoxy that I have known mental emancipation.[4]

Yet we are creatures who in our falleness, in, if you will, our wrongheadedness, are still able to give thanks and to count the leaves on the morning trees. The fact that damnation is a real possibility for us is merely the reverse side of the risk of glory, so that we can thank our neighbor for a cup of water because he need not give it to us. The structure of the cosmos is such that we have both the water and the cup along with the power to give it where we need not, or to refuse to give it where we ought. If damnation were not possible in little things, there would be no great ones. This is why ordinary lives are, before God, as important as heroic ones. Thus, the first thing we need to know about ourselves is our philosophy, whether we live in a world where damnation is possible because thanksgiving can be refused.

Thinking: A Perilous Occupation

In his *Autobiography*, Chesterton recalled why he titled his collection on Kipling, Shaw, and Wells precisely *Heretics*. It was, he said, because each of them "erred through an ultimate

---

[4] Chesterton, *Orthodoxy*, p. 363.

or religious error".[5] This title naturally led to the challenge, irresistible for Chesterton, to tell us not what he disagreed with, but what his own theology was about. This latter statement he called *orthodoxy*, though he confessed he was not wholly happy with that title until he gradually realized there was something very "provocative" about it. He began to realize that in the modern world, there was only one "unpardonable heresy" and that was classic Christian orthodoxy. Everyone praised him or joked with him until they found out that he "really meant what [he] said".[6]

What he meant by *orthodoxy* was substantially what was in the Creeds as the Church understood them. These Creeds are the foundation of our dignity, and our dignity is undermined somehow every time we seek to change one iota of their content. Indeed, the very effort to change them is itself an instrument in the process of weaving or fashioning another sort of man from the one the Creeds describe. Ultimately, to change the man, you must first change the Creeds. This is why thinking is such a perilous occupation, for in changing your mind, you may well end up changing the world. We can be murdered for our beliefs, but we can more easily be destroyed by our doctrines. And while the martyr ought to know for what it is he dies, the rest of us ought all the more to know what it is for which we live. For the former, faith may be enough, but for the latter, doctrine is needed if we are also to have our dignity.

[5] G. K. Chesterton, *The Autobiography of G. K. Chesterton* (New York: Sheed and Ward, 1936), p. 179.
[6]Ibid., p. 180.

Who Will Be Our Teachers?

Thus, we have a gifted nature, a human nature which, as Eric Voegelin remarked in his essay "The End of Modernity", does "not change".[7] But we also have a "second nature", what we choose to be, to know. For this we need a teacher, and for this teaching, as Leo Strauss wrote, "yet the greatest minds utter monologues . . . and they contradict one another regarding the most important matters".[8] But this very contradiction among the greatest minds means that we ourselves must judge among the great teachers who do not always, or even mostly, live in our own lifetime. We must then learn from the books of the great thinkers. This means, evidently, that we must decide among the great teachers, among the great books, who will be our teachers about the order of things, for great teachers contradict one another. We must search among the great books to find those that do not contradict reality, for those that guide us to what is given to us.

How do we choose? Leo Strauss suggested that we can do this only through our own thought thinking about itself, by our own grasping that we do ourselves have a mind with a given proper functioning. From this, therefore, we conclude with Strauss:

> This experience [of thinking] is entirely independent of whether what we understand is pleasing or displeasing, fair or ugly. It leads us to realize that all evils are in a sense necessary if there is to be understanding. It enables us to accept all evils which befall us and which may well break our hearts in the spirit of good citizens of the City of God. By becoming aware of the dignity of the mind, we realize the true ground of the dignity

---

[7] Eric Voegelin, *The New Science of Politics* (Chicago: University of Chicago Press, 1952), p. 165.

[8] Leo Strauss, "What Is Liberal Education?" in *Liberalism: Ancient and Modern* (New York: Basic Books, 1968), p. 7.

of man and therewith the goodness of the world, whether we understand it as created or uncreated, which is the home of man because it is the home of the human mind.[9]

This observation, of course, brings us directly to the central Chestertonian theme of our being homesick at home; of how the Christian doctrine of the resurrection of the body relates to the Aristotelian notions of the impossibility of friendship with a First Mover, who is "thought thinking on itself"; of whether the object of revelation is also truth, doctrine; of the way, the truth, the life; of whether our dignity includes our doctrines and our dogmas, our right thinking about the order of things that need not be in the first place, that is, about the freedom of a God who need not create.

And in this context of whether we can or will bear the whole truth about ourselves in the order of things, a theme that we find most often expressed in the writings of John Paul II, Leo Strauss is known also for one other famous doctrine, one quite similar to Chesterton's experience when the "heretics" discovered suddenly that he was serious about orthodoxy. In his essay "Persecution and the Art of Writing", Strauss presented his well-known thesis about the great teachers who carefully present and conceal the truth in their own writings. They must do this in a cautiously constructed manner both to conceal the truth from dangerous public officials and to reveal it to serious "recruits", who come to see in the writings a path to the truth of things.[10]

[9] Ibid., p. 8.

[10] Strauss, *Persecution and the Art of Writing*, pp. 22–37. See also Strauss *Thoughts on Machiavelli* (Chicago: University of Chicago Press, 1958), p. 168, where Strauss begins to discuss recruits to his project in political philosophy to replace Machiavelli's recruitment. See John Paul II, *The Whole Truth about Man: John Paul II to University Faculties and Students* (Boston: St. Paul Editions, 1981).

Though it could be argued, perhaps, that Chesterton's "paradox" style is a form of "secret writing", since it disarms the critic to think Chesterton not to be dangerous to the established public order, still Chesterton as a Christian was as much concerned that truth have a public expression as that it be preserved by some elite or academic mind. When Chesterton really did convince his critics that he did believe in classical "orthodoxy" as it is found in the Creeds and in Aquinas, he became the real "heretic". That is, he was no longer accepted as a part of the public realm of intelligence. He was not executed, like a Socrates, but he was isolated, even by Christians embarrassed that their truth was really what it claimed to be. In this sense, Chesterton continues to be a sort of sign of contradiction, since he stands for a Christianity that changes the world by not changing its own Creed over against a neomodernism that would save the faith by changing its dogmas to conform to the ever-changing doctrines of the world.

What I wish to suggest, then, is that Chesterton's use of paradox was indeed a form of "secret writing", not so much to conceal the truth, but to engage the mind of the searcher, to find recruits for the truth who may not, in the beginning, suspect or be willing to admit that truth is what they search for. Further, the comprehension of evil as a necessary mental exercise, leading to the dignity of the mind and to the proper location of the City of God, the only adequate home of man, classic Chestertonian themes, directs us to the relation of the doctrine of truth and the doctrine of human dignity in the thought of G. K. Chesterton.

Perhaps the best example of this is found in those lines near the end of his *Autobiography* where Chesterton recounted, prophetically, the relation of orthodoxy, human dignity, and the coming of the absolute genetic state. "But anybody reading this book (if anybody does)", he wrote,

> will see that from the very beginning my instinct about justice, about liberty and equality, was somewhat different from that current in our age; and from all the tendencies towards concentration and generalization. It was my instinct to defend liberty in small nations and poor families. . . . I did not really understand what I meant by Liberty until I heard it called by the new name of Human Dignity. It was a new name to me though it had been part of a creed nearly two thousand years old.
>
> In short, I had blindly dreamed that a man should be in possession of something, if it were only his own body. In so far as materialistic concentration proceeds, a man will be in possession of nothing, not even his own body. Already there hover on the horizon sweeping scourges of sterilization or social hygiene, applied to everybody and imposed by nobody.[11]

Right thinking, right opinion, orthodoxy are, as Strauss implied, the proper grounds of human dignity. Aquinas had pointed out that the vision of God is in part an act of our graced intellects. Thus, although the salvation of man includes the whole person, an error of intellect nevertheless is ultimately an undermining of human worth. Ideas will carry on. Argumentation will be carried to its ultimate conclusion, if not by us, then by someone else. "Good will" alone will not save us.

[11] Chesterton, *Autobiography*, pp. 354–55. See also Chesterton's *Eugenics and Other Evils* (San Francisco: Ignatius Press, 1987); James V. Schall, "The Rarest of All Revolutions: G. K. Chesterton on the Relation of Human Dignity to Christian Doctrine", *The American Benedictine Review* 32 (December 1981): 304–27.

Here I wish to suggest that G. K. Chesterton is one of the great teachers. In his books, we necessarily come to grips with one of the ultimate minds whereby we must locate the other greatest of minds. In Cicero's *De Amicitia,* there was a remarkable passage in which Cicero was speaking of his own dialogues (the *De Amicitia,* the *De Officiis,* the *De Senectute*). He remarked that "expositions of this kind seem to carry special conviction when they are placed in the mouths of personages of an earlier generation, especially when those were eminent men" (vol. I, bk. 4). My own generation was not fortunate enough to have met Chesterton personally, so we have had to meet him through his books (now fortunately being republished by Ignatius Press). The discourse of mankind with the greatest teachers does not cease because those who speak to us are dead.

"Tradition refuses to submit to the small and arrogant oligarchy of those who happen to be walking about", Chesterton quipped in *Orthodoxy.* "All democrats object to men being disqualified by the accident of birth; tradition objects to their being disqualified by the accident of death."[12] This observation was Chesterton's way of making Strauss' point about the location of the greatest minds. The precise point, where the great teaching of Chesterton most clearly comes into play, focuses on the way faith and reason come together in the same person. For faith and reason will eternally be separate unless somehow, somewhere they are both addressed to and exist in the same mind.[13]

The key passage to illustrate this unity is found in the preface to *Orthodoxy,* where we read:

---

[12] Chesterton, *Orthodoxy,* p. 251.

[13] See Stanley Jaki, *Chesterton: A Seer of Science* (Urbana: University of Illinois Press, 1986); "Chesterton's Landmark Year", in *Chance or Reality, and Other Essays* (Lanham, Md.: University Press of America, 1986), pp. 63–77.

It is the purpose of the writer to attempt an explanation, not of whether the Christian faith can be believed, but of how he personally has come to believe it. The book is therefore arranged upon the positive principle of a riddle and its answer. It deals first with all the writer's own solitary and sincere speculations and then with all the startling style in which they were all suddenly satisfied by the Christian Theology. The writer regards it as amounting to a convincing creed. But if it is not that, it is at least a repeated and surprising coincidence.[14]

This extraordinary passage addresses itself directly to the Straussian problematic of whether faith is needed for reason, so that the content of reason is somehow corrupted when it is arrived at within a faith context.[15]

Chesterton's approach to this issue was rather empirical. He somehow, as he told us in *Orthodoxy,* had a sense of Christianity both from its objectors, who seemed willing to use any weapon against it, and from his feeling that if Christianity did not exist, he would have had to have invented it for himself.[16] This affirmation is almost the only time in modern literature, I think, that "atheism" has been successfully combined with Christianity. Theologically, in any case, we cannot say that the truths of faith can be all reasoned *to* by our own minds. But they can be reasoned *from,* as it were, so that the Incarnation, for example, is the answer to philosophical questions that cannot be adequately confronted without it, or at least, are not met without it.

---

[14] This preface is not found in the Ignatius Press edition; it is in the Doubleday Image edition of *Orthodoxy* (New York, 1959), p. 6.

[15] See Strauss, *Natural Right and History,* p. 164; "The Mutual Influence of Theology and Philosophy", *Independent Journal of Philosophy* III (1979): 111–18.

[16] Chesterton, *Orthodoxy,* chap. 6; *Heretics,* chap. 20. (Both of these volumes are now continued in vol. 1 of *The Collected Works of G. K. Chesterton,* published in 1986 by Ignatius Press, San Francisco.)

Pondering the Creed

Thus, Chesterton was able to write near the end of *Orthodoxy:*

> But I may pause to remark that the more I saw of the merely
> abstract arguments against the Christian cosmology, the less I
> thought of them. I mean that having found the moral atmo-
> sphere of the Incarnation to be common sense, I then looked to
> the established intellectual arguments against the Incarnation
> and found them to be common nonsense.[17]

What is important here is Chesterton's insistence on telling us
how he took the logical arguments against the Incarnation
very seriously as themselves expressions of world views that
sooner or later did affect human dignity, because they were
errors of intelligence. The Creed, then, is not only something
to be recited, but also something to be thought about.

Flannery O'Connor caught some of this in her *Mystery and
Manners,* where she wrote:

> Dogma is an instrument for penetrating reality. Christian dogma
> is about the only thing left in the world that surely guards and
> respects mystery. The fiction writer is an observer, first, last,
> and always, but he cannot be an adequate observer unless he is
> free from uncertainty about what he sees. Those who have no
> absolute values cannot let the relative remain merely relative;
> they are always raising it to the level of the absolute. The
> Catholic fiction writer is entirely free to observe. He feels no
> call to take on the duties of God or to create a new universe. He
> feels perfectly free to look at the one we already have and to
> show exactly what he sees.[18]

[17] Chesterton, *Orthodoxy,* p. 347.
[18] Flannery O'Connor, *Mystery and Manners* (New York: Farrar, Straus,
and Giroux, 1969), p. 178. See also Dorothy Sayers, "The Dogma Is the
Drama", in *The Whimsical Christian* (New York: Macmillan, 1978),
pp. 23–29.

Heretics was devoted to literary philosophers, like Shaw, Kipling, and Wells, who, for all their brilliance, were forced to absolutize their constructs because dogma did not save them to see this world. They were always, to use Flannery O'Connor's phrase, raising the relative to the level of the absolute.

Almost prophetically, then, Chesterton concluded *Heretics* with the dogma that we will eventually need faith even to look at what we already are looking at.

> We who are Christians never knew the great philosophic common sense which inheres in that mystery until the anti-Christian writers pointed it out to us. The great march of mental destruction will go on. Everything will be denied. Everything will become a creed . . . we shall be left defending, not only the incredible virtues and sanities of human life, but something more incredible still, this huge impossible universe which stares at us in the face. We shall fight for visible prodigies as if they were invisible. We shall look on the impossible grass and the skies with a strange courage. We shall be those who have seen and yet have believed.[19]

Anyone familiar with Stanley Jaki's *The Road of Science and the Ways to God,* with its exact historical thesis that it was, in the end, Christian theology that enabled us to see precisely this incredible universe and not merely our minds, or nothing at all, cannot but marvel at Chesterton's sure foresight.[20] For he realized that the "heretics", for all their good will, were not in fact orthodox, were not in fact able to see the world and the grass growing up to the blue skies.

---

[19] Chesterton, *Heretics,* pp. 206–07.
[20] See also Jaki's study of science in Chesterton, *Chesterton: A Seer of Science.*

Chesterton and Paradox

Chesterton, we can readily admit, does not easily lend himself to footnotes, to the apparatus of standard academic discourse. Few of us refer to Chesterton by the device of exact citation. We constantly catch ourselves remarking, "as Chesterton said somewhere". Then we go ahead and cite him fairly accurately, because he did teach us, because his teaching is the great contradiction of the other great masters. Usually, we give Chesterton credit by ignoring his page numbers. "If a thing is worth doing, it is worth doing badly", we quip, wishing we had really said it first, but glad that we did not, for it is somehow a greater thing to discover what is already discovered, to discover England, to think it is really the end of the world.

Chesterton remains even today one of the most quoted and quotable writers in the English language.[21] Though not a few persist in professing annoyance at the infinity of paradoxes, I confess to finding them amusing, memorable, alerting. Yet the point of Chesterton's amusement was always near the meta-physical heart of reality, as when he discovered in *Orthodoxy* that the reason why the sun comes up each day may not be dull determinism, but delightful chance and the joy of repeating what is itself an utter amazement. Each of us, I suppose, can give something of a personal or autobiographical account of our encounters with Chesterton's teaching us about the structure of reality, about what he called sanity. I do not merely mean that we may have visited Beaconsfield or Edwards' Square, or should we be old enough, to have heard Chesterton lecture or converse. Rather, we each have our own intellectual

---

[21] See the book, *The Quotable Chesterton,* ed. George Marlin, et al. (San Francisco: Ignatius Press, 1986). C. S. Lewis is quoted almost as much as his friend Chesterton, see *An Anthology of C. S. Lewis: A Mind Awake,* ed. Clyde S. Kilby (San Diego: Harcourt-Harvest, 1980).

history that leads us somehow from heresy to dogma, from odd doctrine to sanity.

I grew up at a time when it was out of fashion, even wrong, to read or especially to like Chesterton. Of course, I never even heard of him until I was about twenty-two or so, but that was a different problem, as it took me that long to begin to understand what it meant to have a Catholic intelligence in the first place. Chesterton's "brand" of Catholicism, as it was called, was said to be out of date. Science, history, ecumenism, theology, and even philosophy were all said to conspire to make of him a quaint Englishman, who will perhaps endure because of his Father Brown stories.

Let me confess, however, I have never read any of Father Brown except for a brief short story or two. I dislike mystery stories, however noble the art. To be sure, I have cited time without number Chesterton's remark that we should commit our murders all the time, but by writing about them, in mystery stories. This is, after all, Plato's point: that knowledge of evil is not evil, but good. Chesterton was quite sure that one of the great arguments for being a Christian was that it enabled us to understand the real nature and depths of evil in ourselves and in the world. The Crucifixion was the end of the Incarnation, even when the Resurrection followed it.

The Final Joy

We should not, I think, take Chesterton's reason for joining the Church lightly. "When people ask me . . . 'Why did you join the Church of Rome?' the first essential answer . . . is, 'To get rid of my sins'."[22] We are true to his witness only if we take him quite literally as a man who did know the reaches of evil

[22] Chesterton, *Autobiography*, p. 340.

in himself not only as a possibility according to which he could imagine unimaginable murders for his Father Brown stories, but as a statement of fact. Chesterton knew quite well that denying the possibility or actuality of human evil implied a basic heresy: that of reducing each man and woman to ultimate insignificance, to a being in this world with nothing serious to do, nothing final to accomplish.

And so in this context Chesterton discovered his "Ethics of Elfland", wherein,

> There had come into my mind a vague and vast impression that in some way all good was a remnant to be stored and held sacred out of a primordial ruin. . . . All this I felt and the age gave me no encouragement to feel it. And all this time I had not even thought of Christian theology.[23]

But that we cannot save ourselves did not mean that there was nothing to be saved from, did not mean that there was nothing more than what we create.

Chesterton knew, of course, that intellect was capable of deceiving us. The heart, even in its sins, was often less dangerous than intelligence gone wrong. At the end of *The Catholic Church and Conversion,* he confessed: "I have much more sympathy with the person who leaves the Church for a love affair than the person who leaves it for a long-winded German theory to prove that God is evil or that children are a sort of morbid monkey."[24] The arrogance of the twentieth century, Russell Kirk had noted, suggests a corrupting power more than human at work in the cosmos. The answer to this power lies not in a cessation of thought, but in thinking rightly.

---

[23] Chesterton, *Orthodoxy,* p. 268.

[24] G. K. Chesterton, *The Catholic Church and Conversion* (New York: Macmillan, 1926), p. 115.

Religious and philosophical beliefs are, indeed, as dangerous as fire, and nothing can take from them that beauty of danger. But there is only one way of really guarding ourselves against the excessive danger of them, and that is to be steeped in philosophy and soaked in religion.[25]

But with what reason? And with what philosophy?

I began these reflections with a reference to Professor Leo Strauss and his concern to protect at least a place for revelation over against civic life and the philosophers who could not bear the truth. Strauss knew, not unlike St. Thomas, that only a very few could be expected to be truly wise. Even fewer could bear the truth once they found it. Strauss worried about Socrates in Athens, whereas Christians worried about Christ in Jerusalem before Pilate. I suggested that Chesterton's preface to *Orthodoxy* is the proper link of faith and reason, the account of how one man came to believe, of how the riddles actually experienced in our lives are solved by the dogmas, of how the Christian philosophy is very strange if indeed it is not true.

In his book on Thomas Aquinas, Chesterton directed himself to the limits of reason and the needs of faith.

> Something in his [Aquinas'] character ... led him rather to exaggerate the extent to which all men would ultimately listen to reason. In his controversies, he always assumes they will listen to reason. That is, he does emphatically believe that men can be convinced by argument, when they reach the end of the argument. Only his common sense also told him that the argument never ends.[26]

Chesterton went on, with obvious reference to Aquinas' discussion in the *Summa Theologiae* (I–II, 91, 4), about whether divine law was necessary to observe and know the natural law.

[25] Chesterton, *Heretics*, p. 203.
[26] G. K. Chesterton, *St. Thomas Aquinas*, in *Collected Works*, vol. 2, 1986, p. 434.

Essentially, Chesterton argued that so many sidetracks and interferences, so many interesting but dead-end digressions, would come up that the arguments for most men would never be able to reach their final conclusion.

Where did this leave the common man?

> St. Thomas takes the view that the souls of all the ordinary hard working and simple-minded people are quite as important as the souls of thinkers and truth-seekers; and he asks how all these people are possibly to find time for the amount of reasoning that is needed to find truth. . . . His argument for revelation is not an argument against reason; but it is an argument for revelation. The conclusion he draws from it is that men must receive the highest moral truths in a miraculous manner; or most men would not receive them at all.[27]

In the context of modern political and moral philosophy, this is a most remarkable conclusion, for it accounts not only for the ease with which "heretics" are heretics, but it also respects the province of mind and its connection with reality. The mind does not become an instrument incapable of truth and truth-seeking.[28] That is, human beings as persons actually are connected to ultimate things.

Yet, in maintaining that we could know the world and its order and cause by ourselves, with our own personal powers, if they are presented to us, Chesterton avoided the secret writing and the elitism that might somehow lead to a two-truth thesis or deny to most men the highest things. "The fact

---

[27] Ibid., pp. 434–35.

[28] "According to Aquinas, the object becomes a part of the mind; nay, according to Aquinas, the mind actually becomes the object. But, as one commentator acutely puts it, it only becomes the object and does not create the object. In other words, the object *is* an object; it can and does exist outside the mind, or in the absence of the mind. And *therefore* it enlarges the mind of which it becomes a part." Ibid., p. 541.

is", Dorothy Sayers wrote, "that in this Christian country [England] not one person in a hundred has the faintest notion of what the Church teaches about God or man or society or the person of Christ."[29] G. K. Chesterton, in *Heretics* and *Orthodoxy,* not only spelled out what it means in terms of human dignity not to know these doctrines, but also freed us to know them, to know them by argument or by revelation, to see for ourselves how they do answer the riddles that our lives present to us.

Chesterton teaches us, in other words, to be philosophers ourselves when the great teachers disagree about the highest truths. On the basic doctrines and dogmas of our dignity and freedom, it strikes me, G. K. Chesterton in his books remains the greatest of teachers, for not only is his creed convincing in having been already discovered some two thousand years before his time, but it is a "repeated and surprising coincidence" that does answer the final riddles of our existence. Our doctrine does ground our dignity. Our heretics can and do lead us to orthodoxy. Evil is finally saved not when we do it, but when we think it and know it is evil. We, as Christians, do not care

---

[29] Sayers, "The Dogma Is the Drama", *The Whimsical Christian,* p. 35. The following books treat the religious condition of Christianity:

1. A. N. Wilson, *How Can We Know? An Essay on the Christian Religion.*
2. James Hitchcock, *Years of Crisis.*
3. Malcolm Muggeridge, *The End of Christendom.*
4. Hans Urs von Balthasar, *A Short Primer for Unsettled Laymen.*
5. Joseph Ratzinger, *The Ratzinger Report: Interview with Vittorio Messori.*
6. Ann Roche Muggeridge, *The Desolate City: Revolution in the Catholic Church.*
7. James J. Thompson, *Fleeing the Whore of Babylon: A Modern Conversion.*
8. George Kelly, *The Battle for the American Church.*
9. Michael Novak, *Confessions of a Catholic.*
10. Paul Johnson, *Pope John Paul II and the Catholic Restoration.*

only for "the communion of mind with mind", for we know we are to be saved by more than thought. Yet our own thought thinking on itself is not entirely unlike Thought Thinking on Itself, as Aristotle called it, not unlike the Word made Flesh. Our minds are not only connected with the whole universe; they are also connected with ourselves.

The final discovery is that we are given not only the cosmos but ourselves, not only the universe but the Author of the universe. This was for Chesterton the final truth that put every experience he had into its proper order.

> The mass of men have been forced to be gay about the little things, but sad about the big ones. Nevertheless (I offer my last dogma defiantly) it is not native to man to be so. Man is more himself, man is more manlike, when joy is the fundamental thing in him. . . . Joy . . . is the gigantic secret of the Christian.[30]

The final heresy is that we made ourselves; the final joy, the final orthodoxy, is that we are given something more than we ever could have imagined.

[30] Chesterton, *Orthodoxy*, p. 364.

Seven Books of G. K. Chesterton, besides
Orthodoxy *and* Heretics,
Not to Be Missed,
Even Though He Wrote about a Hundred More,
Not to Be Missed Either

1. *The Autobiography of G. K. Chesterton.*
2. *St. Thomas Aquinas.*
3. *Charles Dickens.*
4. *What's Wrong with the World?*
5. *What I Saw in America.*
6. *The Thing.*
7. *The Man Who Was Thursday.*

Chapter Ten

On Evil and the Responsibility for Suffering

(These considerations on evil and suffering were occasioned by Jeffrey Burton Russell's
Lucifer: The Devil in the Middle Ages.*)*

No topic is more intellectually fascinating, perplexing, or agonizing than that of evil. "But choice of a mean is not possible in every action or every feeling", Aristotle wrote in the second book of *The Ethics*. "The very names of some (actions) have an immediate connotation of evil." Modernity has often been a brave thesis which, so it hoped with its belief in progress, promised a more perfect, a more charitable human estate. But on arriving at this better world in which reason or science replaced faith, we suddenly find our children terrorized in grammar schools by "peace" studies graphically picturing "doomsday", or "the day after" some bomb or other. "Apocalypse", as I have written elsewhere, is now a "secular enterprise".[1] The fires of hell are the daily fare of modern ideologies. At times, religion itself appears so tame by comparison that even clerics seem to have become vocal pacifists so they would not be outdone on the descriptive terror front.

No examined life, of course, is worth living unless it includes an account of evil as a part of its own history, beginning with itself and extending to that of the cosmos. Yet evil remains a mystery, a maddening one, however careful we are to clarify

[1] James V. Schall, "Apocalypse as a Secular Enterprise", *Scottish Journal of Philosophy* 29, no. 4 (1976): 357–73.

its core, an endeavor, as Plato reminded us, i[...]
paradoxically, good. Even if we should [...]
own "doing" of it, we should still "kno[...]
reflection on our own deeds or those of [...]
misconceiving evil, moreover, is heavy. W[...]
presence, surely the temptation of philosoph[...]
which this significant book of Jeffrey Burton [...]
we end up by trivializing human (and di[...]
standards so that nothing makes any difference [...]
Belsen, differs from Mother Teresa's Calcutta [...] by virtue
of subjective preference or mere external power. When we
hypostatize evil, however, in the noble hope of ridding ourselves of it forever, we tend to identify evil with specific
persons, nations, classes, or even angelic beings, to justify their
eradication in order to eliminate evil completely, so that our
own lives may be pure. The classic doctrine that evil was
rather a "privation" than a substance was designed, in part, to
prevent this dangerous result.

On the other hand, experience suggests that Gulags bother
some of us very little, while others seek to remove, say, South
Africa from the face of the earth on the ground that the
ultimate cause of evil is somehow located there. Indeed, one of
the things that strike us about discussions of evil in modern
times as opposed to those in medieval treatises and traditions is
that evil is today more and more political, while for the
medievals, it was personal and spiritual. In any case, we are not
so made that we can easily leave this topic of evil alone, even if
we must, in our logic, eventually accuse the divinity of having
made the world rather poorly because of the amount of evil
evidently found within it. In fact, this latter charge seems to be
the conclusion to which Professor Russell's remarkable book
argues, albeit reluctantly.

Lucifer is the fourth in a series of studies of the history of evil by Jeffrey Burton Russell. (His previous books were *Witchcraft in the Middle Ages, The Devil: Perceptions of Evil from Antiquity to Primitive Christianity,* and *Satan: The Early Christian Tradition.* We should also mention Richard Kenneth Emmerson's *Antichrist in the Middle Ages.*) One naturally hesitates to suggest that "witchcraft" is again in vogue, but these studies at least suggest that the topic remains a live one, one that can lead us to abiding questions fundamental to our existence. Russell's erudition is most commendable, while his concern for the subject itself is most anguished.

Indeed, after finishing this thorough book, one cannot help but wonder at times whether Russell's studies in the history of evil are not themselves manifestations of his own ruminations over this basic "problem" of reality. The manner in which he works his own "logic" into his conclusions makes this book seem not so much a "history" of evil, but rather a scholarly autobiography about how one man accepts or rejects the various explanations of evil that have arisen during the course of history. There is nothing wrong with this, of course, but it does give a certain slant to the work, even a certain poignancy. For Russell seems to leave himself, in the end, with the unsettling conclusion, after all is said and done, that this world ought not to have existed at all, if it is going to be as it is.

In this observation, initially, I am reminded of a passage in G. K. Chesterton's *Autobiography,* where he recalled his maternal grandfather, an old Wesleyan lay preacher. His grandfather, on hearing the younger men of his time easily criticize the general thanksgiving of the prayer book by arguing that "a good many people have very little reason to be thankful for their creation", remarked trenchantly, "I should thank God for my creation if I knew I was a lost soul."[2] I venture to suggest that no place for such a view exists in Professor Russell's

---

[2] Chesterton, *Autobiography,* p. 12.

metaphysics. For Russell's intellectual agony was precisely about a creation in which it is impossible both to suffer *and* to give thanks. "God remains responsible", Russell concluded, "for a world in which the amount of suffering greatly exceeds that necessary for the existence of human free will".[3]

Just how we are to calculate this "amount", to be sure, remains itself obscure. And on the hypothesis—the only one that makes the universe interesting and full of risk—that free will causes so much evil but remains the very price of existence at all, we might hesitate to prefer nothingness or, even less, an alternate creation in which it is precisely our very kind who could not erupt into being in the first place.

Russell's thesis began, on the surface, rather like several short stories of Flannery O'Connor: with a vivid newspaper account of several wanton instances of sadism and uncontrolled slaughter. Violence is described in the media for its own sake and seems to result from a perverted will. Russell used this sort of account to accuse the modern mind of superficiality, of neglecting to face honestly the vast amount of evil that evidently exists in the world before our very eyes, often by our own hands. Russell did not imply that such accounts of evil do not get on the police records or in the press, but that they are simply explained away, so that they have little or no effect on our sensibilities. Our theories have made us dull to the depth of evil in the world. Psychology, sociology, and even political theory leave us mostly blind to what really happens. In a sense, our anthropomorphic theories have so made us think we could get rid of evil by ourselves that we have refused to face the fact that we have not and cannot.

Thus, Russell proposed that such violence, which he seemed to take as itself a sign of evil, along with such popular culprits as nuclear weapons, ought to force us to refocus ourselves on the

[3] Jeffrey Burton Russell, *Lucifer: The Devil in the Middle Ages* (Ithaca, N.Y.: Cornell University Press, 1984), p. 309.

reality of evil. This time, however, evil is not something spiritual or abstract, as it supposedly was in earlier eras, but something in our own very midst. In this context, however, Russell recognized that the discussion about evil is an ancient one in all societies, so that our age, if anything, is peculiar in not recognizing the necessity to account for evil. In this sense, Russell argued that evil has a concrete "history" so that we must know and respect this tradition, even if it includes devils and witches, before we can adequately confront the issues presented by the abidingness of evil in human history and the presumed inadequacies of its previous, satanic representations.

In the end, however, Russell is no Machiavellian who tells us to lower our sights before the human enterprise of goodness, but he does maintain a lawyer's brief against God about his responsibility for evil. Yet, "the idea of the Devil is a metaphor; so is the idea of God, in the sense that anyone's view of God—Christian, Muslim, Hindu, or whatever—is a metaphor for that which passes understanding".[4] If it is any consolation, Russell holds that "physics too is a metaphor". But all of this reflection leads us to wonder what metaphor, then, can bear such a burden? All of this makes the older metaphysics seem rather more attractive by comparison. When Augustine and Aquinas called evil a real lack of a good, they did not intend a metaphor, however exalted.

No matter how he argued the tradition, Russell kept coming back to the same conclusion, namely, that God is responsible, even if we have to locate, like Nicholas of Cusa, evil in the Godhead itself, where we also purport to find a drive to overcome it. Russell's main concern was, clearly, contained in his concluding chapter, "The Existence of the Devil":

> The Devil is a metaphor for the evil in the cosmos, an evil that is both in God and opposed by God; he represents the transconscious, transpersonal evil that exceeds the individual human

[4] Ibid., p. 307.

evil will; he is the sign of the radical, unmanageable, yet ultimately transcendable evil in the cosmos. We may well be in need of another name for this force. Let it be so, if one can be found. But let it be one that does not evade, blur, or trivialize suffering.[5]

This conclusion, it seems, takes us back to the real problem in Russell's own theory—to wit, the identification of evil with suffering or pain. Strictly speaking, Russell's "devil" may not, as he is described, have anything to do with "evil" at all.

The question is not, then, whether God ought to have created a cosmos in which there was genuine free will—its denial, in one sense, even in the Deity, resolves the problem of "responsibility"—but one in which there was little or no suffering. Russell in fact seems intent on saying that there should be less evil rather than none at all.[6] Meanwhile, "violence can be understood as the evil infliction of suffering".[7] The operative definition seems to be, "The conscious and deliberate inflicting of suffering is the heart of violence and moral evil."[8]

This definition, no doubt, raises certain questions that Yves Simon dealt with in his *Philosophy of Democratic Government*.[9] Simon argued that there was a sense in which something could be "violent" and quite legitimate, self-defense, for example. The "heart of violence and moral evil" must have standards against which to define what deviates, to define what is evil. Russell's concern seems to be rather with the sufferer, not the cause of the suffering. His accusation against God is primarily rooted in the "amount" of pain or suffering, not in the "amount"

[5] Ibid., p. 311.
[6] Ibid., p. 309.
[7] Ibid., p. 21.
[8] Ibid., p. 21.
[9] Yves Simon, *The Philosophy of Democratic Government* (Chicago: University of Chicago Press, 1977).

of chance or free will that might cause evil. Thus, if I am killed by lightning, while lightning does what lightning normally does (hence, killed by chance), or by a robber doing enthusiastically what a robber does, the focus is on my fate and suffering, not on the "cause". In this sense, Russell's real problem seems to be with free creatures and chance—with finiteness—rather than with suffering, which, as Aristotle said, has its own purpose.

Russell, of course, surveyed carefully the theories of evil that seek to relate free will and divine omnipotence and knowledge. His analysis of Aquinas and the general tradition of redemption by a Suffering Servant or a Man-God was again governed by the principle "cancer is an evil because it causes suffering".[10] If evil is a lack of good in what ought to exist, God still seems to will a world in which such a lack can appear and continue. This is the accusation: "Thomas' God, then, does not will natural evil, but he accepts it as the necessary price for the existence of the cosmos. Is that existence worth so much suffering, or is so much suffering compatible with the idea of a good God? Thomas assumes so. Not everyone would agree."[11]

Of course, Professor Russell himself is one of those who would not agree. On what grounds? On the grounds that Thomas' "privation answer" fails to offer an explanation for natural evil. Why? Because "it is possible to conceive of a diverse cosmos that contains and limits suffering to a much greater extent than does this cosmos".[12] As an example of this position, Russell used this somewhat curious, sacrificial example: "The mouse, for example, might not have to suffer fear or pain but instead find happiness in offering itself up to a weasel." That is to say, when spelled out, Russell evidently suggested, in refutation of Thomas, that if a mouse were created to be a

[10] Russell, *Lucifer,* p. 196.
[11] Ibid., p. 198.
[12] Ibid., p. 198.

being capable of voluntary self-sacrifice, it would be a better universe. But if a mouse could "by nature" do such a thing, it would be a "rational being" in fact, and some "mouse"-Aeschylus would grasp that it learns "by suffering". Russell, in other words, has "re-created" the world that already exists in order to reject this very same world that does exist.

No doubt, the figure of Lucifer or Satan (they are sometimes the same, sometimes not), especially since Milton, has been a rather jaunty, ever attractive one. Lucifer tends to steal the show whenever he appears on stage. But whatever the literary tradition may make of Lucifer, the problem remains. Something is wrong with and in the world, with and in ourselves. Russell's constant identification of evil and suffering makes it almost impossible for him to accept any kind of universe in which suffering exists. Even when he suggested that some alternate universe in which less suffering exists is conceivable, still, given its existence in fact, Russell would have the exact same problem that he does with the present one.

On this point, even though Russell cited C. S. Lewis only once, and this in connection with *The Screwtape Letters,* one wishes his study might have shown some more evidence of Lewis' *The Problem of Pain,* since there the relation of "suffering" to evil is most nuanced. The Suffering Servant underwent pain but was not evil. And the higher order in which suffering, just or unjust, is finally resolved cannot be judged, as Plato saw, without some stance on the immortality of the soul, or, for Christian theology, the resurrection of the body. Without these two doctrines, the problem of evil and suffering may be insolvable, but to exclude them as not pertinent to the question of whether this particular cosmos should have existed in the first place because of suffering in it is a reductionist position. That is, it excludes in principle what may in fact be the clear answer to the problem.

In a related reflection, Professor R. C. Zaehner analyzed the Charles Manson murders, ones similar to those with which Russell began his treatise. Zaehner concluded that these murders were rooted in genuine philosophy, in the belief that in the One, "good and evil, order and disorder" are reconciled, so that Manson's acts were ultimately not wrong. Zaehner's conclusion is rather close to Russell's:

> For many Charles Manson personifies what Bonhoeffer calls the "wickedness of evil". Maybe, but on his own premises, he was scarcely illogical. He had won his flash of enlightenment the hard way and he had learned that in Hindu mysticism and in Zen, the enlightened man who has realised himself as the Absolute . . . is beyond good and evil. "If God is One, what is bad?" he is quoted as saying. And again, as an assiduous student of the Bible, he knew that God had commanded genocide in ancient times and that the Word of God would return in the last days, "his cloak soaked in blood" and himself designated "to tread out the wine of Almighty God's fierce anger".
>
> Perhaps he was a little fanciful in identifying himself with this Rider of the Apocalypse. Interpret it as you will. Say with Lucretius if you will: *tantum religio potuit saudere malorum;* or take the Zoroastrian way out and insist that evil is and must be a principle independent of the absolute hostile to God. Alternatively, if you believe in God at all, you must accept the Jewish paradox in some form and simply admit that the "wickedness of evil" must somehow proceed from the very heart of God and that what God excuses in himself, he hates in us.[13]

And Michael Harrington took this position further by arguing in *The Vast Majority* that even if Christ, the Man-God, did suffer horribly for three hours on the Cross, this could in

---

[13] R. C. Zaehner, *The City within the Heart* (London: Unwin, 1980), p. 44.

no way be comparable with the starving millions throughout history.[14]

And yet, when we pursue all of this, we return to the initial problem that begins with the possibility of there being anything other than God. If we grant that two Gods are intrinsically contradictory, unthinkable, we must grant that for finite creatures other than God to exist, they must bear their own limited being. The "accusation" continually rephrased by Russell, and he meant it sincerely, intellectually, is that this particular world ought not to have existed. Or if it does, God cannot be God. God is thus "responsible" for any "suffering", whether moral or natural, because he made this world that "might" have been made otherwise. (C. S. Lewis also treats in his space trilogy — *Out of the Silent Planet, Perelandra,* and *That Hideous Strength* — other possible forms of redemption and cosmos). I am quite willing to grant the possibility of some other cosmos or some other redemption. The old argument about whether this is the "best possible world" need not detain us except to enable us to grant that this is a "possible" world because obviously it already is.

We have to assume, therefore, that the "amount" of actual suffering in human and cosmic existence was not a surprise to an omniscient being. What was the real alternative that exists for this particular world? It is either no existence at all, or existence with the kind of beings and capacities we possess, ones which by their working out result often in suffering. Any other "possible" world would not in any way include precisely "us". When a tree falls on a wolf to deprive it of one of its legs, all the laws of being that make us possible are merely doing what they do, as is the pain in the leg of the wolf doing what it ought to do.

Absolutely to prevent this pain from ever happening, then,

[14] Michael Harrington, *The Vast Majority* (New York: Simon and Schuster, 1977), p. 253.

we have to think out of existence both the wolf and the tree, along with the wind or ax or lightning or old age that caused the tree to fall in the first place. And in the case of human suffering caused by human freedom, which bears a true reality, to remove it, we would have to demand a world in which this autonomous freedom did not exist. That is, we would demand a world in which there were no real human beings. Does this mean then that the "cause" of evil is God, especially since God is the origin of all beings, including fallen angels? It means rather, I think, what Aquinas thought it meant, namely, that God is the cause of all "being" and that "evil", which cannot be ignored, is a privation, not an entity or a source in God. Evil is a privation by and in beings, rational and irrational, doing what such creatures do "do", as Machiavelli would have had it.

How is all this admitted suffering redeemed? In blaming God for creation in the first place? In demanding another form of "being" after the genetic engineers or the philosophical revolutionaries? Or are we beings born to immortality, as Plato thought, whose very existence ought to lead to the choice of the highest things? It is possible to imagine, following Russell's remark, not only a world in which there would be "less" suffering, but a world in which "evil" existed with no physical suffering. This seems to be more or less what the angelic world was conceived to be by the great scholastics. But if we are to concentrate on suffering, then of course we must ask a different kind of question: namely, does suffering lead to the highest things?

Earlier, I mentioned Flannery O'Connor. Her short story "A Good Man Is Hard to Find" dealt with the slaughter of a grandmother and her family by a misfit, who turned out to be a member of the same family. It is a gruesome story in its way. Yet, its whole purpose was not so much to lament the evil of human suffering and slaughter but to remind us that our salvation is to be found through these very things, or at least it can be. In a letter to Cecil Dawkins on May 21, 1959, Flannery O'Connor made the following brief, amused remark on this story, a story she loved to read to shocked college students and professors:

> I cannot remember if I told you what Jesse Stuart said to a friend of mine after I had read "A Good Man Is Hard to Find"—at Vanderbilt. He said he didn't know why I ended it that way. Didn't I realize the audience identified with the grandmother? I should have kept it going until the cops got there and saved the grandmother.[15]

This seems to me to be more or less Russell's basic feeling about suffering in the world, that it would be a much better world if misfits could not kill their grandmothers.

Flannery O'Connor saw it rather in a different way, as she put it in another letter (April 14, 1960):

> It's interesting to me that your students naturally work their way to the idea that the Grandmother in "A Good Man" is not pure evil and may be a medium for Grace. If they were Southern students, I would say this was because they all had grandmothers like that at home. . . .
> . . . Grace, to the Catholic way of thinking, can and does use as its medium the imperfect, purely human, and even hypocritical. Cutting yourself off from Grace is a very decided matter, requiring a real choice, act of will, and affecting the very ground of the soul. The Misfit is touched by the Grace that comes through the old lady when she recognizes him as her child, as she has been touched by the Grace that comes through him in his particular suffering. . . . In the Protestant view, I think Grace and nature don't have much to do with

[15] Flannery O'Connor, *The Habit of Being: The Letters of Flannery O'Connor* (New York: Viking, 1978), pp. 333–34. See Howard Fickett and Douglas R. Gilbert, *Flannery O'Connor: Images of Grace* (Grand Rapids, Mich.: Eerdmans, 1986).

each other. The old lady, because of her hypocrisy and human-
ness and banality, couldn't be a medium for grace.[16]

This, I think, is the issue presented by Professor Russell's
analysis: whether a finite world in which real evil and suffering exist can in some way also be touched by a higher
purpose.

In conclusion, we could say that Russell's *Lucifer* is but
another treatise not on evil, as it seems initially to be, or even
on suffering, but on the relation of reason and revelation. The
problem of evil is, no doubt, one of the central themes that
mankind has agonized about over the ages. Civilizations will
differ pretty much because of what they believe about evil.
Russell did us an inestimable service in tracing this record of
how evil has been looked upon in our tradition. But I think
that Chesterton's Wesleyan grandfather was closer to the heart
of things when he was willing to thank God for existence even
were he a lost soul. The concern that I have for Russell's
worthy study of evil, then, is that by concentrating on "suffering"
instead of evil, he has made suffering into an accusation against
God, only to have lost the real question of evil which a
"Lucifer" originally brought up—that is, the possibility of a
free creature choosing itself over a higher good, a choice with
its own necessary consequences not only for itself in spiritual
and physical suffering, but for the whole cosmos.

C. S. Lewis has, I feel, set down the proper way to look at
suffering—no matter how "much" or how "little" of it we
grant to be acceptable:

> The tendency of this or that novelist or poet may represent
> suffering as wholly bad in its effects, as producing and justify-
> ing every kind of malice and brutality in the sufferer. And of
> course, pain, like pleasure, can be so received: all that is given to

[16] O'Connor, *The Habit of Being,* pp. 389–90.

a creature with free will must be two-edged, not by the nature of the giver or of the gift, but by the nature of the recipient.[17]

The nature of the recipient, not the nature of God, is the locus for the proper thinking about evil and suffering. Whether it would be better for the recipient not to exist is the real theme of *Lucifer.*

Yet, in classical thought, Lucifer is a being who remains, even in his own choice of himself, as Aquinas held, substantially good. All "evil" is dependent on what is good, on simply *what is.* The only radical alternative to *what is,* is what is not, not some other form of creation conceived merely in terms of whether there might or might not be less suffering.

Eight Books on Evil and Suffering

1. C. S. Lewis, *The Problem of Pain.*
2. Jacques Maritain, *St. Thomas and the Problem of Evil.*
3. Alfons Deeken, *Growing Old and How to Cope with It*
4. Henry Fairlie, *The Seven Deadly Sins Today.*
5. Paul Vitz, *Psychology as Religion: The Cult of Self-Worship.*
6. Peter Kreeft, *Making Sense out of Suffering.*
7. Frederick Sontag, *God, Why Did You Do That?.*
8. William Kirk Kirkpatrick, *Psychological Seduction.*

---

[17] C. S. Lewis, *The Problem of Pain* (New York: Macmillan, 1978), p. 107.

Chapter Eleven

The Obscure Heart of Ideology

(This chapter is an analysis of the book
The Coercive Utopians,
by Rael Jean Isaac and Eric Isaac.)

Understanding what is going on in one's own society, in the
world itself, is never easy. We are creatures who can deceive
and be deceived, even by ourselves. This teaching about our
human condition once stood at the heart of moral and religious education and preaching. This education and preaching
first looked to the human soul, not to political structures, to
explain evil and disorder in their ultimate depths. The desire
for the good, moreover, does not, by itself, produce the good.
Indeed, the desire for the good by itself is what makes evil
possible in our kind, since, as the classical writers on the
subject tell us, evil is always chosen, albeit willingly, under
the appearance of some particular good. The great Gnostic
dream, revised in modern social analysis and again proposed to
an unwary generation, places evil in the organs of collectivities, classes, corporations, and other demons, apart from personal responsibility and insight into oneself and one's ultimate
destiny.

Moreover, as Aristotle suggested, the greatest tyrannies invariably will be concocted not by poor and simple folk, but by the
more astute and intelligent insofar as these deviate from the
good as it is given in reality. The more or less undisciplined
citizens in the democracies, unable clearly to recognize where
the sophisticated sirens might take them, not even really wanting to know, can be led almost voluntarily into the worst

regimes and be told by the pedants who led them there that this utter corruption is good and holy.

Why, then, in the discussion of this issue, do we find the peculiar expression "coercive utopians"? The Isaacs wrote:

> Most of the groups we will describe are utopian because they assume that man is perfectible and the evils that exist are the product of a corrupt social system. They believe that an ideal social order can be created in which man's potentialities can flower freely. They are "coercive" because in their zeal for attaining an ideal order they seek to impose their blueprints in ways that go beyond legitimate persuasion.[1]

Put in terms of Professor Leo Strauss, we have again a generation that has lost its understanding of the "moderation" that is required of the public order and the individuals in it if they are not to destroy themselves by seeking to impose on this world visions proper to metaphysics and religion.

What is being played out, then, in much of our society, which often does not want even to acknowledge what is going on, is precisely this civic deception by an alienated elite, very often ironically but not unexpectedly the sons and daughters of the older oligarchs and moderate clerics. They have not yet, perhaps, found a single tyrant (leader, hero), but it is early, and they do follow movements. They do reject things that sane and normal men and women by experience and good sense hold dear—children, family, property, self-motivation, reward, fairness, growth, risk, and truth. There are many future candidates for "darkness at noon" among us.

The Coercive Utopians is a meticulous account of this process of intellectual alienation. But it is also an explanation of how this process could happen, so that it is likewise an essay on the

[1] Rael Jean Isaac and Eric Isaac, *The Coercive Utopians: America's Power Players* (Chicago: Regnery-Gateway, 1983), p. 2.

condition of religion and moral philosophy. Indeed, the Isaacs have provided an explanation of how religion and moral philosophy themselves can come to embrace the very ideologies from which they were thought, perhaps naively, to protect us. We need to know in detail the character, the names, the motives of that segment of the elite that has culturally confused its wondrous ideals with what can or ought to be. This blunt and fascinating study by the Isaacs is, therefore, very welcome. It helps show why there is a small but growing concern that many of our best and brightest, even in religion—some would say, especially in religion—have opted for a closed agenda that is anything but compatible with the tested values and experiences we have learned to rely on because they correspond with reality.

This book is, if you will, another chapter in our civilization's relation to what it thought it heard in Plato. It is, likewise, as Igor Shafarevich noted in *The Socialist Phenomenon*—a book that could easily be a fit companion volume to this one—a reconfirmation of the suspicion of Shafarevich that a certain kind of mind chooses death over the messiness of real life and politics. That is, it chooses to eliminate the very reasons why finite man is unique in the universe and peculiarly himself. What man already is, in the thinking of the coercive utopians, is seen to be itself an evil. Therefore, a "new man" is constantly posited, a man formed frighteningly out of none of the norms of classical philosophy or revelation. I suspect, with Professor Allan Bloom, that Plato wrote *The Republic* to teach us what "pure justice" might be like in practice, with certain extraordinary consequences in family, property, and state, so that we would not in fact choose it in this life if we could avoid it. Yet the truth is that intellectuals and dons, lay and clerical, who have in fact given up in practice a transcendent faith or a realist metaphysics, inevitably turn on the real world to "refashion" it in their own earnest, self-generated image of what civilization and therefore reality "ought" to look like.

This way, of course, has always proved to be lethal for the majority of mankind. Evidently, the people who unfortunately live under this world reformism, once in power, learn, willingly or forcibly, what such a system might actually look like in practice. And they are genuinely surprised that such "interesting", even "noble" ideas—as they thought—have led them here, if indeed they can bear to see the truth. The Solzhenitsyns of this world, no doubt, exist as a grace, to warn us in advance; but, as the Isaacs noted, the current media and academy are not at all much interested in telling us about this. All of this ideology, moreover, arises from a personal rejection of the elements of reason and revelation that implied that a Gnostic self-salvation was not what mankind was really about.

The "coercive utopians"—whom I myself have usually dubbed, more narrowly, the "liberal fascists"—are those sincere men and women in new-left academies and think tanks variously named and accounted for by the Isaacs, or Naderites of various hues, in environmental and peace movements, all of whom have more or less come to believe that America in particular and modern civilization in general is all wrong somehow and the origin of all public and private evils. It might be noted also that this is quite different from the thesis of Voegelin and Strauss, who also see a fundamental disorder in the "modern project" itself. The "coercive utopians", in fact, are logically bringing to an extreme conclusion precisely those ideas of modern political and moral theory that were variant positions from the classical and revelational traditions.

The Isaacs are aware that, whatever the real relation of all this is to Marxism, itself a part of this modern project, it will in all likelihood lead to the worst forms of Marxism, even while professing anarchism, by destroying the spirit and power of anything that might actually prevent its takeover. Most of the "coercive utopians" described carefully by the Isaacs would claim to reject the brutal consequences of the Soviet Union and see no relation between their own ideas and how the Soviet Union arrived at its own sad state. This is a train of thought that a Solzhenitsyn would find quite amusing.

This book performs a service of double value. The first service might be called documentary, the second philosophic. The Isaacs have given a coherent, detailed account of who these "coercive utopians" are, their organizations, their interrelationships, and their methods, presuppositions, and relation to the major ideologies of our time. They pull no punches. They give names and genealogies. Hannah Arendt remarked that practical truth often seems utterly unbelievable, so that we need a minute record of particular dates, actions, places, names. How this is done for movements will vary, but the Isaacs have managed, I think, to demonstrate how this can be carried out.

The Isaacs, secondly, go on to suggest why these alienated clerics, scions, and academics come to set themselves against the values and accomplishments of the best in the modern (and ancient) world. I found this the more important part of the book, but it depends, for its full force, on the particular descriptions of the movements and the actors in them. The Isaacs show how these movements embody revivals of certain anarchistic and utopian premises that have gnawed at the heart of modern thought since Joachim of Flora and are now working themselves out in a final effort to present a coherent, incarnated, this-worldly utopia, built, point for point, on a rejection of the contents of reason and revelation about what it is to be human in precisely this universe. Some readers will probably be surprised that religious people,

who often play such an important part in this narrative—
Protestants, Jews, and Catholics—seem to contribute more and
more to this essentially Gnostic enterprise of perfecting this
world.

The Isaacs' book, however, is an occasion for another kind
of reflection. One of the most curious aspects of this story of
the "coercive utopians" is the contribution of Christians to it,
either as actors or followers. I have been struck recently in
regard to the peace movements, another well-covered activity
of the "coercive utopians" in the Isaacs' book, that much of the
most hardheaded, acute, and perceptive criticism of the implications of pacifism in the churches has come from Jews. Indeed,
I would suspect that the present growing alliance of many
Christians with the "coercive utopians", Marxists, anarchists,
or whatever is a major factor in confirming a Jew's suspicion
that Christianity cannot be true. This takes on double meaning
when it is recalled that the "coercive utopians" of fifty and a
hundred years ago were usually Jewish, at least in leadership.
What has intervened in the meantime is the existence of Israel
as a particular state. That is to say, the Jewish intellectual is
going in the direction of realism, whereas the Christian
intellectual, beginning historically from particularity in the
Incarnation, is going in the opposite direction: toward abstraction and collectivities.

In this sense, then, the very existence of Israel has served to
sober the mystic ideologue in the Jewish tradition—the Isaacs
note this earlier propensity—in the direction of what works,
of what actually happens. We need, in this sense, in connection
with the Isaacs' comments on the American bishops' peace
pastoral, only to read an Albert Wohlstetter or Edward Luttwak,
or especially Joseph Cropsey's essay "America as a Regime", to
realize who preserves the tradition of reason and realism in this
area, once the almost undisputed position of Augustine and

Aquinas.[2] Ironically, it is the Christian intellectual, no longer grounded in any piety or duty to real places, regimes, or people, who has begun to spin off ideal solutions for this world. So long as Christians were still rooted in Augustine or Aquinas, they retained the realism that could account for this world and its limitations, while properly locating the Kingdom not of this world. From a classical Christian view of political theory, it is now conceivable, in view of the Isaacs' book, that the earthly "mystery" of Israel, of which Maritain and von Balthasar spoke, may be able, by its sober realism, to prevent the Christians from embracing a this-worldly utopianism that denies the fundamentals of faith and reason.

What I found especially valuable in *The Coercive Utopians* is the lively intelligence to look beyond the immediate to see where very noble ideas actually lead. Whether it be in promoting the Sandinista "vision", the wilderness, appropriate technology, antipollution or antinuclear technology, pacifism, or human rights, many on-the-surface quite incontrovertible hopes of social morality, the Isaacs see and trace where such ideas actually lead in practice, for all the high rhetoric. And they lead, as the classics already suspected, to an anti-human utopia, a utopia designed to replace the best practical state and the transcendent Kingdom of God. One might hope, I suppose, that this fascinating, sobering book would be on the shelf of every bishop, academic, and TV commentator. But it is not likely that the Isaacs' frank message will be much allowed to be heard in its full force, since few people see why the "coercive utopians" are not benefiting mankind.

---

[2] Joseph Cropsey, "America as a Regime", in *Political Philosophy and the Issues of Politics* (Chicago: University of Chicago Press, 1980), pp. 1–15. See also George Weigel, *"Tranquillitas Ordinis": The Present Failure and Future Promise of American Catholic Thought on War and Peace* (New York: Oxford, 1987).

The Isaacs feel that the sole sure way to prevent such ideologies from gaining further control of the bureaucracies, the press, and the universities is by careful exposure to what these ideologies are in fact proposing. Thus far, practically all the effective efforts to "stem the utopian tide" have come from obscure individuals, often themselves victims of this utopianism in which by their own choices they once believed. They have finally realized how ideas come to exist in movements and how such movements work to destroy what already exists. "If the silent majority remains silent and passive", say the Isaacs, "the articulate, committed minority will determine their future".[3] So long as the Soviet involvement in the nuclear freeze, for example, or the participation of certain Christians in revolutionary violence, or the antiprogressive nature of environmentalism go unnoticed and unaccounted for, the future utopian ends will probably come about in coercion. There are those who are now prepared to "save" mankind from itself. These are the most dangerous persons in our society. The Isaacs have pointed out their existence and their intentions. This is no small service.

Finally, the Isaacs do not hesitate to suggest, at least, what the alternatives to the utopian visions might be:

> There are alternative, pragmatic approaches to all the problems the utopians address, precisely in the wrong way. There are alternative "market strategies"... to deal with problems of pollution.... Greater safety and health will not come through ever more regulation that makes products ever more costly, but through the recognition of the basic principle that "richer is safer". And the poor will not become richer through "decentralization" or "appropriate technology" but through expanding production.[4]

[3] Isaac and Isaac, *The Coercive Utopians,* p. 309.
[4] Ibid., p. 310.

In the past, religion and philosophy have been accused of ignoring man's earthly task by concentrating on his ultimate status before the One or God. In trying to correct this apparent alienation, the passions and energies that formerly went into questions of trancendence now go rather into the enterprises of this world. The result has been not an improvement of the world, but an attack on its very sanity and foundations. Ironically, the immediate salvation of the world itself requires that religion and philosophy return to their true nature and goal. The Isaacs' book is as good an account as any of why.

Eight Books on the Topic of Utopianism and Coercion

1. Igor Shafarevich, *The Socialist Phenomenon.*
2. Hannah Arendt, *The Origins of Totalitarianism.*
3. J. L. Talmon, *The Origins of Totalitarian Democracy.*
4. Eric Voegelin, *Science, Politics, and Gnosticism.*
5. Aleksandr Solzhenitsyn, *Solzhenitsyn at Harvard.*
6. Michael Novak, *Freedom with Justice: Catholic Social Thought and Liberal Institutions*
7. Jean-François Revel, *How Democracies Perish.*
8. Paul Johnson, *Modern Times: The World from the Twenties to the Eighties*

Five Books about Art and Beauty

1. Jacques Maritain, *Creative Intuition in Art and Poetry.*
2. Etienne Gilson, *Painting and Reality.*
3. Armand Maurer, *About Beauty: A Thomistic Interpretation*
4. Jacques Maritain, *Art and Scholasticism.*
5. Gerardus van der Leeuw, *Sacred and Profane Beauty.*

Chapter Twelve

The Mortality of Immortal Men

*(These remarks are based on two books about the English
writer Hilaire Belloc: A. N. Wilson's biography,*
Hilaire Belloc, *and John P. McCarthy's*
Hilaire Belloc: Edwardian Radical.*)*

A.

From various reviews and comments about it, I was prepared to dislike this new book about Hilaire Belloc, the
great English essayist, whose wonderful book *The Four Men*
has recently been reissued by the Oxford University Press
in paperback, edited by this same A. N. Wilson. At first, I
found the biography rather distasteful in tone, particularly
its meticulous endeavor, willful almost, to find Belloc all too
human, restless, often even rude. But by the time I reached the
following delightful passage, a hundred or so pages into the
book, when I realized that Wilson too, as I did, thought *The
Path to Rome,* the travel and whimsical essays, the humorous
poems, the reflections on our lot, to be the best things in
Belloc, if not in our literature, I was ready to change my
mind.

> Dining one night with the Jesuits at Campion Hall at Oxford,
> he [Belloc] was asked by a skeptical fellow guest how he could
> possibly believe that the bread and wine at the Mass were
> transformed into the actual body and blood of Our Lord.

Belloc replied that he would believe that they were changed
into an elephant if the Church told him so.[1]

To this tale, Wilson added, amusingly, "It was the Jesuits, not
the skeptic, who were scandalized by this very characteristic
reply." Belloc was the one who understood "the crucial importance of believing in the truth of Catholic doctrine".[2]

Perhaps, in the light of this story, it is worthwhile to dwell
upon this point: doctrine in the eyes of Belloc, the Jesuits, and
the skeptic. Belloc held that "Catholicism was the only true
alternative . . . to Atheism."[3] And he wrote to Chesterton in
1921, "I am by all my nature of mind skeptical".[4] Why, we
might wonder, was it the Jesuit, not the skeptic, who was
scandalized? The answer to this is hinted at in a letter Belloc
wrote to Professor Phillimore about the same time (1920): "It
is essential for us to impress it upon our contemporaries that
the Catholic is intellectually the superior of everyone *except the
skeptic* in all that region cognate to and attached to that which
may be called 'Intellectual Appreciation'—pure intelligence."[5]
The skeptic was not scandalized because he understood perfectly well the validity of Belloc's remark and the sense of its
inner logic.

Throughout the rest of this book, one gets the impression
that Wilson himself invariably is on Belloc's and the skeptic's

---

[1] A. N. Wilson, *Hilaire Belloc: A Biography* (New York: Atheneum,
1984), p. 108. For other looks at Belloc, see Robert Speaight, *The Life of
Hilaire Belloc* (New York: Farrar, Straus, and Giroux, 1957); J. B. Morton,
Hilaire Belloc: A Memoir (London: Hollis and Carter, 1953); Frederick D.
Wilhelmsen, *Hilaire Belloc: No Alienated Man* (New York: Sheed and
Ward, 1954).

[2] Wilson, *Hilaire Belloc*, p. 254.

[3] Ibid., p. 251.

[4] Ibid., p. 250.

[5] Ibid., p. 243.

side, in the name of both faith and reason, over against what
has happened in the Christian system after Belloc's time.

> The Catholicism in which he was nurtured, and of which he
> was the most eloquent champion, is unlike the Catholicism of
> the Second Vatican Council. It was "triumphalist", baroque,
> certain, glorious, and hard. Pius XII was the last Supreme
> Pontiff of the Church to maintain this Faith in its fullness, and
> with the supreme confidence of his five predecessors. After that,
> a very different order of things would come into being; an order
> which Belloc would, in many particulars, not have recognized
> as Catholic at all. At Pius XII's coronation, no one would have
> guessed that Europe, however scarred and changed, would more
> or less survive the coming conflict; that there would be some
> kind of visible continuity between the Europe of 1939 and that of
> the 1980s; but that the one thing which would be changed out of
> all recognition was the infallible and unchangeable Church.[6]

To understand this book, we need to understand that this is
Wilson, not Belloc speaking. That is to say, we can wonder
about Wilson's own agenda in writing *Hilaire Belloc*.[7]

One of the underlying tensions of the book, appearing
again and again, then, is Wilson's supposition that the Church
Belloc knew and the Church we now have are no longer the
same institution—though Wilson did hint that Belloc's Poland
and John Paul II may conspire to return in the older direction.
Recounting, for example, Belloc's love of the French country
Mass, Wilson added, with wit and perception, "Now [1985],
he [Belloc] would be lucky to find a morning Mass at all. In
many French villages, it is offered only weekly, and in the
evening, often to the accompaniment of song, and an extempore

[6] Ibid., p. 358.
[7] Wilson spelled out his own position in his *How Can We Know?: An
Essay on the Christian Religion* (New York: Atheneum, 1985).

commentary on the latest world news."[8] Wilson continued, "modern Christianity has taken on the characteristic of a sect." Again one wonders if Wilson's main theme in this book is really Belloc. Again, "Belloc would probably have found the new vernacular Mass and the *religion* which gave birth to it . . . " unpleasant.[9] And Wilson doubted that Belloc's "faith would have survived the Second Vatican Council". Passages such as these cause us to wonder if we are still talking about Belloc, the man of doctrine, or about Wilson.

Yet, in so many ways, this is an endearing, wonderful book about a very great man. "His greatness really consisted not even so much in what he said as in what he was", Wilson wrote.[10] "There is no one else in the history of the world remotely like him." Such are remarkable words if we are to think that Wilson is somehow debunking Belloc by recounting all his foibles. On the surface, Wilson's Belloc is iconoclastic and muckrackish. Belloc's prejudices, errors of judgment, faults, and vulgarities are recounted with minute accuracy, even annoyance. One wonders why. To be sure, they were part of Belloc, the human being, "the very great man". But in Wilson's view, Belloc always turned out, on the important issues, to be largely correct.

Jewish critics in particular have been tempted to look on the surface of Belloc's presumed "anti-Semitism" to see in Wilson an ally in attacking Belloc wherever this anti-Semitism supposedly occurs. But this view turns out to be a very strange affair in the book itself. Wilson's careful judgment of Belloc's real position was that Belloc did understand the reality in a way no one else did in his time. Belloc was concerned about settling the Jewish problem fairly. The failure to recognize the nature of the problem and the nature of the solution, not Belloc's view, was what led to the later disasters. A rabbinical reading

[8] Wilson, *Hilaire Belloc,* p. 107.
[9] Ibid., p. 253.
[10] Ibid., p. 383.

of Wilson, for all its merciless detailing of Belloc's awful language, would lead to another conclusion about the situation itself and its causes.

One would expect to find G. K. Chesterton here, but he hardly appears. Belloc missed GKC's baptism, while Chesterton is described at his death as a "childishly charming soul". Wilson never cited Belloc's famous assessment of Chesterton, particularly that Chesterton was too charitable—though Wilson did recount that at Chesterton's funeral, Belloc apparently sold the "exclusive" rights to his views on GKC four times. Again, one suspects Wilson of being more of a Bellocian than meets the eye. None of the gigantic sanity and intelligence of *Orthodoxy*, or how Belloc related to it, is even hinted at by Wilson, even though *Orthodoxy* was written in 1908.

In Wilson's life, Belloc is eternally restless and lonely, yet he had at the same time myriads of friends, male and female. In the course of Belloc's long life, there were gradually taken from him many of these: his American wife, sons in both Wars, drinking companions, intellectual friends. Belloc lectured every place, including, on April 3, 1923, to "the Public Speaking Class of St. John's College, Brooklyn". Belloc hated parliament, parties, socialism, capitalism, Prussianism, Oxford dons, and newspaper magnates. Many grew to hate him in return. One of his stories was among the first ever to appear on television, and Wilson thinks Belloc would have been terrific on television. No doubt he is right, if he were allowed to speak frankly. We can think of Malcolm Muggeridge or William F. Buckley, Jr., in this connection. Many hold that he wrote too much. He agreed, but only added that he did it to keep from starving, to keep a certain style of life, as Wilson recounted. Belloc loved a fight. "He delighted in the idea that everyone else was wrong and he was in the right."[11]

[11] Ibid., p. 363.

Wilson holds that Belloc's light verse is perhaps the best in the language. Belloc's best, for Wilson, are not his histories or apologetics or novels or economic tracts, but his travels, his profound awareness in his essays of the poignancy of our human existence, whose meaning the Faith, its doctrines, illumines, even when it does not console, as it did not Belloc himself. "Life was very sorrowful, and few have had a stronger sense than Belloc that our theological condition here is best defined in the *Salve Regina,* which speaks of us 'mourning and weeping in this valley of tears'."[12] This sense of melancholy is, I think, only capable of being grasped by those who hold the dogmas of the faith, of the Incarnation in particular. Laughter (and good red wine), the promotion and evidence of joy, are especially also our lot. There is no need to wonder why melancholy and friendship go together in this world. They are companions, with laughter; hence the poignancy, hence the melancholy, hence the loneliness.

Visiting his old French army unit at the ill-fated Maginot Line in 1939—he still thought the French army the best in the world—Belloc wrote: "It is an astonishing thing to come back to the same atmosphere and tradition after a gap of just on to fifty years. It is the only pleasant accident to mortality I have known, and had an air about it of the immortal."[13] The immortal is confronted only in those ultimate experiences of our mortality, in friendship, in war, in time, in particular things no one else knows but ourselves. Belloc went to the Holy Land after his lecture tour in the United States in 1935. In a letter to Katherine Asquith—"He deeply cared for women"[14]—Wilson recounted one of the most beautiful passages in our tradition:

[12] Ibid., p. 366.
[13] Ibid., p. 363.
[14] Ibid., p. 316.

That is great poetry and therefore, justly interpreted, sound truth: sound theology. Not that God Himself can suffer, but that God was so intensely, so intimately Man in the Incarnation, that the memories and experiences of Divinity and Humanity are united therein: and through it, the worst pain of the creature is *known,* by actual experience of our own kind, by the Creator. We are, of all our miseries, much the most afflicted by Mortality: and that means not mere Death—least of all our own, which may be but a blessed sleep between the good troubled life and the good untroubled life of beatitude—but the impermanence of all things, even of love: the good-byes and the changes that never halt their damning succession: the unceasing tale of loss which wears down all at last. *That* is mortality. *That* is the contradiction between our native joy and our present realities, which contrast in the curse of the Fall.[15]

It is this passage, I suspect, that led Wilson to write this book, this passage that assured him of Belloc's final greatness, in spite of all.

Such, then, is the essence of our theology, as it is the essence of our lot, that our joys and sadnesses are bound together in the Man-God, as in ourselves, that both suffering and joy give us intimations of the vale beyond the tears. In this matter, I believe I can do Wilson one better, merely to reconfirm his own feeling about Belloc, in a passage I have thought about often, cited many times, read even more—indeed, Belloc's essays are best appreciated when they are read to our friends, aloud. This is from Belloc's essay "A Remaining Christmas", in J. B. Morton's—Morton was at Belloc's deathbed—collection:

Man has a body as well as a soul, and the whole of man, soul and body, is nourished sanely by a multiplicity of observed traditional things. Moreover, there is this great quality in the unchanging practice of Holy Seasons, that it makes explicable,

[15] Ibid., pp. 338–39.

tolerable and normal what is otherwise a shocking and intolerable and even in the fullest sense, abnormal thing. *I mean, the
mortality of immortal men.*[16]

No wonder Belloc celebrated a traditional Christmas at King's
Land, no wonder, as his friend G. K. Chesterton said, we are
homesick even at home.

Wilson, I think, has written a much more perceptive and
profound sort of book than many are willing to admit. He did
not hesitate to say, "There is no one else in the history of the
world remotely like him." What is remarkable about Belloc
himself is not his genius, prejudice, laughter, wit, hatred, song,
wisdom, or loneliness. It is rather that all these things belong
to one human being, to the mortality of immortal men, for
whom nothing in this vale of tears suffices, however lovely it
is.

Let me conclude these remarks with another passage that
Wilson did not mention, though it is one he would like, I
think. It is from Belloc's 1923 essay on the Cathedral at Seville,
in Spain. This is, perhaps, how Belloc would have addressed
himself to Wilson's worry that Belloc's religion has disappeared
from the face of the earth, a sad, melancholy event, because
Wilson hinted that the skeptic, not Belloc, was right about
why we believe what we believe. Belloc wrote, on the contrary,

> A man in the Cathedral of Seville understands the end of his
> being. He is, while standing there on earth, surrounded by
> stones and rocks of the earth, with his own body in decay and
> all about him in decay—he is, in the midst of all this material
> affair, yet in some side-manner out of it all; he is half in
> possession of the final truths. Nowhere else in the world, that I
> know of, has the illimitable fixed itself in the material. Divinity
> is here impetricate.

[16] Hilaire Belloc, "A Remaining Christmas", in *Selected Essays of Hilaire
Belloc,* ed. J. B. Morton (Baltimore: Penguin, 1958), p. 213.

It is not only proportion that does this at Seville—it is also multiplicity. It is not only that mark of true creative power—the making of something more than that you meant to make—it is also that other mark of creative power—diversity, endless breeding, burgeoning, foison, which everywhere clothes this amazing result.[17]

In other words, the loneliness of our mortality does not prevent, but indeed suggests, our sense of immortality, our wonder at the extraordinary creativity of reality, its diversity, its wonderment that a Belloc could even exist, with his laughter and his sadness. This is what Mr. Wilson's book has brought us to think about, and we are grateful.

B.

In taking a rather different look at Belloc, this time through John McCarthy's book, I mean to suggest that Belloc is himself someone we ought to let educate us, for he will take us through paths, as we have seen, that we could not otherwise find. Thus, I want to begin with another favorite passage from another essay in the Morton collection, one called "London and the Houses in It", an essay written in 1909. It begins

In every decade men growing older deplore the disappearance of this or that sanctuary of isolation and silence, but in the aggregate they never disappear; something in the very character of the people reproduces them continually, and if any man will borrow the leisure—even a man who knows his London well—to peer about and to explore for one Saturday afternoon, in one square mile of old London, how many such unknown corners will he not find![18]

[17] Belloc, "On the Cathedral of Seville and the Misanthrope", in *Selected Essays*, p. 184.
[18] Belloc, "London and the Houses in It", in *Selected Essays*, p. 109.

That aspect of education that Belloc often leads us to is precisely what I like to call "the recovery of unknown corners", the spirit of wonder about the places in which men live, the deep mysteries we always find there.

John McCarthy began his preface to *Hilaire Belloc: Edwardian Radical* with this comment: "My interest in Hilaire Belloc began when I read *The Servile State* while a student."[19] How many of us can say something similar! Perhaps we did not first discover *The Servile State* or *The Redistribution of Property* but *Europe and the Faith* (still the most superficially "refuted" book by a certain sad type of Christian intellectual) or *Danton* or *Survivals and New Arrivals* or, if we were lucky, *The Path to Rome*, a book still so precious that we find it hard to believe anything so wonderful could be written by a mere man—a book whose major thesis is that only a mere man did in fact write it. Its only real rival is Belloc's own *The Four Men*. But I have always felt that *The Servile State* was a much more significant book than we have suspected.[20] *Hilaire Belloc: Edwardian Radical* is a welcome reminder of just why.

To comment dispassionately on anything about Belloc I find difficult, however, as I perceive John McCarthy did. For Catholics of our generation, Belloc was still much more of a folk hero, a man who made us think our faith was in fact thinkable. Only later, as we found ourselves unaccountably older, were we told that we must take a stand for or against Belloc and his style of Catholicism. Usually we were judged harshly if we did not disagree with him. No doubt we must be "objective", and this is what McCarthy set out to be, earnestly, successfully. Still, in being so objective, I missed some of the Belloc I remembered.

---

[19] John P. McCarthy, *Hilaire Belloc: Edwardian Radical* (Indianapolis, Ind.: Liberty Press, 1978), p. 11.

[20] See James V. Schall, "Freedom, Property, and *The Servile State*", *The Chesterton Review* XII (May 1986): 185–94.

This book was not designedly about Belloc the Catholic, or Belloc the traveler, or Belloc on the *Nona,* or Belloc the poet, or Belloc the historian. Nevertheless, in one small instance, I found it difficult to forgive John McCarthy for rather "summarizing" my favorite passage in *The Path to Rome,* and in general for his giving us too little of the mystical sanity of Belloc.

This is McCarthy's rendition of a passage in which Belloc told us what the traditional Mass meant to him and his culture:

> Instead, Belloc believed that man could "be fairly happy . . . and, what is more important, decent and secure of our souls", only by gaining that "feeling of satisfaction" which results from doing what "is buried right into our blood from immemorial habit" and "what the human race has done for thousands upon thousands of years": traditional and natural activities such as hunting, drinking "fermented liquor with one's food — and especially deeply on feast days", going to sea, dancing, and singing in chorus. Another wise thought, he insisted, was that "every man should do a little work with his hands".[21]

This, however, is the complete text of the same passage in Belloc himself:

> And the most important cause of this feeling of satisfaction is that you are doing what the human race has done for thousands upon thousands of years. This is a matter of such moment that I am astonished people hear of it so little. Whatever is buried right into our blood from immemorial habit that we must be certain to do if we are to be fairly happy (of course no grown man or woman can really be very happy for long — but I mean reasonably happy), and, what is more important, decent and secure of our souls. Thus one should from time to time hunt animals, or at the very least shoot at a mark; one should always drink some kind of fermented liquor with one's food — and es-

[21] McCarthy, *Hilaire Belloc,* p. 77.

pecially deeply upon great feast-days; one should go on the water from time to time; and one should dance on occasions; and one should sing in chorus. For all these things man has done since God put him into a Garden and his eyes first became troubled with a soul. Similarly some teacher or ranter or other, whose name I forget, said lately one very wise thing at least, which was that every man should do a little work with his hands.[22]

We should not "summarize" such magnificent lines, I think.

For a long time, in any case, Catholic intellectuals have felt comfortable in treating Belloc as a kind of embarrassing oddity, I suspect mostly because he was adamantly Catholic. John McCarthy touched this delicately when he remarked, near the end of his book, "The post-Vatican II Catholic Church would have broken his heart."[23] Yet Belloc loved the Poles and the Irish—for him, the two peoples added to Christendom from outside the boundaries of the old Roman Empire—so that, I suspect, John Paul II, with his warmth and with his decisions, would have been much to his liking, as he has not been with the intellectuals after Vatican II.

Nonetheless, and this is John McCarthy's thesis, the intellectual tenor of our time in social philosophy has tended to vindicate Belloc against his various critics. Many of the things Belloc stood for have become the common fare of post-liberal social thought. Therefore, it is worthwhile to recall "the prophetic and subtle character of so much of his [Belloc's] social and political commentary".[24]

In this context, one might note, though John McCarthy did not do so, the relation of much of Belloc to E. F. Schumacher's

[22] Hilaire Belloc, *The Path to Rome* (Garden City, N.Y.: Doubleday Image, 1959), p. 39.

[23] McCarthy, *Hilaire Belloc,* p. 339.

[24] Ibid., p. 339.

Small Is Beautiful. And Catholic radicals in the Third World have missed something very significant when they unfortunately "opted for socialism", as their clerical apologists like to call it, instead of the much more viable and pertinent theories of property and craft for which Belloc argued. Had, say, Julius Nyerere read *The Servile State* before launching into *Ujamaa* and socialism, the world would have been better for it, especially Nyerere's own country. Belloc was right, however we account for it: *the* political issue of the twentieth century was to be "the servile state", so that Belloc is well worth the attention of a generation that has felt it "chic" and heady to reject in retrospect much of what Belloc rejected in prospect.

To understand Belloc, of course, it is today necessary to do exactly what McCarthy set out to do for us, namely, to place him within the Edwardian period and the way it perceived its own problems. "Tell me what you are against, and I will tell you what you stand for." Thus, in the case of Hilaire Belloc, when we see why he was against the plutocrats, the party system, the Prussians, the Webbs, the "Jews", as we saw earlier in the case of A. N. Wilson's book, it becomes much clearer what he did hold.

Belloc has been too easily accused of "anti-Semitism", whereas, as McCarthy also carefully pointed out, Belloc was quite sympathetic to Jews, but he did not feel constrained, as we undoubtedly do today, to exempt a rich or powerful Jew from criticism when he abuses wealth or power just because he is a Jew.[25] In a sense, anyone who does not criticize a Jew, or any one else who in fact abuses wealth or power, for fear of being called "anti-Semitic" is undoubtedly much less respectful of Jews as human beings than someone like Belloc who did criticize what he held to be wrong. Belloc felt that wealthy capitalists abused

[25] Ibid., pp. 261–66.

their trusts and responsibilities, both Gentiles and Jews. To call this view prejudice is quite dubious.

Indeed, one of the most interesting things about Belloc—in the light of our contemporary neoconservatism and the experiential realization that socialism, which alternative Belloc instinctively rejected as it grew out of the British liberal left, leads to tyranny—is that Belloc was also most clearly against "capitalism". No one on today's socialist left can condemn "capitalism" more eloquently than Belloc could and did.

In this sense, Belloc legitimately belongs, as John McCarthy pointed out in connection with Belloc's relation to Leo XIII, to a social tradition that is neither capitalist nor socialist. He was for incentive and feared the state. He believed in the value of communal life but knew how wealth could abuse the poor. The loss of Catholics in their own tradition does not excuse them from blindness to the contemporary pertinence of Belloc's analysis.

Another interesting aspect about Belloc in this connection is his relation to the United States. Like Chesterton, he believed it to be the last of the medieval monarchies, because one man, with assemblies and with intermediate organizations, not oligarchies, ruled. And this man generally ruled people with property. And property for Belloc was not so much agricultural land but one's own house and craft. Co-ownership of necessarily larger organizations, as to Leo XIII and Pius XI, seemed most sensible to Belloc. Arguing for a strong ruler, Belloc, like others, misjudged Mussolini, but one still wonders what the Italian ruler might have turned out to be without his German friend to the north. As Belloc had little use for the Teutons in general, he was not surprised to see how it all did turn out.

Nonetheless, what Belloc did realize in the United States was the need for legitimate political authority exercised by a ruler not dependent on oligarchical sources. This ruler was needed as much for the common man as it was needed against socialist and capitalist abuses. What is of perhaps some interest here is a comparison of Belloc's *The Contrast,* his book on the United States, with Chesterton's *What I Saw in America,* Jacques Maritain's *Reflections on America,* and Father Bruckberger's *The Image of America.* All of these should then be compared with the pervasive anti-Americanism and anticapitalism of contemporary liberation theology, with all the nuances. The result of such a comparison, I think, would suggest that the instincts of Belloc in the pre-World War I period of British politics, so well related by John McCarthy, were prelude to the present situation wherein socialism has led to bureaucratic tyranny, reducing the citizen to the serf-like status of Belloc's fears and wherein liberal capitalism had to be reformed of its abuses but retained for its contributions to helping precisely the poor. With the young French left now admitting much of this—which would have warmed Belloc's Gallic heart—not to mention Margaret Thatcher, we are in a position to see if a kind of "productive distributivism", not unlike the reformed "neo-capitalism" of an Irving Kristol, a P. T. Bauer, a Willard Beckermann, or a Michael Novak, might not just work best for the major needs of our time.[26]

In this sense, Belloc could well provide for Catholic libera-

[26] See. P. T. Bauer, *Reality and Rhetoric: Studies in the Economics of Development* (Cambridge, Mass.: Harvard University Press, 1984); Irving Kristol, *Two Cheers for Capitalism* (New York: Basic Books, 1978); Michael Novak, *The Spirit of Democratic Capitalism* (New York: Simon and Schuster, 1982); Wilfred Beckermann, *Two Cheers for the Affluent Society: A Spirited Defense of Economic Growth* (New York: St. Martin's, 1975); Charles Murray, *Losing Ground* (New York: Basic Books, 1984); George Gilder, *Wealth and Poverty* (New York: Basic Books, 1981); Peter Berger, *The Capitalist Revolution: Fifty Propositions about Prosperity, Equality, and Liberty* (New York: Basic Books, 1986); Lawrence Harrison, *Underdevelopment Is a State of Mind* (Lanham, Md.: University Press of America, 1985).

tion a much needed "path to Rome". John McCarthy has cleared much of the underbrush.

However, as I mentioned earlier, Belloc is, for some of us, at least, rather like a drug, a habit we do not in the least want to break. The shortcoming of McCarthy's book—and it is also its very strength—is his sticking to the historical record to elucidate for us just what Belloc argued and why he reached the conclusions he did in his era.

Yet, in the end, I cannot resist one—no, two—last memories of the Belloc we cannot forget, if we be sane. The first is about what has come to be known, alas, as "equal" rights, found in a most wonderful essay on Jane Austen:

> [Jane Austen] says of one of the men in her books that one of the women in her books who came across him paid no attention to what a certain gentleman thought on any matter, because she did not care enough about him—not in the sense of affection, but in the sense of attention. So speaks this ambassadress from her own sex to mine, and I will not be so ungenerous as to leave her without a corresponding reply.
>
> My dear Jane Austen, we also do not care a dump what any woman thinks about our actions or our thoughts or our manners unless they have inspired us to—what shall I call it? It need not be affection, but at any rate attraction, or, at least, attention. Once that link is established, we care enormously: indeed, I am afraid, too much.[27]

And the second passage I want to cite is about what we have to choose, that incredible faculty of free choice given to us all to form our lives:

> Look you, good people all, in your little passage through the daylight, get to see as many hills and buildings and rivers, fields, books, men, horses, ships, and precious stones as you can

[27] Belloc, "Jane Austen", in *Selected Essays,* pp. 196–97.

possibly manage to do. Or else stay in one village and marry in it and die there. For one of these two fates is the best fate for every man. Either to be what I have been, a wanderer with all the bitterness of it, or to stay at home and hear in one's garden the voice of God.[28]

And so Belloc was like his character, a traveler, "with all the bitterness of it". Too, he was a boatman, and a man who loved home. And so he knew his restlessness had only one resting place in this world—our very home, to which all men aspire and which they all should own, wherein they love and rest.

Belloc, then, stood for the recovery of such unknown corners, of London, of any city, for any man and for any woman, for those we love, no doubt, too much. John McCarthy, like A. N. Wilson, recounted in his book the social structures and philosophy in which Hilaire Belloc thought such things might happen in this warm, imperfect world, this beloved world in which we can be, at best, as he said, only tolerably happy. Ultimately, Belloc knew, our happiness was not here, even at home. We have tended to forget this, so that an essential part of the sort of education that I should like to discover is concerned with Belloc, who sensed in his own way so much of what it is we most need.

Ten Books by Hilaire Belloc Well Worth Reading

1. *The Path to Rome.*
2. *The Four Men.*
3. *The Cruise of the "Nona".*
4. *Selected Essays of Hilaire Belloc.*
5. *The Servile State.*
6. *Cranmer: Archbishop of Canterbury.*

---

[28] Belloc, "The Death of Wandering Peter", in *Selected Essays,* p. 75.

7. *The Crusade.*
8. *Letters from Hilaire Belloc.*
9. *On Nothing.*
10. *Survivals and New Arrivals.*

Chapter Thirteen

Oddness and Sanity

*(This chapter presents reflections on Henry Veatch's
book,* Human Rights: Fact or Fancy?*)*

When I first received Henry Veatch's book on human rights, I
sat right down and read it. It is a special work, special to those
of us who have long admired and relied on Henry Veatch as a
source of inspiration, wisdom, and, indeed, humor. When I
had almost finished this book, David Forte, from the law
school at Cleveland State University, dropped by. Forte was a
student, as were so many, of Henry Veatch. I said, "You know,
as I read the book, I could just hear Henry speaking." Forte
laughed and agreed.

In this book, Henry Veatch's vivid, incisive mind is fully
engaged, as is his wit. "Is it any wonder", Veatch asked himself,
after stating clearly the objection to his own position (Veatch
has indeed read St. Thomas who insisted on this method),

> that modern moral philosophers have, seemingly almost to a
> man (or woman), eschewed any effort to find a basis for ethics
> in fact or in nature? How, then, can I hope to do what others
> have largely given up trying to do? Is this perhaps not so much
> a fools' paradise as a case of "fools rushing in where angels fear
> to tread"?[1]

Henry Veatch is no fool, but he simply delights in our human
condition in which foolishness is possible.

Henry Veatch is now happily retired, living on the campus

---

[1] Henry B. Veatch, *Human Rights: Fact or Fancy?* (Baton Rouge:
Louisiana State University Press, 1985), p. 213.

of Indiana University in Bloomington, where he once taught. He was the chairman of the philosophy department at Georgetown for a decade or so. Veatch's books on Aristotle—*Rational Man* and *Aristotle: A Contemporary Appreciation*—are marvels of clarity and good sense, a just reflection of the spirit of Aristotle himself. The books of Henry Veatch serve to do something the older scholastic authors attempted to do, namely, to keep the perennial questions of philosophy before us in all their force. Veatch has also written widely on modern logic and on the nature of scientific inquiry. Indeed, one of the important contributions that this present book makes is to show that the modern scientific enterprise does not and cannot, on its own premises, obviate the philosophical endeavor as such, particularly that involved in ethical and political discourse.

Veatch, like Aristotle, has a marvelous capacity to cite from historical example or from literary incidents that illustrate his point. I recall a couple of years ago reading for the first time Jane Austen's description of Sir Walter Elliot in *Persuasion.* Nothing is quite so amusing, so it was a delight to find Sir Walter appearing again and again in Veatch's book as an example of Aristotle's less-than-perfect man. Veatch's admiration for Jane Austen is unbounded, itself a sign of deep sanity.

At a time when most of the seminaries, theologates, universities, and graduate schools have given up much serious consideration of natural law, we find suddenly a vigorous, articulate endeavor to inquire whether the modern objections to this tradition are really valid. The argument takes us right to the heart of the revival of natural law that we associate with the work of Germain Grisez and John Finnis, themselves responsible for so much vigor in this area. Veatch, while admiring their work, has reservations and argues that ultimately, they too abandon a solid natural law basis in their argument. The basis of the problem seems to arise from natural science.

> I suspect that Grisez-Finnis have perhaps uncritically accepted the standard view of nature that has been regnant ever since the seventeenth century, according to which all distinctions between right and wrong, good and gad, "ought" and "ought not" are totally absent from the natural world.[2]

As is clear, this controversy is of the utmost importance. And it is in such apparently esoteric, obscure controversies that the future of civilizations and institutions lies, in the endeavors of good men to understand the truth of things.

Henry Veatch, in this handsome new, readable book, has the capacity to cut away from the traditional forms of scholarship and, in his own words, present the essence of the debate, its history, its import, its conclusions. Veatch has spent a lifetime with these issues. Here, we have the spare presentation of what it is all about. Veatch constantly asks: What is the argument? Can it be held? He does not waste words, yet his words are vivid. His examples, like Aristotle's, are graphic, homey. Bass fishing comes up more than once in Henry Veatch's reflections.

Three things in particular struck me about Veatch's argument. (1) He has met head-on the enigma about modern Thomists that Leo Strauss had pointed out in his *Natural Right and History,* namely, their uncritical acceptance of modern science as a basis to separate ethics from nature. In this connection, it is also well to mention, in support of Veatch's view, the book of Veatch's friend, Leon Kass, *Toward a More Natural Order: Biology and Human Affairs,* and Stanley Jaki's many works on the realism of science, such as *The Road of Science and the Ways to God*

[2] Ibid., p. 103.

and *Cosmos and Creator.*[3] I felt that Veatch's conclusions at the scientific level would have been strengthened by Jaki's positions.

(2) Veatch has understood the problem posed by modern natural rights. One of the great issues, broached by Jacques Maritain (whom Veatch did not cite), was whether modern rights theory could be reconciled with a natural law theory. Veatch is very cautious here. He finally grounds rights in a theory of self-development based on the real given being of human reality. Veatch, following his friend Iredell Jenkins, is most circumspect about so-called "positive" natural rights. He sees the totalitarian implications that this concept usually entails. Moreover, Veatch's sensible defense of property and entre-preneurship is unique and reasonable. For someone who says that he does not know much about economics, Veatch comes to the most commonsensical of economic conclusions—one Aristotle and Aquinas already had foreshadowed. Veatch too recognized the place for charity, for something beyond justice and distribution.

(3) Veatch positively argues that natural law theory, when carefully spelled out, is valid and can be upheld. But to do this, one must patiently recount the teleological, deontological, and libertarian arguments as they have appeared in modern philoso-phy, not merely the Benthams, Lockes, Kants, but the Rawlses, the Nozicks, Hayeks, and Gewirths. This is one aspect of philosophical discourse that Henry Veatch conducts very well.

In a sense, Veatch himself has been in a lonely position since all the momentum of academic and media opinion has gone against the view that Aristotle still makes sense, as does Aquinas.

[3] Leo Strauss, *Natural Right and History* (Chicago: University of Chicago Press, 1953); Leon Kass, *Toward a More Natural Science: Biology and Human Affairs* (New York: Free Press, 1985); Stanley Jaki, *The Road of Science and the Ways to God* (Chicago: University of Chicago Press, 1978); Jaki, *Cosmos and Creator* (Edinburgh: Scottish Academic Press, 1980).

But Veatch holds what he does because of argument. There is a kind of intellectual strength in Veatch that is uncommon, I think. He wrote, amusingly,

> Thus the mere fact that the predicted consequences of, say, Einstein's hypothesis do in fact occur no more proves the truth of that hypothesis than it might be supposed that I could prove myself to be a true genius merely on the grounds that any and every genius is bound to act oddly at times, and I certainly do act oddly, not just some of the time but perhaps even all of the time.[4]

My own suspicions are, following Aristotle, that there is another conclusion from this in the case of Henry Veatch: that at a time when all other positions are eminently dubious or foolish, the one sensible one will look decidedly odd. This latter is how I see Henry Veatch. In this case, oddness and sanity combine.

The only problem I had with this book concerned Veatch's curious hesitancy to affirm the rights of defective children within his own argument.[5] I do not see why his basic position leads to a problem. Simply because someone, because of accident, cannot fully develop in fact, does not imply that the objective being given does not determine what it is. Nature sometimes fails, but it is still what it is.

In conclusion, this book is a kind of milestone, one that ought to be carefully read in every seminary, university, graduate school, rectory. I cannot think of a better gift to one's local bishop, caught floundering in the throes of academic confusions. Veatch's use of Scripture, his awareness that natural law and rights do not close off something more than either of them can account for, is implicit throughout the book. This is a wise

[4] Veatch, *Human Rights,* p. 231.
[5] Ibid., pp. 195–96.

book by a wise man. Louisiana State University Press has done us an enormous service in presenting it. Henry Veatch teaches at every step. He does not get distracted, but he does get amused. He will go wherever the argument will go, even if no one else will follow him. If this be "odd", as he implies it might be, let us thank the Lord that such oddness is among us.

Nine Books on Natural Law:

1. Henry Veatch, *Human Rights: Fact or Fancy?*
2. Jacques Maritain, *The Rights of Man and the Natural Law.*
3. Heinrich C. Rommen, *The Natural Law.*
4. E. B. F. Midgley, *The Natural Law Tradition and the Theory of International Relations.*
5. Johannes Messner, *Social Ethics: The Natural Law in the Western World.*
6. Alexander Passerin d'Entreves, *The Natural Law: An Historical Survey.*
7. Peter Stanlis, *Edmund Burke and the Natural Law.*
8. Maurice Cranston, *What Are Human Rights?*
9. Frederick D. Wilhelmsen, *Christianity and Political Philosophy.*

Six Books by Stanley L. Jaki:

1. *Brain, Mind, and Computers.*
2. *The Road of Science and the Ways to God.*
3. *The Origin of Science and the Science of Its Origins.*
4. *Uneasy Genius: the Life and Work of Pierre Duhem.*
5. *Cosmos and Creator.*
6. *And on This Rock: The Witness of One Land and Two Covenants.*

Four Other Books by Henry Veatch:

1. *Rational Man: A Modern Interpretation of Aristotelian Ethics.*
2. *Aristotle: A Contemporary Appreciation.*
3. *Two Logics.*
4. *For an Ontology of Morals.*

Part Three

Have You Thought about It This Way?

Schall's Unlikely List of Books to Keep Sane By—Selected for Those to Whom Making Sense Is a Prior Consideration, but a Minority Opinion

1. G. K. Chesterton, *Orthodoxy*.
2. Dorothy Sayers, *The Whimsical Christian*.
3. J. M. Bochenski, *Philosophy: An Introduction*.
4. Hilaire Belloc, *The Path to Rome*.
5. Christopher Derrick, *Escape from Skepticism: Liberal Education as If the Truth Really Mattered*.
6. E. F. Schumacher, *A Guide for the Perplexed*.
7. C. S. Lewis, *Till We Have Faces*.
8. Gilbert Meilaender, *The Theory and Practice of Virtue*.
9. Eric Mascall, *The Christian Universe*.
10. Flannery O'Connor, *The Habit of Being: The Letters of Flannery O'Connor*
11. Henry Veatch, *Rational Man*.
12. Josef Pieper, *In Tune with the World: A Theory of Festivity*.
13. Aleksandr Solzhenitsyn, *Solzhenitsyn at Harvard*.
14. Julian Simon, *The Ultimate Resource*.
15. Stanley Jaki, *The Road of Science and the Ways to God*.
16. Raymond Dennehy, *Reason and Dignity*.
17. Marion Montgomery, *Reflective Journey toward Order*.
18. Eric Voegelin, *Conversations with Eric Voegelin*.

19. M. Krapiec, *I–Man: An Outline of Philosophical Anthropology.*
20. C. S. Lewis, *The Four Loves.*
21. G. K. Chesterton, *St. Thomas Aquinas.*
22. Josef Pieper, *The End of Time.*
23. Yves Simon, *The Philosophy of Democratic Government.*
24. Christopher Dawson, *The Making of Europe.*
25. James Boswell, *The Life of Samuel Johnson.*

To Which It Might Be Added, with No Guarantee of Further Sanity

26. James V. Schall, *The Praise of "Sons of Bitches": On the Worship of God by Fallen Men.*
27. _____, *The Distinctiveness of Christianity.*
28. _____, *Redeeming the Time.*
29. _____, *Far Too Easily Pleased: A Theology of Play, Contemplation, and Festivity.*
30. _____, *Unexpected Meditations Late in the XXth Century.*

Introduction

In this third section, I want to discuss rather substantive things, both intellectual and spiritual. Here I want to say something about the humanities, about devotion, prayer, something more, again, about permanent things. Previously, I have talked about how to study and about some books I have found of importance and, through them, about authors from whom I have learned much and about issues that need confronting. I insist in a way that there is *another sort of learning* that deliberately takes account of what a friend of mine calls "the higher order concerns".

Indeed, let me cite this friend more fully:

> Over my lifetime, a few of my conversations have been elevated, have reached some essence of truth. I am not so skeptical as to think that we only come up against contradiction. I believe there are truths that can be known, and that is the reason why we exist, to discover them. At least that is why I think I exist, that seems to be the single most important thing I will do while I exist.

No doubt, we learn from those who think that what they teach is of importance. Yet we have constantly to ask whether what is taught is of value and if so, in what context. My friend was right in realizing that the pursuit of truth transcends our education and is at the center of our lives.

There is an indefinable excitement to the highest things. Nothing is wrong with practical education, with learning a profession, a task, a skill. But these things, in the tradition, are not of ultimate value, even though we can find the highest things in every place and walk of life. Sometimes, it seems, there is a sort of studied neglect of what is beyond use. Indeed, the very idea that there are things beyond use is itself a classical idea that is too little recognized. This relationship of what things are for use and what beyond use remains the permanent value of Josef Pieper's famous book, *Leisure: The Basis of Culture,* a wonderful book that cannot be read too often.

I have frequently mentioned the fact that many books, like many dramas and paintings, for example, ought to be read or seen more than once. There is something narrow, even self-defeating, in reading a great work only once. We have time limits, I know, in what we can read simply because we are mortal and do not have all the time there is in which to pursue what we might wish to read or reflect on. In fact, one of the reasons Aquinas gave for the necessity of revelation was precisely the fact that, since most of us have so little time in which to pursue the highest things, we need a revelation to direct us to that which is truly ultimate.

No doubt I wish to encourage the love of books, the idea that every home should have book shelves, that every young man and woman should think of his or her own personal library, of things once read and kept because they were read. Yet there are millions and millions of books. We must select. This selection process is one of the meanings of a liberal education, of an education that knows and reads that which is highest and best. On the other hand, we live in an age that is reluctant, if not hostile, to the idea that some things are better than others, some things closer to the heart of *what is.*

But if we follow the spirit of our age, we will soon become lost in the trivial, the unimportant, the uninteresting. This is why we need a guide: to realize that some things are important to read simply because they are good or true. This latter sense is what I wish to emphasize here: that there are things that we must read and know just because they are true. To miss certain things is not only something of an intellectual tragedy, it is also a void. We are not moved by ourselves but must somehow come into contact with what causes us to wonder, to seek to know something just for itself, for its own sake, as the Greeks used to put it.

To be in an institution of higher education does not mean by itself, unfortunately, that a student will confront the highest things. This book, in part, has been based on this observation, on the realization that it is necessary to transcend the system, often, to arrive at some understanding of the higher order of things. But the Aristotelian word *wonder* remains the spirit and context of what is said here. As many writers have realized over the centuries, the idea with which Aristotle began his most profound work, *The Metaphysics*—the idea that we desire by nature to know and that what incites us is not need or pleasure but just the curiosity or desire to know the truth about something—is itself one of the most profound things we can learn. It is in this sense that I talk about *another sort of learning*, about the idea that often our education prevents us from knowing the highest things and that, therefore, we must do something to supply what is no doubt lacking to us.

Fourteen Books by Josef Pieper

1. *Leisure: The Basis of Culture.*
2. *In Tune with the World: A Theory of Festivity.*
3. *On Hope.*
4. *The Four Cardinal Virtues.*
5. *Scholasticism.*
6. *The Silence of St. Thomas.*
7. *Enthusiasm and the Divine Madness: On the Platonic Dialogue "Phaedrus".*

8. *Death and Immortality.*
9. *Reality and the Good.*
10. *Problems of Modern Faith.*
11. *The End of Time: Meditations on the Philosophy of History.*
12. *Happiness and Contemplation.*
13. *What Catholics Believe.*
14. *A Guide to Thomas Aquinas.*

Chapter Fourteen

The Recovery of Permanent Things

At one time, the literary genre called "the Christian essay" was in great vogue. Belloc, of course, was a master of this form, as were Dorothy Sayers, Newman, and Maurice Baring. Such essays arose in an era whose concern was perhaps more to distinguish Christianity from the rest of mankind rather than, as in our own time, to state how Christianity is "like" other philosophic sects, cultures, and religions. In Christian essays, the Creed was presupposed, a part of an essay's own very fabric.

Maurice Baring, in 1938, wrote a letter in French to an Abbé friend at Notre Dame de Paris. In it, he recounted an anecdote once told by the painter Burne-Jones, who, I believe, did the lovely wall restoration of the Reformation damage to Waltham Abbey. The very audacity of the story presupposes distinctly Christian things. A priest in Avignon, it seems, once was hearing confessions, when a young man at last reached the confessional. He confessed so many sins that the priest protested loudly. "But you would have had to live for centuries to do so much evil!" "I have lived for thousands of years", the young man replied. "I fell from heaven at the birth of the world, and I would wish to go back." The priest, good theologian that he was, answered that such would be quite possible, so he said to the young man, "Repeat after me—'God alone is great and perfect'. But the young man went away desolate, still damned."[1] This sense of the abiding framework of Christian

[1] Laura Lovat, *Maurice Baring: A Postscript* (London: Hollis, 1947), p. 72.

orthodoxy, its permanent reality, even in French, even in Avignon, the old papal enclave, recounted by an English painter, again repeated by a British diplomat once in the Court of St. Petersburg, this constitutes the very fabric of the classical Christian essay.

In one of her letters, dated August 2, 1955, Flannery O'Connor, herself no stranger to the Christian essay, wrote, "One of the awful things about writing when you are a Christian is that for you the ultimate reality is the Incarnation, the present reality is the Incarnation, and nobody believes in the Incarnation; that is, nobody in your audience."[2] And yet, as Flannery O'Connor hinted, there is an "audience" for the Incarnation, so that it behooves us to wonder where that gathering might possibly be. Such an audience exists, I wish to argue, among the potential philosophers and among those who are still touched by "permanent things", which are still somehow alive in this world, this world called, in Christian belief, without apology, "a vale of tears".

"The essence of social conservatism is preservation of the ancient moral traditions of humanity", Russell Kirk wrote.[3] Those who would keep such traditions are not today coterminous with those who call themselves Christians. And that the "poor would always be with us" was not necessarily in this orientation a sign of hopelessness, but rather the locus of some higher contact with truth and being. The Beatitudes of the New Testament indicated primarily what would happen to us if we lived the faith. There are, then, abiding enigmas that arise in the very context of life and thought that are in a real

[2] Flannery O'Connor, *The Habit of Being: The Letters of Flannery O'Connor*, ed. Robert and Sally Fitzgerald (New York: Viking, 1978), p. 92.

[3] Russell Kirk, *The Conservative Mind* (Chicago: Regnery-Gateway, 1967), p. 6.

sense "answered" in grace and faith.[4] And the answer given is an appeal to and instruction of precisely our intelligence.

Students who still read Aristotle—there are happily not a few—are often struck by his discussion of friendship, a subject to which they are normally much attracted as a locus of ultimate meaning in human life.[5] Yet in the very midst of this Aristotelian discussion, we find these disturbing words from the most reasonable of all men: "When one party is removed to a great distance, as God is, the possibility of friendship ceases" (1159a5). The context of this passage was that of equality and inequality. No friendship between God and man—yet, Aristotle had just taught that friendship was the highest human reality we can know, wherein our potentialities are most exercised. The average student who may possibly have read Aristotle will, today, be unlikely also to have read the *Gospel of St. John*, so he will be a member of that wider audience that does not believe in the Incarnation. Yet how odd it is to find in John that we are no longer to be called by God servants, but friends (15:14-15). The distance is narrowed. New possibilities exist.

Christianity is also a "city-oriented" religion. Hostility to the city, so deep in part of our tradition and often in our contemporary sociological and development theories, easily makes us forget that Socrates barely ever left Athens. The city is the place of the great gathering, where a Roman law was hammered out from a bewildering number of individual conflicts and standards. And it is a place of solitude too. "Sir, if you wish to have a just notion of the magnitude of this city",

---

[4] See John Paul II's Address to the French Youth, June 1, 1980, as well as his Address on Aquinas to the Angelicum University, Nov. 17, 1979, in *The Whole Truth about Man: John Paul II to University Students and Faculties* (Boston: St. Paul Editions, 1981).

[5] See James V. Schall, "Friendship and the End of Human Life", *Redeeming the Time* (New York: Sheed and Ward, 1968), pp. 216-27.

Samuel Johnson said, in 1763, of one of our civilization's universal, most particular cities,

> you must not be satisfied with seeing its great streets and squares, but must survey the innumerable little lanes and courts. It is not in the showy evolutions of buildings, but in the multiplicity of human habitations which are crowded together, that this wonderful immensity of London consists.[6]

Every man thinks of London in different ways, Johnson went on, the politician, the glazier, the mercantile man, the dramatic enthusiast; even "a man of pleasure" sees it "as an assemblage of taverns, and a great emporium for ladies of easy virtue".

But there is more for the intellectual man. London strikes him symbolically "as comprehending the whole of human life in all its variety, the contemplation of which is inexhaustible". The city is the approach to the whole of life's variety, of its inexhaustible contemplation. And here, as in friendship, we address our audience for ultimate realities, those who still repeat in their hearts, "God alone is great and perfect."

Near the end of *The City of God*, St. Augustine wrote:

> In the everlasting City, there will remain in each and all of us an inalienable freedom of the will, emancipating us from every evil and filling us with every good, rejoicing in the inexhaustible beatitude of everlasting happiness, unclouded by the memory of any sin or sanction suffered, yet with no forgetfulness of our Redemption nor any loss of gratitude for our Redeemer (XXII, 30).

Sanctions and sins, but no memory of them, the desire to go back, the Redeemer, the Incarnation — such are indeed Christian themes.

[6] James Boswell, *Life of Samuel Johnson*, vol I (London: Oxford, 1937), pp. 281–82.

There are to be no abstractions in the City of God, only friends. The Polish Pope teaches:

> We are not dealing with the "abstract" man, but the real "concrete", "historical" man. We are dealing with "each" man, for each one is included in the mystery of the redemption and with each one Christ united himself forever through this mystery. Every man came into the world through being conceived in his mother's womb and being born of his mother ... (*Redemptor Hominis,* no. 13).

Incarnation, Redemption, these begin in tininess, in the least of our brothers, in the innumerable little lanes and courts.

One of P. G. Wodehouse's most fascinating women was Roberta Wickham. Of her, we read that she "wouldn't recognize the quiet life if you brought it to her on a platter with watercress on it. She's all for not letting the sun go down without having started something calculated to stagger humanity."[7] Where is the audience? What is ultimately calculated to "stagger humanity"? Friendship and the incalculable variety, the City composed of no abstractions, "every man comes into the world through being conceived": from such does the audience begin to form.

Western civilization is unique, Christopher Dawson wrote in his remarkable *Religion and the Rise of Western Culture* (1950), because of its "missionary character", a character that in some sense predates the assimilation of the Judaeo-Christian tradition into it.[8] This particular culture was incited by a "continuous series of spiritual movements" caused largely by the dynamic division and tensions between religious and cultural

[7] P. G. Wodehouse, *How Right You Are, Jeeves* (New York: Avon, 1976), p. 113.

[8] Christopher Dawson, *Religion and the Rise of Western Culture* (Garden City, N.Y.: Doubleday Image, 1957), pp. 11–25.

leadership over against the structure and requirements of the political order. Both God and Caesar, not *either God or Caesar* — such were the invigorating yet separating sources of spiritual motion. Indeed, the fact that religion could now affirm positively that there *were* things of Caesar, this was more novel than for Caesar to recognize, vaguely albeit, the things of God. And in this tradition, it was spirit that moved matter, not the other way around, as so much modern thought has tried, mostly without success, to believe.[9]

This civilization, divided as it was — Greek and barbarian, Gentile and Jew, Roman and Hun, No Strange Gods and Incarnation — nevertheless, in its Greek, Jewish, Stoic, and Christian origins did claim to be, in some elemental sense, "universal". There was one cosmos, one natural law, one brotherhood, one Church, one Empire. Aristotle, Plato, and Thucydides taught us not merely how the Greeks thought and acted, but rather how to think and act at all, how man is to think if he is to think, how he is to act if he acts rightly. There was not one mind at Athens, another at Rome, another at Mecca, another at Peking. Anyone who still teaches the great Greek thinkers can sense the hush when students suddenly recognize what these ancient men were about. Israel, Christ, Athens, Jerusalem, Rome, and Aachen were designed also to be universal — as were their later offspring in London, Paris, and New York — so that the dynamism they placed into the world was precisely unsettling, challenging for everyone, a dynamic ordered toward the noble, the best, the right, no matter what the historic conditions or compromises, provided only that we did not forget, in the process, those "in the multiplicity of human habitations which are crowded together", for whom such "wonderful immensity" exists.

[9] Ibid., chap. 1.

Thus, of the Tower of Yahweh, Isaiah heard, "*All* the nations will stream to it, peoples without numbers will come to it" (2:2). And when he heard, when he knew of his own wretched state, of "so many crimes", this same Isaiah heard the Lord ask, "Whom shall I send?" Isaiah answered, "Here I am, Lord, send me" (6:8). Our condition of imperfection, our centuries of doing so much evil is here, astonishingly, found to be a motive for *action,* not for stagnation, passivity. Paul of Tarsus rushed to all the ancient cities as one sent, even though the least of the Apostles, the least of those "sent". "Come to Macedonia and help us", he heard, while looking at Europe (Acts 16:9). A cosmos, a mission, a goal, a civilization sought to return to that to which it had never yet arrived. The alpha and the omega, the beginning and the end. "Well", Socrates recalled, "and were we not creating the ideal of a perfect *polis?*" "To be sure." "And is our theory a worse thing because we are unable to prove the possibility of a city being ordered after the manner described?" To this enigma, Glaucon responded in words we still repeat, "Surely not."

So the theory remains within the culture, even though it may not be realized, hence the dynamism, the possibility and the power of unsettling existing societies. Let me recall again the young Hungarian priest in Rome who remarked to me, "We are not allowed to read Plato at home." "Why not?"—this I still ask my students. Those who know already begin to be part of *the audience.* You cannot ask about the best if you are already in "the best". Yet this missionary drive for the best, for what ought to be, for the city Socrates erected at least in speech for all who yet presume to think, this has made it difficult to live in this world. Real cities—Athens, Rome, Jerusalem, and London—these have killed Socrates, Cicero, Christ, and Thomas More.

Irving Kristol grasped the sense of the problem: "The influence of Christianity, with its messianic promises, made the distinction between 'the best' and 'the legitimate'."[10] And yet, as we have recalled, Christians are also readers of St. Augustine, the man, as Hannah Arendt taught in *The Life of the Mind,* who most revealed to us the nature of the will.[11] And it was Augustine who made it abundantly clear that the pursuit of "the best" could coexist with "the legitimate", but only if the former be properly located in the Parousia, the latter within the difficult, sinful circumstances we do find in this world. Carl Becker, J. B. Bury, Paul Hazard, and Robert Nisbet have traced the history of what happens when this distinction is not respected, the history of what is still called "The Enlightenment", perhaps even yet the major temptation of the modern mind.[12]

Thus, not unexpectedly, we find Machiavelli, the founder of "modern" political thought, described as an Augustinian realist without the City of God. Machiavelli it was who asked us systematically to "lower" our sights and our ideals, to rid ourselves of the classical and Christian concerns for "the best", both in theology and in politics. Yet we live in an era in which Machiavelli's successes—"the best" has, in Hegelian fashion, become, properly refashioned, *what is*—have come to be curses

[10] Irving Kristol, *Two Cheers for Capitalism* (New York: Basic Books, 1978), p. 174.

[11] Hannah Arendt, *The Life of the Mind,* vol. 2 (San Diego: Harcourt, 1978), pp. 84-110. See also Mary T. Clark, *Augustine: Philosopher of Freedom; A Study in Comparative Philosophy* (New York: Desclée, 1958); Vernon J. Bourke, *Will in Western Thought* (New York: Sheed and Ward, 1964).

[12] Robert A. Nisbet, *History of the Idea of Progress* (New York: Basic Books, 1980). See Carl L. Becker, *The Heavenly City of the Eighteenth-Century Philosophers* (New Haven, Conn.: Yale University Press, 1932); J. B. Bury, *The Idea of Progress* (New York: Dover, 1932); Paul Hazard, *European Thought in the Eighteenth Century* (New York: Meridian, 1963); Christopher Dawson, *Progress and Religion* (London: Sheed and Ward, 1938).

in their turn. And these curses, to understand them properly, arise because we are looking out for "the best" in our world as if it were somehow our "due". Furthermore, this is not our *due* merely as a result of "hard work" in the Max Weber tradition of the Protestant Ethic—we are only vaguely Pelagians—but almost as a gift without a giver. Standard political philosophy today, which is undergoing a most curious flowering in the name of Aristotle's "distributive justice", hardly has a thing to say any longer about why or how something exists to be redistributed in the first place.

We have, moreover, gone beyond the distributism of an Eric Gill, which was a "production", quality, personal concept, rooted ultimately in the Christian notion of creation and Aristotle's notion of art. We go toward redistribution as if the problems of production and their relations to justice and benevolence have somehow disappeared. Paul's "if a man will not work, neither let him eat" has been replaced by a sort of secular version of the old Communion Antiphon, "Take and receive". Indeed, there is something to be said for the idea that this "multiplication of the loaves" and their common sharing have been taken out of the context of the Mass and located in the world, almost as if the bread we eat is produced as miraculously as the original loaves and fishes. Theoretical neglect of production has left us searching for the "collective sin" that explains maldistribution. Clearly, we do not understand, as P. T. Bauer has remarked, that "profit" is earned. Distribution follows production and does not exist outside of it.

To attribute all our evils to some system's malfunctioning, some social sin, no doubt, is a dead-end street, not merely because production and innovation still lie at the heart of any possible distribution, let alone any redistribution, but because contemporary redistribution theories, particularly those of Marxism or Rawls, are based upon a denial of "the legitimate", so

that only "the best" is allowed full existence. And this "best",
unlike that of Augustine, is now found, supposedly, coming to
be in this world as something that *must* exist if man is to be
man. We actually think we must "invent" man, a notion quite
powerful in genetic and sociological theory. Man, the human,
is thus not a given, as in Aristotle, but only an eventual
end-product. The radical historicist version of this thesis asks
not about the "supernatural", but rather about what ought the
"supernatural" to "do" for this world, so that the validity of
the supernatural is defined and conditioned primarily by its
worldly performance, which is itself held to be known as the
product of a worldly science or knowledge.

No one is more important, in this context, than the late
Leo Strauss, whose theoretical challenge to particularly Christian
thought, as I suggested earlier, has hardly been understood,
let alone competently argued, in Christian intellectual circles.
In his *Thoughts on Machiavelli*, Strauss set down the agenda
of this issue: "There are fundamental alternatives which are
permanent or co-eval with man. . . . Our critical study of
Machiavelli's teaching can have ultimately no other purpose than
to contribute towards *the recovery of permanent things.*"[13] And,
from a classical Christian view, the most important permanent
thing to be "recovered" is precisely Augustine's City of God
and, therefore, the separation of "the legitimate" and "the
possible" from contemporary theorizers of "the best" as a
this-worldly project. These latter are substantially those who
want to achieve their goals in the now by the "redistribution"
of what already is, on the tragic assumption that what we
have *already* called forth is all we can call forth, so that the
order of human happiness is merely a question of equality in

[13] Leo Strauss, *Thoughts on Machiavelli* (Chicago: University of Chicago
Press, 1958), p. 14.

apportionment, fashioned by certain radical programs and systems.

Such is, furthermore, too often what is meant by "public policy analysis" today. Thus, without ever telling why, in spite of his initial polemic against Max Weber's ill-fated "fact" and "value" dichotomy, Martin Rein stated in his *Social Science and Public Policy* that "I regard the primary subject matter of social policy as egalitarianism — that is, concern with the equitable distribution of social goods".[14] Robert Nozick's *Anarchy, State, and Utopia* is, of course, an attempt to suggest that the gain of some is *not* necessarily the loss of others.[15] In any case, it is no wonder that Irving Kristol could exclaim of such egalitarian propositions: "To the best of my knowledge, no serious political philosopher ever offered such a proposition before. It is a proposition, after all, that peremptorily cast a pall of illegitimacy over the entire political history of the human race."[16] But, of course, that is the very point, the claim that we do now have available to us "the best", if we simply "restructure" ourselves and our societies properly. In Russell Kirk's sense, thus, there is simply no "ancient moral tradition of humanity" to preserve.

To be sure, there are more sober voices in our general culture. "I used to hold", Graham Greene remarked at age seventy-four, "the view that perfect evil walked the world where perfect good can never walk again. But there was also the hope that the swing of the pendulum would insure that

[14] Martin Rein, *Science and Public Policy* (New York: Penguin, 1976), p. 140.

[15] Robert Nozick, *Anarchy, State, and Utopia* (New York: Basic Books, 1974). This book is constantly compared with John Rawls, *A Theory of Justice* (Cambridge, Mass.: Harvard University Press, 1971). See also Hadley Arkes, *The Philosopher in the City* (Princeton, N.J.: Princeton University Press, 1981).

[16] Kristol, *Two Cheers for Capitalism*, pp. 171–72.

justice would be done. Now I am less sure that the pendulum will swing in that direction."[17] But if we live in a world where justice will not be well done, where egalitarianism is a theoretic illusion arising out of certain identifiable errors of cognitional and ethical theory, where does that leave "the permanent things" to be remembered, the fundamental alternatives rooted in man?

Paul Sigmund has followed with attention the fate of Catholic social theory in recent years. "It would be unfortunate if Thomistic theories no longer give rise to new social and political foundations", he argued in his Calgary Aquinas Lecture,

> because, along with marxism and the liberal humanism of the Enlightenment, Christianity has been a principal source of symbols and motivations for the transformation of society, especially in times of crisis, and the Thomistic formulation of Christian social and political theory remains one of the more appealing, moderate, and flexible ways to relate the Christian message to contemporary politics and society. More fundamentally, the belief that it exemplifies that human beings can perceive a purposive order and essential regulative principles for their life in community is one that has attracted men throughout the ages — and if that belief disappears one has reason to fear for the future of democracy — or even of our civilized life altogether.[18]

The major reason for this decline of moderation as a first principle of Christian thought deserves attention. Except perhaps for John Paul II and someone like Eric Mascall, there has been a strange silence about Aquinas, aside from those circles currently trying to make him into a Marxist. But both Augustine and Aquinas knew we can only be "moderate" in politics if politics is not itself the location of "the best".

[17] *New York Times,* Feb. 3, 1980.

[18] Paul Sigmund, "Thomistic Natural Law and Social Theory," Toronto, 1979, p. 76.

The late John East and Garry Wills have thought the attention given to Thomism, especially in its "neo-Thomistic"
formulations, has been misplaced, so that a return to Augustine
is really the correct approach. "It is the Thomists who are
likely to think of world government as a matter of form,
structures, mechanics, and legalisms to be rationally constructed
and directed from above", East wrote,

> while the Augustinians will argue that all government, includ-
> ing world government, is not an abstraction imposed by edict;
> rather it must be a product of a sense of community arising
> from organic forces, rooted in living, evolving social tissues.
> Armed with such realism, the student of Augustine has no
> illusions about the utopia of the world state. He is prudent,
> cautious, and restrained. As with Augustine, he is braced for
> the interminable conflicts of world politics; for pressure, tension,
> and "power politics" are inherent in the nature of things human,
> and no panacea of human construction can eliminate these
> realities.[19]

This approach would already question the very structure of
contemporary theories of justice and equality to refocus attention on the legitimate and the illegitimate, on realities less than
"the best", but free from the dynamism of the "totalitarian
democracies" that J. L. Talmon rightly saw arising in the
process of trying to achieve "the best" in this world.[20]

"An Augustinian view", Garry Wills wrote in his *Confessions
of a Conservative,* "would 'settle for less' in the state's claims on
us, and lower our opinion of the state's ability to enunciate just

---

[19] John East, "The Political Relevance of St. Augustine", *Modern Age,*
spring 1972, p. 174.
[20] J. L. Talmon, *The Origins of Totalitarian Democracy* (New York:
Praeger, 1960).

teaching. It would also discourage people from seeking a political remodeling of our earthly ills."[21] Thus, Machiavelli's lowering of our sights has, when reset within Augustine's *City of God,* the paradoxical effect of restoring permanent things that are not political or achievable by the political or economic processes. It also frees the temporal to be the temporal, and not a pseudo-eternal or "best". And this restores the possibility of the searching for and finding of God in any existing society, where most men and women really are, and not exclusively limiting us to "the best", as our contemporary distributionist theories and liberation theologies tend to do.

Does this mean, however, that the realities that are permanent have no *ordering* effect upon the things political, which latter are, in Thomism, also natural and good? Here, it is important to reject any notion that the Christian theory of grace is an abstraction designed merely to emphasize the "universality" of permanent things. In this context, it is strange to hear J. G. A. Pocock, writing of late medieval political thought, argue that it existed within

> a culture with a very strong bias towards believing that only the universal, the unchanging and consequently, the timeless, was truly rational. This raised in an acute form the problem, which could become crucial, of the intelligibility of the particular, the local, the transitory—and consequently of time considered as a dimension of transitory being.[22]

Again here, we have an *audience* that does not know the Incarnation. Pocock seems unaware of the meaning of Augustine's brooding about time or about the medieval concern about singulars. It is true that the late medieval period began to

---

[21] Gary Wills, *Confessions of a Conservative* (Garden City, N.Y.: Doubleday, 1979), p. 202.

[22] J. G. A. Pocock, *Politics, Language, and Time* (New York: Atheneum, 1973), p. 81.

see a revival of Greek categories in the Renaissance. But the abiding Christian concern, its "permanent thing", was precisely with the particular, the local, with the Son of Man born in Bethlehem, when Caesar Augustus was emperor, there and nowhere else.

Hannah Arendt perceptively remarked in *The Human Condition* that Christianity made permanent and eternal that which Greek thought had most difficulty with, namely, the mortality of the particular human being.[23] Maurice de Wulf put the issue quite clearly:

> Every human being has a certain sacred value, an inviolable individuality, and as such he has a personal destiny.... Why, indeed, does the human person possess the right to realize his happiness, of which no state can deprive him? Metaphysics replies: because human personality alone is a genuine substantial reality. On the other hand, any group whatever, the state included, is not a real being; it is simply a group of human persons.[24]

It is this position that most contemporary ecological and radical political theories seek to overthrow in the name of the species or of "humanity", to instrumentalize the individual in the name of a corporate salvation that has its roots in a restructuring of the political and economic order.

This primacy of the collectivity over the individual, moreover, is why we find theories of redemption, like that of Michael Harrington in *The Vast Majority,* that seek to replace Christ, the Incarnation, with suffering humanity as the locus

[23] Hannah Arendt, *The Human Condition* (Garden City, N.Y.: Doubleday Anchor, 1959), sec. I.

[24] Maurice de Wulf, *Philosophy and Civilization in the Middle Ages* (New York: Dover, 1932), p. 223. See also the author's "The Reality of Society in St. Thomas", in *The Politics of Heaven and Hell: Christian Themes from Classical, Medieval, and Modern Political Philosophy* (Lanham, Md.: University Press of America, 1974), chap. II.

of salvation.[25] This is why we have theories of Christology that locate redemption not in the Cross but in the structural refashioning of society to eliminate human suffering from this world. Simply put, there is arising in this area the notion that redemption ought *not* to have taken place in the way it did. There is, in other words, a desperate search for a redemption other than the Christian one.

The "audience" for Incarnation, however, lies with those who await the recovery of "permanent things", in which the realization that human society symbolizes but *is* not the City of God, that the state is not real being, but a relation of order for mortals who ask, with Augustine, in his *Confessions,* "Whence could such a creature come but from Thee, O Lord? Or shall any man be skillful enough to fashion himself?" (I, 4) The modern age thinks it is becoming so skilled. True Christianity says, with Aquinas, that we are from another, even in our being, even in our happiness.

God alone is great and perfect, the multiplicity of human habitations, the intensity of London, every man comes into the world by being conceived in his mother's womb. . . .

"The aspect of London, as the man who knows it grows older, begins to take on characteristics of permanence and characteristics of change, both of which are comparable to those of human life", Hilaire Belloc wrote in his Christian essays of 1909, very appropriately called *On Everything.* "It is perceived that certain qualities in the great soul of the place are permanent". The recovery of permanent things. . . . One of the awful things about writing when you are a Christian is that for you the ultimate reality is the Incarnation. . . . Certain characteristics are permanent. As Leo Strauss said of Machiavelli's project, we too must create our own listeners, our own *audience* for the Incarnation.

[25] Michael Harrington, *The Vast Majority* (New York: Simon and Schuster, 1977).

In his *Lost Lectures* on the 1890s, Maurice Baring wrote, "To those who lived in London during this period, there seemed to be nothing at all unusual about the place."[26] And in another place, another time, they said,

> "Where did this man get all this? What is this wisdom that has been granted to him, and these miracles that are worked through him? This is the carpenter, surely, the Son of Mary, the brother of James and Joset and Jude and Simon? His sisters, too, are they not here with us?" And they would not accept him (*Mk* 6:2–4).

The narrowing of the distance to God, the falling from heaven at the birth of the world. . . . Whom shall I send? Come to Macedonia and help us. . . . Something calculated to stagger humanity, the inexhaustible contemplation, the assemblage of taverns where nobody believes in the Incarnation—the "recovery of permanent things"—of such matters are still Christian essays, of such is the Christian reality composed.

Eight Collections of Essays and Letters Not To Be Missed

1. Christopher Derrick, *Joy without a Cause.*
2. Herbert Butterfield, *Herbert Butterfield: Writings on Christianity and History.*
3. Russell Kirk, *Enemies of the Permanent Things: Observations of Abnormity in Literature and Politics*
4. Flannery O'Connor, *The Habit of Being: The Letters of Flannery O'Connor.*
5. Evelyn Waugh, *The Letters of Evelyn Waugh.*
6. Flannery O'Connor, *Mystery and Manners.*
7. J. R. R. Tolkien, *The Letters of J. R. R. Tolkien.*

[26] Paul Horgan, *Maurice Baring Reconsidered,* (New York: Farrar, Straus, and Giroux, 1970), p. 125.

8. W. E. Williams, ed., *A Book of English Essays.*

Two Books by John Cage

1. *A Year from Monday.*
2. *Silence.*

Chapter Fifteen

What Is a Lecture?

Maurice Baring, as I mentioned in the previous chapter, wrote a book I once happily read, called *Lost Lectures*. Actually, I suppose, he originally gave them as lectures and later someone found them. Now, lectures are not quite the same things as essays, such as H. V. Morton's collection of Belloc's essays, which I have also mentioned. Nor are they exactly sermons, like those of Ronald Knox or John Donne. Certainly, they are not letters, such as those marvelous ones of Flannery O'Connor, J. R. R. Tolkien, or Evelyn Waugh. Nor are they precisely addresses such as C. S. Lewis' *Weight of Glory*.

If we take a look at some published lectures, such as Gabriel Marcel's Gifford Lectures on *The Mystery of Being*, which he gave at the University of Aberdeen in 1949 and 1950, or Etienne Gilson's Richard Lectures at the University of Virginia in 1937, entitled *Reason and Revelation in the Middle Ages*, we can see, I think, that lectures are in a class all by themselves, sort of rare flowers that ought to be carefully protected from extinction, particularly from television and talk shows, which have almost nothing in common with a good lecture. And, preferably, a lecture should be heard, one should be there, such as I was recently at the Henley Park Hotel, across from the Washington, D.C., Edmund Burke Memorial, where Russell Kirk lectured on "Why We Still Study Burke".

Frankly, I am a fan of a good lecture, and I love to be invited to give a formal lecture, if given the time to compose it at my leisure, to a curious audience, and for an "occasion". It does not have to be a "big" occasion either, but it has to be an occasion, nonetheless. Thus, a lecturer needs to have a topic, a purpose for pursuing something, some idea or course of thought, for no other immediate reason than itself—something which, to the audience, will be out of the ordinary, unexpected, yet with enough earnestness, even with its humor, to claim, at least to seek, the truth.

Lecturers, too, ought to give memorable, intriguing, or lofty titles to their efforts, like the one Marion Montgomery told me he was going to give to his upcoming Lamar Lectures: "Possum and Other Receits for the Recovery of 'Southern Being'". Who could possibly not want to hear such a lecture, especially were he also to recall the first person singular of the Latin verb *posse,* and its relation to *esse,* Southern or otherwise? At first, indeed, when I read the title of Montgomery's proposed lecture, I thought there was a mistake, that word *receit.* I looked for it in several dictionaries, and it did not appear. Finally, recollecting, somehow, that the word sounded right and that Marion Montgomery always chose just the right word, I finally found it as an "obsolete word" in that old standby, the O.E.D., the *Oxford English Dictionary,* probably our last hope against feminist destruction of language, and probably too, against the destruction of being, again, Southern or otherwise.

The word *lecture,* however, has acquired at least one pejorative, but legitimate, secondary connotation, as in the sentence "Alfred E. Neumann was 'lectured' by his father on how to behave at grandmother's house." The slang expression, "I was really 'read out' by my dean", is close to this meaning. Nevertheless, the word *lecture,* in itself, is a noble one. A lecture is a discourse, before some hopefully interested audience, but one never knows, which is read out loud in order to set forth some considered opinion or pondered topic.

The past participle of the Latin word *legere* is *lectum.* The word meant to collect or gather things together, like grapes.

Then it came to mean to choose, as to select judges. Finally, it meant to read or peruse books, to read aloud what, presumably, the lecturer has especially chosen or selected, for the "occasion", for what falls or happens at a particular time. This is why lectures need dates on them and the name of the places in which they were originally given. Leo Strauss' *Natural Right and History* was the annual Walgreen Lecture at the University of Chicago in 1950. (Alas, my edition of this key series of lectures does not give the exact place in which they were given, the hall, or the exact date, a fault, in my view.)

In Fowler's *Modern English Usage,* the following bemused entry is pertinent to our topic:

> *Lectureship, — urership.* The first (lectureship) is an irregular formation [my *Random House Dictionary* gives this entry, *lectureship,* with no hint about its irregularity], as a parallel for which the *Oxford English Dictionary* quotes the now obsolete *clergyship* [though a person can be clergy better than he can be lecture]; but it is long-established, and those who use the second (lecturership) instead perhaps make it in momentary forgetfulness that the irregular form exists.

Thus, we might suggest that what is happening here is that a "person" who is "better clergy" ventures, in an irregular state of "momentary forgetfulness", to write an essay about a "lecture" or on "lecturing". Thus, I believe that an essay written not to be originally read aloud is not a "lecture". Likewise, a written essay becomes a formal reality, a *lecture,* only when it is intended to be read aloud to an audience who listens to it. A lecture, thus, is addressed to living beings out there in the hall or room, people whom the lecturer can observe, the audience listening and watching him.

All this came up recently because I was invited to give, so I thought, a lecture at a small conference on some sufficiently obscure metaphysical issue. There were four papers to be read. Each writer was expected to present a written text of his address for future publication. My proposed lecture was about fourteen double-spaced pages, perhaps a forty to forty-five minute effort. The topic was one I liked, solemn, but one lending itself to some wit, some originality, some surprise, or at least, so I thought.

Consequently, in my text, I had woven some stories, some asides, some ironies, some references to the classics, unexpected conclusions. It was a lecture I was relatively happy with before I gave it. I did not quite know the audience, to be sure, but I anticipated reading my text to literate people who would understand the overtones and the undertones, the allusions, the solemnity and the humor, which I had tried to put into the endeavor. I have been to hundreds of lectures in my day. There is nothing better than a good one, and I am vain enough to want those who do me the honor to listen to me to enjoy what I say and even, hopefully, learn something, some aspect of a common truth to which we are all open because of what we are. At the same time, though, I would hope for an attention, an active listening, from my audience. I know the gazings out the window when the audience has lost interest, usually because my lecture deserves such response.

Anyhow, this was my state of mind when I got to the conference. Right away, after some initial introductions of other speakers and members of the organization, a very nice lady wanted to know if I had the text of my lecture. Well, as that is precisely one of those things one does not leave home without if he is to deliver it, I assured her that I indeed had this gem clutched in my very hands and planned to leave it with the conference director, as per request, when I had finished presenting it to the audience. She next told me that she wanted to "reproduce" it ahead of time, so the attendees could have it while I was giving it. This request, of course, seemed like a perfectly awful idea to me, so I politely tried to reassure her that I would give it to her when I had completed the lecture. Then, if any of the bewildered audience would actually be so rash as to want a copy, she could reproduce it later for them.

The next thing I knew in this saga was that the director of the conference quietly asked me to give the precious text of Schall's reflections as a courtesy to the audience. Well, who can be against courtesy? So I reluctantly gave the lady the copy to reproduce. Thus, when the actual meeting gathered in the hall, everyone was already provided with the same text that I was about to present. I had feared this was going to be closer to a Mitch Miller sing-a-long than a formal lecture. All I needed was to have it projected on a screen with the little bouncing balls, something, incidentally, that could have been done, as this conference room was equipped with just about everything in the communications technology world, except direct mind reading.

As it turned out, only one other speaker had his text in reproducible form in advance. The first speaker talked from notes—it was a good talk too. He spoke into a microphone that recorded it all for posterity. The fourth speaker, who followed me, had at least fifty pages of text, none reproduced in advance, while the second speaker, whose text we had, had about thirty pages. So the second speaker began. Sure enough, everyone in the audience, but me, took out his copy of the very lecture being presented. It was somewhat like a test on whether the speaker could read his own document properly and pronounce the words. All in the audience had pencils provided, so they were able to mark the text. When the poor speaker turned the page, the audience reciprocated.

At a lecture, I usually doodle, jot things down, reflect actively when I listen to a speaker who has something to say.

That is, I feel I have the honest duty to pay attention, to watch the speaker, not rigidly, of course, but fairly. I do not want to "read" simultaneously what the lecturer is saying, because this distracts from the very reality of a "lecture", of something being read, something originally prepared by a man or a woman I have implicitly consented to listen to. There is a spiritual relationship between the speaker and the hearer that is sacred somehow—word passing from one being to another, the kind of activity in which all is gain, words upon souls.

So there I was becoming more and more annoyed that this particular audience, because of advanced information systems, such as photocopying, would never really "hear" me out, would not give me the license to vary the text, adapt it, add a story, drop something, surprise them. The literary whole that is the entire lecture in its intended effect would be broken. The audience would know what was coming next. I had planned, for example, to begin with a passage from Plato. I had anticipated reading it slowly, without telling them from whence it came, so the hearers might ponder it with fresh curiosity. But no; there it was in front of them on the photocopy, the very citation plus the exact reference. There could be no wonderment about what this might mean, this "clergy" giving a "lecture". The audience would know in advance. There was to be no momentary "forgetfulness", alas. And my stories and jokes, so literate, so woven into the argument—the audience could each read the punch line before I got to it. I would see grins on faces before the point of amusement was reached. And my intricate, yet, I hoped, lucid argument—there it was, all laid out for everyone to mark up with pencils independently of my voice. The punch lines came to the eyes of the readers before they came to the ears of the hearers.

I think I did mention that I preferred the audience all to listen, rather than read, my lecture. One or two did, so I could catch that fleeting eye that is so important in speaking to a human gathering. But I was disappointed. This was not really a "lecture" as I had written it—to be read, elegantly, I hoped, to a group of unknown listeners. It turned out that I knew one or two of them. I like to include the audience in a lecture a bit, not overdoing it. I want them to know I am glad they are there. But I also want to demand something of them: that is, that they hear my argument, what I have carefully written to be read aloud to them, something they know I worked on, something that came from all I know, somehow.

Yet, on reflection, I suppose it is wrong to blame technology or conference organization for this problem. After all, I am dealing with literary etiquette. No one is forced to read a printed text even if he has it. I myself appreciate having a copy of a lecture when it is over, especially when it was given a century before my lifetime. That is to say, I can always read lectures previously read aloud to a live audience, even if given before my own lifetime, such as, say, Hegel's *Lectures on the Philosophy of History,* given in 1822. We derive a certain comfort, I think, in recalling that a live audience heard these momentous words.

Yet I must admit that not everyone shares my view of the lecture. Samuel Johnson, for example, a man for whom I have the highest regard, thought a lecture was just a substitute for a book or printed text. On April 15, 1781, an Easter Sunday, Boswell recorded this passage:

> We talked of the difference between the mode of education at Oxford, and that in those Colleges where instruction is chiefly conveyed by lectures. *Johnson.* "Lectures were once useful; but now, when all can read, and books are so numerous, lectures are unnecessary. If your attention fails, and you miss a part of a lecture, it is lost; you cannot go back as you do upon a book." Dr. Scott agreed with him. "But yet (said I), Dr. Scott, you

yourself gave lectures at Oxford." He smiled. "You laughed (then said I), at those who came to you."

No doubt, a "lecture" is not the best way to teach or learn regularly. As I think, a lecture ought to be mainly an occasion. Yet we should have them. We need the opportunity to be addressed, to be spoken to. Likewise, we need the chance to set forth, in public, seriously, yet as effectively as we know how, what it is we hold. But I am the last to believe that our public lives exhaust the essence of what we are. In fact, the origin of what we can say in public must lie somewhere in the depths of our private lives and loves.

The lecture, in conclusion, then, unlike debate, unlike conversation, is something some one of us writes down considerately to tell us. We need to hear of the highest things, so there is a certain seriousness of purpose, of topic, to our speaking formally to one another. But, such is the mystery of the relation between joy and sadness, between tragedy and comedy, that I am not so sure that the more profound lectures are not rather those full of humor and delight, though I am grateful for both kinds.

Nathan Scott wrote:

> The great difference . . . between the tragic man and the comic man is something that arises out of their different ways of dealing with the burden of human finitude. For the tragic man it is a profound embarrassment and perhaps even a curse, for he would be pure intellect or pure will. . . . But the comic man is unembarrassed by even the grossest expressions of his creatureliness: though the world may not be all dandy, he has no sense of being under any cruel condemnation; nor does he have any sense of desperate entrapment within a caged prison.[1]

Those who lecture to us enter into a trust. Lecturer and listener

[1] Nathan Scott, "The Bias of Comedy and the Narrow Escape into Faith", *The Christian Scholar*, spring 1961, p. 93.

are each finite. The pull of pure truth seems pitted often against the laughter that pervades our pretensions to know *what is*. *The Gospel of St. John* begins with the famous words, "In the beginning was the Word". And Adam is said to have "named" all the creatures. Word upon word. In the end, truth is not merely given in the structure of things, but it needs to be "spoken" and "heard", by ourselves, among ourselves. At its best, this is what a lecture is.

Twelve Collections of Lectures and Reflections

1. Maurice Baring, *Lost Lectures.*
2. C. S. Lewis, *The Weight of Glory and Other Essays.*
3. Gabriel Marcel, *The Mystery of Being.*
4. Etienne Gilson, *Reason and Revelation in the Middle Ages.*
5. J. M. Bochenski, *Philosophy: An Introduction.*
6. Frank J. Sheed, *Theology and Sanity.*
7. Malcolm Muggeridge, *Jesus Rediscovered.*
8. John Henry Newman, *The Idea of a University.*
9. Hans Urs von Balthasar, *New Elucidations.*
10. Jean Guitton, *Man in Time.*
11. Josef Pieper, *Problems of Modern Faith.*
12. John Paul I, *Illustrissimi.*

Fourteen Books on the Value and Defense of Human Life

1. Joseph Sobran, *Single Issues: Essays on the Crucial Social Questions.*
2. George Gilder, *Men and Marriage.*
3. Ellen Wilson, *An Even Dozen.*
4. John J. O'Connor, *In Defense of Life.*
5. William Brennan, *Medical Holocausts.*
6. Julian L. Simon, *The Ultimate Resource.*

7. John and Sheila Kippley, *The Art of Natural Family Planning.*
8. Carl Anderson and William J. Gribbin, *The Wealth of Families.*
9. Christopher Derrick, *Too Many People? A Problem in Values.*
10. Dietrich von Hildebrand, *Marriage: The Mystery of Faithful Love.*
11. Henry Hyde, *For Every Idle Silence.*
12. Gabriel Marcel, *Creative Fidelity.*
13. Allan C. Carlson, *The Family in the Modern World.* (Periodical published by the Rockford Institute.)
14. James V. Schall, *Christianity and Life.*

Chapter Sixteen

On Devotion

According to a calendar found by the *New Yorker,* an outfit in California — where else? — called the Siddha Meditation Center conducted a workshop once a week in order to forge a link between "creative experience" and meditation. After such "meditation", it seems, one should be able to write better screenplays for Hollywood films and TV shows. All of this, furthermore, was designed to help the potentially creative meditator and playwright — "This is an incredibly unique opportunity for you to learn to 'honor yourself, respect yourself, and love yourself'." The *New Yorker* was right to have been amused by this. Needless to say, a case can be made for the fact that we already know too well how to honor and respect ourselves. Much classical prayer life, in fact, was concerned with this very problem and sought to direct a healthy attention to something not ourselves.

After I read this delightful account of what must be a classic misunderstanding of what meditation is all about, and not forgetting at the same time that some philosophic and religious systems did put ourselves at the very center of reality, I chanced on a question in Aquinas entitled, appropriately, "Whether Contemplation or Meditation Is the Cause of Devotion?" (II–II, 82, 3). And on reading this article, sure enough what seems most striking about meditation within the Christian tradition, at least, is that meditation and devotion are not directed at ourselves or our skills, but rather to God, to something definite, to *what is.*

Moreover, Christian devotion, although it is not self-centered, nevertheless does not forget that the one who contemplates or meditates remains a distinct, independent being, whose faculties or powers can take him out of himself, but which do not deny that he ought to remain precisely himself. Christians do not hold that through devotion a human being becomes a "god" or the cosmos or some other reincarnated creature. Each person remains the limited human being he is created to be, not by himself. This is why we are also told to love our neighbor "as ourselves". But we are told to do this largely on the assumption that the First Commandment—"thou shalt love the Lord thy God"—will be in danger of neglect because of our excessive love of our own selves.

We live in an age, no doubt, loathe to make distinctions when they imply that religious or philosophic differences make a real difference in how we live and can live. We want to say that love of self or love of neighbor is sort of self-explanatory; if not positively virtuous, at least it is harmless. And yet it makes a world of difference what we mean when we speak of such things. The point was made by Chesterton in one of his Father Brown stories, one called, "The Wrong Shape", in which the following passage is found:

> "When that Indian spoke to us", went on Brown in a conversational undertone, "I had a sort of vision, a vision of him and all his universe. Yet he only said the same thing three times. When he first said, 'I want nothing', it meant only that he was impenetrable, that Asia does not give itself away. Then he said again, 'I want nothing', and I knew that he meant that he was sufficient to himself, like a cosmos, that he needed no God, neither admitted any sins. And when he said the third time, 'I want nothing', he said it with dazzling eyes. And I knew that he meant literally what he said; that nothing was his desire and his home; that he was weary for nothing as for wine; that annihilation, the mere destruction of everything or anything. . . . "[1]

[1] G. K. Chesterton, *The Pocket Book of Father Brown* (New York: Pocket Books, 1943), p. 41.

In Christian metaphysics, there is a real sense in which the love of self verges into the love of nothing.

When Augustine spoke of the "two loves" that built the "two cities", then, he knew that the essential spiritual choice that each person has, why he is given life at all in the first place, is the choice between himself and God as the cause of *what is,* of reality, of especially his own being. The temptation to nonexistence, to death over life, is one that follows from the choice to construct our own universe instead of choosing to receive the one given to us as the greater reality, even for ourselves.

If I read the first book of Aristotle's *Ethics* correctly, that wise man argued that we all act for some purpose in all we choose to do or make. During the course of our days, our lifetime, we put into existence by our choices many different actions, ones originating in us. These fall into recognizable patterns, however particular each action of whatever virtue or vice might be as it proceeds out of us. Moreover, all of these actions put together in that story or pattern of our lives are grounded in some final, central choice or definition of what it is we are about in all we do or make. In this sense, we, having been given ourselves, refashion or recreate ourselves by what we in fact do with those activities that properly proceed from us. The ultimate wars of the world are over the differing kinds of ultimate choices or definitions of happiness we might put forth into reality. Aristotle recognized that all possible alternatives could result in the right choices, no matter what we did. We had to understand and seek out what the human reality as given to us indicated; that is, what it indicated that real happiness consisted in for a human being such as man finds himself to be. For Aristotle, this was the steady contemplation of the truth in things as it reflects the truth from which it originates in the First Mover.

The modern notion of "pluralism" has come to mean not merely the fact that there is a wide variety of ways to embody the real virtues we can incorporate in ourselves, but that there are no "ends", no "happinesses", other than the ones we choose on the basis of, ultimately, the love of ourselves. Modern society is an arrangement, an order, whose very purpose is to declare the impossibility of arriving at any morally or metaphysically binding truth. This means that society becomes an arena of ultimate indifferences, where each "life-style", each sort of "choice", plays itself out with equal right and dignity just because it is "chosen". The modern idea is that "You have your end and I have mine and, in the end, isn't all that variety nice?" Truth, in fact, has come to be looked upon as an enemy of modern society because it hints that there is something wrong in our world if truth does in fact exist, something that we can define and act for or against.

Aristotle would have found this world in which truth could not be affirmed to be a curious one. He said that pleasure and wealth and fear were goods, but not the highest ones. Without denying the objective worth of all the other things that we could put our trust in, Aristotle still thought there was a highest good that was not the product of our own choice or making. And further, since such an end was something of reality, not just subjective, a wish or imagination, it was something we ought, insofar as we could, to select, want, embrace. Our reaction to the highest reality, for which we were given our very intelligence as part of our own being, Aristotle called contemplation, our effort to know what, ultimately, could not be otherwise. It was the search for this reality, Aristotle thought, that should guide us in all else we do.

Thomas Aquinas often spoke of activities such as holiness, meditation, religion, and devotion. Clearly, these in some sense were intended to imply some relation between ourselves and the highest things. Aquinas held that there was much in Aristotle that could be legitimately accepted by a believer once he recognized that this "truth" is somehow also active in regard to each of us. Indeed, our own highest activities, which we should learn are within us by self-reflection, ought to be related to this truth or reality revealing itself to us through the world to which we are somehow open in our very being and knowledge.

Sanctity or holiness was essentially the relating of all our actions and deeds to God so that we were recognizably whole beings, aware of our own finiteness, of our own internal unity and its relation to the highest things. The "devout" person thus was someone who understood that the right order of his own life was to offer precisely himself to God, so that each action might reach its immediate and ultimate object of being, so that it might reach beyond nothing. Meditation was our own inner effort to see both that and how this was so. Meditation is the awareness that ultimately the order of reality must be put together in us also, by us, to relate ourselves to what is not merely ourselves. Devotion centered more on our own will, meditation on our intelligence or understanding. Once we knew the truth, we were, in a sense, freed. But we each had to direct our own activities to the highest things. In this, we had to remember that it remained always possible for us to direct all reality, as we grasped it, to ourselves, to worship ourselves, to be "devoted" to ourselves. The nature of devotion, then, implied not merely our awareness of our own powers and capacities, but also the fact that our own very being is directed out of ourselves, that our own being is insufficient for the sort of reality we recognize that we are constituted for and directed to by what we are.

I bring this up because I think there is an abundance of misplaced devotion in our world. We can use all of our powers and faculties to direct ourselves to a view of the world that somehow makes us the center of all being. Our world is full of "self-fulfillment" theories and practices, very "spiritual" ones in their own way. At bottom, these positions result in little else but voluntary choices of ourselves as the causes of being, supported by intellectual theories that purpose to explain how this is possible or necessary. We can even choose others and still remain within this self-contained world. Indeed, the most dangerous theories about today are undoubtedly those that see in the state, that is, in the collection of human beings, however defined, the ultimate end to which all else should be directed. This collectivity, however defined, is largely what substitutes for God in our world.

Such a polity or collectivity will not merely decide who can belong to it, but will even decide what a human being is. Those who do not fit our political definitions will be excluded or eliminated. Aristotle had remarked that if man were the highest being, politics would be the highest science. The fact that so many do hold that man is the highest being—and therefore not a very important one, ironically—means that politics can legitimately "do" with us what it sees necessary. Chesterton said in another story that "if you do not fear God, you have good reason to fear man".[2] For many of us, we no longer have a vocation or sense of reality that enables us by our devotion or meditation to transcend how our politics defines us. The polity itself, however, is a form of rule that allows us to define ourselves and makes no judgment on what we are, even concerning the truth of our nature and being.

All of this analysis has certain implications for any Christian-oriented spiritual life. In part, at least, it explains why, in the

[2] Ibid., p. 53.

public forum, Christianity appears more and more to stand not for transcendence, but for polity and ideology, why so many Christians now look upon their religious "vocations" as supporting this or that movement over which there is no judgment except of love of self or love of neighbor. This latter seems at first clearly spiritual until we see that in its roots it is not subject to anything but a theory of what human beings "might" be, rather than a reception of a given existing nature or a revelation about what they are. Devotion and meditation become misplaced and are directed to the individual, usually as a function of a collectivity of some sort. In this sense, what we need to recover is meditation and devotion directed first to God in the realization that all else, however good in itself, has in modern thought become a substitute for God. We need what might direct us to something that we ourselves are not by our own powers and choices.

St. Thomas, thus, said that the external cause of our devotion is God, whereas the inner cause, from our own resources, is meditation or contemplation. Devotion is an act of our wills by which we are prompt to offer ourselves to the divine service, itself our only real and ultimate goal. Yet we cannot do this offering unless we understand what we do. Our wills depend on how we grasp what we should do, so our meditation does cause our devotion, our offering ourselves to God, because we need first to conceive the very idea that we should first serve God. In any right order of thinking, we ought not choose "nothing", nor ought we to choose first to love ourselves or our polity or our self-formulated salvation ideology as the object of our devotion.

What remains rather is the reality of God made known to us not by ourselves, but by God in his dealings with mankind, in his self-outpourings to us in Church, sacrament, and prayer. Much of modern life is, in a sense, a constant effort to suggest to us some "good", some end, less than God as that which bears and incites our service and devotion. The sign that this is so is the willingness to formulate an object of devotion against the criteria of the orthodox view of man, cosmos, and God. Intensity of devotion or sincerity of purpose will not, in itself, be enough to assure us that the happiness we define for ourselves is what we really seek by the structure of what we are. This latter results rather from our reason and its openness to a revelation that is the truth itself, something whose proportions are beyond our imaginings, but not beyond our capacity to recognize that we are being addressed.

In the end, Aquinas asked whether devotion caused joy in us and wondered how it could since the Passion of Christ is what causes us to serve God. In fact, he said, the Passion of Christ does make us sad in a way because of the human defects for which Christ had to suffer to remove from our condition. Yet it does make us joyful too, because this very Passion reveals God's benignity to us by which we are freed from these crimes and defects (II–II, 83, 4, ad 1). I conclude with this, then, on the subject of devotion, because we are constantly looking for some other remedy for our sins than the one given to us in Christ. In this sense, true devotion is also dependent on a meditation on the Passion, on the realization that no other form of salvation really meets the highest thing to which in our personal being we are called and to which we do aspire.

Eleven Books on Prayer, Belief, and Reflection

1. Hans Urs von Balthasar, *Prayer.*
2. Francis de Sales, *Introduction to the Devout Life.*
3. Thomas Verner Moore, *The Life of Man with God.*

4. Ronald Knox, *The Belief of Catholics.*
5. Dietrich von Hildebrand, *Transformation in Christ.*
6. Henri de Lubac, *The Christian Faith.*
7. Gabriel Marcel, *Homo Viator: An Introduction to a Metaphysics of Hope.*
8. Thomas Merton, *No Man Is an Island.*
9. Dom Jean-Baptist Chautard, *The Soul of the Apostolate.*
10. C. S. Lewis, *Reflections on the Psalms.*
11. C. S. Dessain, *Newman's Spiritual Themes.*

Chapter Seventeen

On Prayer and Fasting for Bureaucrats

To suspect that the worst *can* happen is wisdom. To hold that the worst will *not* happen is optimism. To suggest that there is *no* worst to happen in the first place is pure madness.

Anyone who works for a while around that perplexing institution of human form and divine origin, designed in part to minimize the worst—the state, that is, in all its levels—must philosophically reject the idea that there is no difference between a worst and a better. He must do so at the risk, in not so doing, of never being able to be justifiably angry at anything whatsoever that might happen, anything that someone, including himself, might do. He must also, as Aristotle suggested, have had enough experience, even in himself, to know that the worst sometimes does happen, so that he is able actually to account for the world without rejecting it, when he sees what people do to themselves and others.

Illustrative of this approach, perhaps, is the lengthy subtitle to Jeffrey Pressman and Aaron Wildavsky's book *Implementation,* a book in part based upon the genius of Rube Goldberg's famous inventions, reprinted in the book, inventions that, in spite of how the damn contraptions were built or looked, seemed in the end to deliver the goods. This expanded title—itself not at all uninfluential in the title of this very book—comes close to defining the true internal status of anyone trying, however paradoxically, to do good in the nation's capital, here or any place else. It reads, mindful of Barrington Moore's book *Reflections on the Causes of Human Misery and upon Certain Proposals to Eliminate Them,* as follows: *How Great Expectations in Washington Are Dashed in Oakland: Or, Why It's*

Amazing that Federal Programs Work at All, This Being a Saga of the Economic Development Administration as Told by Two Sympathetic Observers Who Seek to Build Morals on a Foundation of Ruined Hopes. Where, after all, are we to go if our hopes are ruined, if our great expectations are dashed even in Oakland? Our Scripture tells us first to seek the Kingdom of God before adding things to Oakland or, especially, Washington. But we are assured by our culture that this is escapism, that there are only two solutions available to us that are solely under our control: the solution that says, "Try harder", and the solution that says, "Reorganize society".

Activism is, no doubt, the religious enthusiasm of our age, perhaps the one real alternative to God in our era. We are no longer capable of distinguishing a person's interior from his exterior life. Salvation depends upon joining the right causes, designed to alleviate the right evil, defined by the right ideology. The older fraternity of a faith received as a gift, but allowing different politics, has been more and more replaced by a community of like-minded followers of a politically universal purpose, where the doctrinal diversities are reduced to insignificance because of the elevation of the cause. The question can arise, therefore, about whether bureaucrats, policy activists, experts, and sundry opinion managers require an interior life that would suggest, beyond the causes, a sense of prayer and fasting to remind them of a reality that is not exhausted or defined by the movements and interests of the world, however fascinating these might be.

The plot is even thicker. "If you walk into an average classroom today," Mark Lilla recently wrote in *Harper's,*

> you may not hear much about Plutarch, but neither will you find students ready for political agitation. Instead, you will find a professor dressed in beat-up corduroys, a flannel shirt, and

work boots, standing before a class of straight-backed students dressed in designer jeans and pressed shirts. The professor will deliver some scholarly-sounding harangue about bourgeois values, the redistribution of wealth, and the depredations of the multinationals, only to have the students, whose minds are probably on getting into business or law school, ask if all this political stuff will be on the exam. The professor is frustrated, the students are bored. And Plutarch goes unread. . . .

Yet of Plutarch, the *Ancilla to Classical Reading* says, "He has indubitably had more European readers than any other pagan Greek and has been the greatest single channel communicating to Europe a general sense of the men and manners of antiquity." Plutarch, of course, is not read because we do not know why we need any "general sense of men and manners of antiquity". Nonetheless, if we leave college or university or seminary or convent to lead our lives with no sense of what Werner Jaeger called *"paideia"*, no sense of the claim of the classics to be a universal culture, addressing itself to man as such, no matter what his accidental qualities, are we fit for anything but a chaos of the now, a myriad of impressions with no clue about how to reduce them to a common order based upon something other than just one more subjective opinion? Is the cosmos, is our society, safe for us if we do not know what the cosmos, what society means?

Salvador de Madariaga, as I have mentioned earlier, said that, on leaving school, every young European student should be given a small book containing the accounts of the death of Socrates and the death of Christ, neither of whom wrote a book. These two men, the best of our kind, were both executed by the state. Yet if in our leisure we have read the actual accounts of Plato and John of the deaths of Socrates and Christ, we cannot but be left with some latent anger that would reorganize states so that such injustices could never happen again. Both Socrates and Christ, however, suggested that this would be a futile effort, that the true destiny of each person is at stake in immortality and resurrection, no matter what sort of polity he lived in. States, in other words, do not consume everything in us.

Yet the modern world seems full of movements in which human beings are to be identified with politics. "The study of the European past is still relevant to modern world history", Christopher Dawson wrote to this latter point, "since Europe was the original source of the movement of change in which the whole world is now involved and it is in European history that we find the key to the understanding of the ideologies which divide the modern world." If we do not know that politics and religion differ, where each leads, we cannot understand the growing politicization of public and private, individual and family life, which is the chief characteristic of our contemporary culture.

In his treatise, *On Duties,* long a staple, seminal book in western civilization, Cicero wrote, "To every one who proposes to have a good career, moral philosophy is indispensable." To be sure, there is some evidence that this Roman emphasis on moral philosophy over metaphysics in the Aristotelian sense was the beginning of this ideological movement of the modern era. But the great Roman orator went on, writing to his wayward son, Marcus, at college in Athens, to suggest that there can be no real conflict between what is right and what is to our own advantage, that, by virtue of our common human bond, we should all do the right things in economics, commerce, war, and politics, never compromising ourselves.

Cicero, in any case, managed to put at the heart of our culture the idea that, in each instance of our practical lives, there was some right action we ought to discover and put into existence as coming directly out of ourselves. To fail in this endeavor to guide ourselves—and human beings do fail, and this too needs to be accounted for—would violate our personal integrity and, simultaneously, corrupt the common order upon which we all depend. This insight, then, is one of the things we should have learned and carried with us when we left our university studies, this sense of a highest order of rightness implicit in each of our actions. Yet, like Marcus, we may have been busy in Athens, or even in Los Angeles or Washington, about many things.

In his *Ethics,* moreover, Aristotle had suggested that young people were largely incapable of knowing many morally true things because they lacked experience, both the experience in themselves and in others, of what human beings actually do. This is why we should first learn, even memorize, many things we really do not know about, so that, when the time comes for us to be able to recognize a truth, we will have the will, capacity, and language to do so. For the most part, we were not, probably, virtuous or prudent when we were high school or college students, in Athens or Los Angeles or anywhere else. No mere academic training can teach us all these things. Prayer and fasting remain somehow required even when we know what we ought to do.

But universities can and ought to have taught us in general what to expect, so that we could, perhaps, recognize both good and evil, including especially our own, when we are finally able to bear the experience from which we, sometimes valiantly, seek to escape.

Thus, a friend of mine wrote once:

> I have trouble with universals when it comes to human behavior.
> For me, I am never absolutely positive of what I will do, a very
> disturbing way to live. I make up my mind. I decide. I will. I
> brace myself. Then, boom—I do the opposite. VERY BAD TRAIT!

St. Paul, of course, said exactly the same thing: "The good I would do, I do not." This realization, too, should be part of the memory we carry with us from our stays in Athens, or in Los Angeles, or in Washington.

We sometimes forget how important ideas are to our spiritual capacity to be citizens in a world only completely explained by religious truths, about which we hear so little, sometimes even in the churches. Flannery O'Connor wrote on November 8, 1958, what is surely the best advice that can be given to anyone who works for or about the public affairs of a nation. "The notion of the perfectibility of man", she remarked,

> came about at the time of the Enlightenment in the eighteenth century. This is what the South has traditionally opposed. "How far have we fallen?" means the fall of Adam, the fall from innocence, from sanctifying grace. The South still believes that man has fallen and that he is only perfectible by God's grace, not by his own unaided efforts. The liberal approach is that man has never fallen, never incurred guilt, and is ultimately perfectible by his own efforts. Therefore, evil in this light is a problem of better housing, sanitation, health, etc. and all the mysteries will eventually be cleared up. Judgment is out of place because man is not responsible.[1]

Needless to say, bureaucrats and politicians who were educated unaware of these consequences will spend lives of frustration and emptiness seeking to build kingdoms to cure the evils of others, and thereby they will usually end up undermining the last dignity that comes from free choice.

A friend of mine says, "College is not meant to improve income. It is meant to improve living." Plato, whom Cicero had read carefully, as must we all if we have any desire to

[1] O'Connor, *The Habit of Being,* pp. 302–03.

understand our kind and our visions, had suggested in *The Republic* that a society in which there was a multiplicity of doctors and lawyers was already a sick society, that constant litigation and consultation were signs of civilizational decay. Complete absorption in the pursuit of justice and health somehow ends up with neither. This passage in Plato about doctors and lawyers is always something edifying to read aloud to undergraduate classes full of premedical and prelegal students. And, of course, business students would have been hoisted out of Plato's Academy, not to mention his republic, as providing only the means of existence, but having little to say about existing well. Law, medicine, and business, however valuable they may be to alleviate our woes and order our flaws, are not the disciplines that most directly teach us about living, about what John Finnis at Oxford called "human flourishing".[2] We should also have learned something of this latter in our education, even if we are doctors, lawyers, or executives. We should also have had an inkling that perhaps the highest things are not learned in any academic discipline at all.

The last time I was in Rome, I was sitting one morning after coffee before the Trevi fountains with a copy of the Milanese daily, *Il Giornale.* Its third page contained a feature essay about an Italian professor who had spent a year teaching at Amherst College in Massachusetts. Naturally, he was teaching his five students about Machiavelli's *Prince,* that most unnatural of books. Professor Cancogni quickly discovered that his young American students were morally incapable of understanding what the Florentine diplomat was driving at. Americans, the Italian professor concluded, were brought up on a utopianism that did not allow, as in Europe, that kind of shrewd practicality

---

[2] John Finnis, *Natural Law and Natural Right* (New York: Oxford, 1980).

that enabled us to get on in the world in spite of our lofty ideals. "At bottom, the American continues to believe", he went on,

> that his country is an open and free space in which each one has the right to pursue happiness, to realize his own ends, and that the state ought to create the least number of burdens for it.
>
> Is this a good? Or an evil? A good, certainly, and it is for this that for over two centuries, America has been the dream of millions of the disinherited who have thought of it as a vast island of rest in the storms of history. But changed as are the conditions now, no longer being an island of security in the bosom of the ocean, having become, namely, but one state among others, I ask myself whether, in giving so much space in the university to political science departments, which teach the techniques of an abstract politics in a world which no longer exists, there could not be a case made for developing a conscience, before a history populated by so many Ramiro de Lorquas, still capable of accomplishing the art of governing a people, however degrading this art may be?

And who was this Ramiro de Lorqua, whose story so horrified the American students? Machiavelli used this story of Ramiro to illustrate how to rule. It seems that he was a governor appointed by Duke Valentino to eliminate his restless opposition. Ramiro proceeded to do this very thing with maximum fear and ruthlessness. Naturally, everyone was cowed into submission. But the duke had one more lesson to teach: namely, who was really boss. So he ordered Ramiro de Lorqua himself to be cleaved in two, with his bloody halves posted in the city square for all the sober people to witness. This duke, Machiavelli hinted, knew how to rule. Recalling this, we will perhaps sympathize with the American reservations about Europe, while still wondering in practice what living in a fallen world really means. Such dichotomies we should have learned about: those relating our ideals to our realities, those asking whether ideals may not cause us to destroy our reality, something Plato himself began our worrying about.

Let me conclude very simply. If the lessons of the world that we learn by living our lives suggest that this world is not enough, that some radical disorder exists in our society as well as in our hearts, we need something akin to prayer and fasting, no matter what our public or professional or academic status might be. I do not mean this to be a pious exhortation; even less do I wish to suggest that our job or duty or service is what openness to the Lord is all about. This latter notion that religion is political action is probably the most subtle of the modern temptations, made no less so by the fact that what we do is indeed valuable, as well as by the fact that so many religious people in particular seem to succumb to it.

There are, I think, as a result, two ways to turn. The first is, paradoxically, to Aristotle. Aristotle was the man who left Athens so that the best of the ancient cities would not twice be guilty of killing its philosophers. That ancient cities killed Socrates and Christ, as Madariaga pointed out, is the first thing we should know about them. As Peter and John said in Acts, we should obey God rather than men. On the other hand, we should know that much of the modern intellectual world is built on the rejection of the Judaeo-Christian, Greek, and Roman classics. It is this modern world, the one built on this rejection, that is increasingly unsatisfactory to many of our contemporaries. Perhaps, as Henry Veatch well argued, it is time to return to an Aristotle whom we have rejected without realizing his wisdom.

We could, of course, also turn to other gods, to Eastern gods, to the ideologies of our modern thought, or we might even rediscover that religion which made us a religious people in the first place. John Paul II has himself become something of an intellectual revolution by insisting that we cannot understand the whole truth about ourselves, about mankind, without attention to the religious claims within our culture, the ones that made it what it is.

As *The Economist* wrote of John Paul II, many people overlook the way he sees the world.

> Watching him in Poland, in Latin America, in Ireland, people have overlooked the invisible part of the goal John Paul has set for his papacy. His chief role, as he sees it, lies beyond the field of human relations. He regards himself as a sort of ambassador of eternity. He is trying to organize a spiritual counter-offensive whose aim is the reconquest of an unbelieving world for the idea of belief in God (April 10, 1982), p. 66.

The Thomist tradition, so familiar to the Pope, suggested that, if we should discover the fullness and correctness of reason, we ought to allow ourselves to be addressed by the events and doctrines of revelation. Ours is particularly, at least at its intellectual center, an age that seems unable to bear this "humiliation" of not being able to learn even itself all by itself. Perhaps Leo Strauss was right: many of us first need to discover what we can know by our own unaided reason, since we never suspect in advance its glories or its limitations.

But if we need Aristotle, I think, we need Augustine more. Augustine was human enough, brilliant enough to realize that Plato's search for a true public order, which corresponded to our inner order and to the good, was not an unworthy one. Augustine freed us, moreover, by insisting that this search that, if we be human, we discover in our restless hearts, after we have met both Ramiro de Lorqua and the pursuit of happiness in this world, has its proper and final answer as a gift from God, after the completion of our very lives among the existing cities. Augustine remains someone to whom we can turn. We are probably lucky if, in our studies, in our workings, we learned not to reject prayer and fasting, let alone Augustine.

Whether we are bureaucrats, doctors, lawyers, or businessmen, even clergy, if we are attentive to what has passed before us and in us, we should have learned that we do not save ourselves. In his essay "On the Profit of Believing", Augustine said, "No one, so long as he is a fool, can by most sure knowledge find out a wise man, by the obeying of whom he may be set free from so great evil of folly." To become aware of such things, of our own folly, it does matter what we have studied, how we have been exposed to what our race has known and done. Yet whether we live such things, I suspect, still has something to do with prayer and fasting, even for bureaucrats. Such as they, in the end, would build on the foundations of ruined hopes, either in Athens or Los Angeles, in Oakland, Washington, or wherever we might be.

Ten Books on Grace and Thought

1. Henry Veatch, *Aristotle: A Contemporary Appreciation.*
2. Herbert Deane, *Political and Social Ideas of St. Augustine.*
3. John Paul II, *The Whole Truth about Man: John Paul II to University Students and Faculties.*
4. Christopher Dawson, *The Historical Reality of Christian Culture.*
5. Gustav Thibon, *What Ails Mankind?*
6. John Navone, *A Theology of Failure.*
7. Henri de Lubac, *A Brief Catechesis on Nature and Grace.*
8. Jean Galot, *Who Is Christ?*
9. Andre Frossard and John Paul II, *Be Not Afraid.*
10. St. Augustine, *Confessions.*

Four Novels, among Millions, the Most Incomplete of Lists

1. C. S. Lewis, *Till We Have Faces.*
2. Jane Austen, *Pride and Prejudice.*
3. Sigred Undset, *Kristin Lavransdatter.*
4. Thornton Wilder, *The Eighth Day.*

(And all of P. G. Wodehouse and Dostoyevsky—and all novels that show us the infinity of particular life, even when they are not very good novels—but do not neglect the best.)

Chapter Eighteen

On the Seriousness of Sports

If we look in classical literature, and in Scripture even, we will find, perhaps unexpectedly, several passages that show a knowledge of or reference to sports. Moreover, these references take sports seriously, philosophically. Let me cite some of them; to begin:

> 1. I assert that in all the cities, everyone is unaware that the character of the games played is decisive for the establishment of the laws, since it determines whether or not the established laws will persist. Where this is arranged, and provided that the same persons always play at the same things, with the same things, and in the same way, and have their spirits gladdened by the same toys, there the serious customs are also allowed to remain undisturbed; but where the games change, and are always infested with innovation and other sorts of transformations . . . there is no greater ruin than this that can come to a city.

> (From Plato, *The Laws,* bk. VII, 797a–c)

> 2. Amusement is for the purpose of relaxation and relaxation must necessarily be pleasant, since it is a kind of cure for the ills we suffer in working hard. . . . Men have been known to make amusement an end in itself. No doubt there is something pleasant about one's chosen end but it is a very original kind of pleasure, and men in seeking pleasure mistake the one kind for the other. For there is indeed a resemblance; the end is not pursued for the sake of anything that may accrue thereafter but always for its own sake.

> (From Aristotle, *The Politics,* bk. VIII, 1339b15–17; 32–39)

3. All the runners at the stadium are trying to win, but only one of them gets the prize. You must run in the same way, meaning to win. All the fighters at the games go into strict training; they do this just to win a wreath that will wither away, but we do it for a wreath that will never wither. That is how I run, intent on winning; that is how I fight, not beating the air. I treat my body hard and make it obey me, for, having been an announcer myself, I should not want to be disqualified.

(From St. Paul, I Corinthians, 9:24–27)

Such analogies, such reflections, from such sources ought to cause us to wonder a bit about sports.

Why, after all, do so many people, in so many countries, watching so many different kinds of sports, throughout our kind's history, attend games, just to be there, looking on, from foot or chariot races or boxing with Paul of Tarsus to cricket, basketball, soccer, and the Belmont Stakes? One popular theory is that people are merely escaping from life, from its seriousness, from the drudgery or the boredom of their daily rounds. Intellectuals, though not the best ones, as our earlier citations prove, often talk this way, as do some clergy, perhaps in fact the most avid sports fans as a group in any society.

Thus, writers or announcers who think sports merely escapism, on being assigned to cover the U. S. or British Open or the Rose Bowl, conceive themselves as social critics. They tell us how silly it is to chase that little white ball around the grass in Akron, Ohio, or that there is not much else to see but the game in Pasadena on New Year's Day anyhow; besides, it gives the hapless folk in Ann Arbor or Iowa City or Columbus a chance to come in out of the cold, even if they never win, which they apparently never do. Sports are thus considered, in this view, a sort of mild drug, like double-strength Tylenol: harmless enough perhaps, but certainly distracting us from the finer things of life. The sports writer, with this background, is at best a cynic, at worst a sort of social reformer, who would prefer to see the boys down at the plant not waste their time and money on such frivolous things. Such a writer really prefers politics without ever having pondered Plato's suspicion that changes in regimes might come first from changes in music and games.

Here, I will argue something else, something that may sound like a rather startling theory, but one held with tenacity. I want to suggest rather that the closest the average man ever gets to contemplation in the Greek sense is watching a good, significant sporting event, be it the sixth game of the World Series, the European Cup soccer finals, the center court at Wimbledon, or the county championships of his daughter's volley ball team. By this, I do not intend to argue or imply, as many do, that sports are a form of idolatry, that the game or the players are some form of divinities, even though the origin of games was often clearly related to worship. Perhaps the closest we get to the sense of what this might have meant is when at the East-West Shrine Game, eighty thousand fans stand silently at Stanford Stadium while the flag is being raised or the "Star Spangled Banner" is played. We all perhaps recall the medieval story of the juggler who could not speak or pray or craft well, but who silently before the altar performed his juggling act. He was more pleasing than the rest to the Lord.

In any case, I take it as a simple fact of experience that the attraction of the game to so many ordinary people, in so many cultures, over so long a period of time reveals something extraordinarily important about us. Moreover, it is a commonplace that many good political and social columnists and thinkers began their writing on the sports pages. My suspicion is that the best of them were not merely biding their time at the green sheet until they could hop over to the editorial page, but rather that they were learning about what fascinates men, about what men think is important, even if they could not exactly explain why, philosophically. As youngsters, I think, we get our first inklings of justice, after our encounters with our own brothers and sisters, playing ball, getting angry that little Jimmy Smith with the new glove for his birthday really did not catch that ball on the fly, but scooped it up and lied about it.

The path to philosophy, in other words, often passes through the comic pages and the peach sports sections, often for the same reason. In a column he wrote in the *Washington Post* about Georgetown University's basketball team, Dave Kindred quipped, after noting that the last names of the Hoya team were Smith, Jones, Floyd, and Brown, that the roster sounded more like a police lineup. Casey Stengel and Dizzy Dean contributed to our language as well as to our sports and humor. Just as the most theological of the comics is probably *Peanuts,* so the most brilliant of the philosophers filled his last book, *The Laws,* with reference after reference to games. Again, I do not think this is at all accidental. We are a whole. What holds us spellbound for a fascinating moment must not be totally unlike what holds us fascinated forever. What makes us laugh must be something not unlike the joy for which, as Chesterton said, we are made.

In an old *Mad Magazine* paperback (New York: Signet, 1959) featuring Alfred E. Neuman in a basketball shirt, I came across a feature providentially called "The Way Off-Side Department" about what was called "Grandstand Football". Since my ambition here is eventually to move us painlessly back to Plato, Aristotle, and Paul, if not to Creation itself, to the viewpoint of the watcher of games, to fans who care, who later go home and read about what they just witnessed, knowing that they could not comprehend it all, let me recall a few of *Mad*'s "All Time Grandstand Football Greats". This is a subject most appropriate for events such as Super Bowl and Orange Bowl games. The first "great" evidently graduated from the University of Nebraska in 1951. His *Mad* name was "Delbert (Biff) Smeed", whose claim to football immortality was that "on the night preceding the Kansas-Nebraska Game, he slept outside Nebraska Stadium waiting for the ticket booth to open, only to discover the next morning that the game was being played in Kansas".

A second "great" was one Barclay Brisk, Notre Dame '24. Barclay became a *Mad* Great Fan by attending nearly one hundred Notre Dame games without ever once yelling, "We want a touchdown". Finally, there was Barney (Rah-Rah) Windlass, from Iowa '55. Rah-Rah became a Grandstand Great by being banned from all scheduled Hawkeye games because he burned the Coach in Effigy—which Effigy turned out to be, according to the *Mad* account, "a small town just outside of Iowa City".

Good sports writers know who are in the stands, know what the drama of watching the game means, even the drama of getting there and buying or, in the case of Delbert (Biff) Smeed, not buying a ticket. These little incidents are likewise worth writing about because the game is worth going to. And not a few coaches have been burned in effigy, while soccer coaches in Barcelona or Milano know how to get out of the stadium as fast as they can when they lose the national championships. We do not go to the game to "yell", to be sure. Rather, we yell because there is something to yell about, even if the little high school cheer leaders, in all their regalia, sometimes do not yet know what it might be. When my cousin's sons played football for Westmont High in Campbell, California, I used to try to figure out if the football uniforms or the band uniforms cost the taxpayer more. There is a story here too, including the fact that without uniforms, there is no game, not to downplay the sandlot games, of course. And what is it we yell about at games? We yell at the game, but I will return to this topic.

I had an Irish friend in St. Louis, with a touch of Greek, to be sure, who wrote to me once one of the most insightful things I have ever read about real sports. Let me recall this passage in full:

> I find this interesting. Not one person in the family has ever played a video game. They will not buy one for their kids and will not play one themselves. A curious reason for this, with which I agree, surfaced. This is not a human game played on a machine. Reason? *Because there is no chance to cheat!* One big choice is removed.
>
> Ed and I watched a Monopoly Game on the video thing that Joe and Helen bought for their kids for Christmas. I instinctively hated it. No money to hold, apartments to place on your "property". No slipping one by your opponent. You don't even get to throw the dice yourself. The damn machine does it for you! This is not my idea of playing a game. As you say, our ability to make the wrong choice is proof of our glory.

We would be slow afoot, as it were, if these remarks of Ann O'Donnell did not give us pause. There is no game if there is no possibility of cheating! Games are played by people. People are free. Therefore, they can either win or lose, play fair or cheat.

To put it the other way around, where there is a possibility of cheating—this is why we yell "Murder the bum!" at referees, even with instant replay—there is high drama. We are being tested about what we are, what we reveal about ourselves in action. I do not, in this exalted discourse, mean to promote cheating. All games need a code of rules, a Hoyle, a Marquis of Queensbury. We need umpires because we cannot trust ourselves. The field judge, who stands outside the play but within the game, is essential. He too is worth writing about. I do mean to suggest, however, that like life itself, perhaps more profoundly because of life, the possibility of breaking rules indicates the seriousness with which we must observe even arbitrary rules in the games we play.

We have all played games, cards or Monopoly, with people who just hated to lose, who will bend rules, cheat, make up new rules, do almost anything to win. Brother George Reilly at Georgetown was telling me of playing a game with his little nephew, who jumped George's counters before the game even started. "You should see him when he loses!" Brother Reilly laughed. Now our first reaction to such people is that there is something crooked about them. We have to teach little winners that they must play according to the rules, play fair. But my own suspicion in such cases is that there is probably something wrong with us. Without a passionate desire to play, and to play to win—"You must run", St. Paul said, "meaning to win!"—there is no game. Did you ever try to play basketball with a player who was just trying to "get some exercise?" The game, as a game, is ruined with such a participant who is only exercising. If you recall the scene in Paris in *Chariots of Fire* in which the British and American athletes for the 1924 Olympics were exercising, it will be clear that exercising is part of the playing, but it is not *the playing itself.* Even when exercise is a sport itself—the parallel bars in gymnastics offer such an example—it only becomes fascinating in competition, where someone can cheat, which is why the highest and lowest scores of the judges are discounted.

Now, it is this combination of arbitrary rules—Plato was right about constantly changing the rules—and the holding of us to them if we are to play that gives sport its seriousness, that gives sports writers something to write about. Howard Cosell was right to be fuming about the death of a Korean boxer in a match, yet Boom-Boom Mancini was not a killer. The game is serious. The sports writer writes about an action that fascinates us in its being played out. It demands exertion, attention, luck, rules, concern about cheating, wonder. When we see something great, a great relay race, even the skillful billiard shot in a beer ad, we first want to hush, then yell, then tell someone about it. This is the dignity of sports writers.

Furthermore, it is this very action of the game itself, how it goes, who plays, which, when it grips us, just for what it is, takes us out of ourselves. This is why Aristotle said that games were very near to the highest things because they too were for their own sakes. They were not merely for something else, which, incidentally, is the root of the real suspicion about *professional* sports: that the game is played for some motive other than the game itself, for the salary of the player. The same suspicion hovers over certain national teams at the Olympics. But the common instincts of the thousands at a Saturday afternoon at Tuscaloosa or the Los Angeles Colosseum are not misplaced. They see something worth seeing. And they do not know how the game will turn out. This is why we like to have it all unraveled on the sports page later on.

Thus, in our fascination at watching a game, in reading about one, we have at least one example of something that clearly need not exist, but which, when it does, fascinates us. Games are not necessary. They are *not for* something else, like exercise. Can we not wonder on this basis, then, whether perhaps the higher, more serious things, such as the players themselves, also need not have existed, but when they do, they consume our attention, because of the stakes, the risk? Since we can cheat and fail, we know that in the highest things we are serious, as Aristotle seemed to have implied.

Plato suggested in the last book of *The Republic* that violators of the rules of life will be punished, even though we ought not, as he taught the young men anxious to know, observe them merely because of fear, but, like the rules of the games, for their own sakes. The rules of tennis are worthwhile because they are what make it tennis and not squash, because we risk the drama of winning and losing, of cheating, of being real actors in real games that come to an end.

In one of Mel Lazarus' *Miss Peach* cartoons, Marcia and Ira were playing in the Kelly School Kindergarten Checker Championship. In the first frame, Ira says across the table to a supremely assured Marcia, "Are you ready?" She answers, "Yes, and may the better girl win." Marcia makes the first move. Ira immediately jumps four other checkers and yells triumphantly, "You have only one more checker left, and it is trapped, which means that on my next move, I win—and with the choice of jumping it with any of my five kings." To this, Marcia responds demurely but firmly, "That's all well and good, Ira, but if you do, I will smack the living daylights out of you." The next two frames have no words. In the first, Ira looks haltingly down at the checkerboard, while Marcia shuts her eyes calmly. In the second, we see some sweat and constraint on Ira's face. Marcia remains the same. Ira then shouts happily, "What do you know, a stalemate!"[1] Even in kindergarten checker championships, we find the drama of fear and cheating.

My theme here has been the seriousness of sports, how sports too are a way of learning about the highest things, how close sports writers themselves are to ultimate things when they describe checker championships, Kansas-Nebraska games, the World Heavyweight Boxing Championships, or Monopoly played by cheaters. Aristotle rightly said that life is more serious than games or sports, even though we participate in

[1] Mel Lazrus, *Miss Peach Again* (New York: Grosset and Dunlap, 1972).

both, life and sports, for the highest reasons, for their own sakes. The day after New Year's one year, the Reno morning paper described the scene at the clubs the day before during the Bowl games. It described the gathering at the Cal-Neva casino, with its three large television sets, as a large, quiet group of mostly men, mostly slouched down drinking beer or smoking, watching without too much emotion. Evidently, like Barclay Brisk, '24 Notre Dame, we do not yell "We wanna touchdown!" much at TV either.

As it so happened, I was one of those men sitting in the Cal-Neva sports lounge on New Year's morning that year, watching the three TV sets. Later, I went home with my brother to catch the Rose Bowl and Sugar Bowl. It is a rare New Year's that I miss watching all the major bowl games. Why? The Reno paper suggested it was partly because everyone there had a couple of bucks on the game, mostly on the loser, as it turned out. No doubt they did. And we should not forget that betting is a game too, one of the four major categories of games, along with context games, imitation games, and vertigo games, like the Big Dipper roller coaster in Santa Cruz. We even stand fascinated just watching before the crap table as we do before the Super Bowl for the same reason: because an event whose result we do not know is playing itself out before our very eyes, a game in which somebody could cheat, and therefore a human game that need not exist at all, like our own lives—need not, but does. This possibility of nonexistence is the essential wonder that the sports writer must catch, just as we must catch it in life itself.

The most famous philosophical passage dealing with sports is again found in Plato, in *The Laws,* the book Plato wrote as a very old man, a book in which Socrates did not appear. Notice how Plato related the seriousness of our lives to play; war and play are related, we should think and play about the noblest things. Here, the dance, in a way, as for C. S. Lewis and Johan Huzinga, becomes the very heart of sports.[2] The Athenian in *The Laws* began:

> I assert that what is serious should be treated seriously, and what is not serious should not, and that by nature god is worthy of a complete, blessed seriousness, but that what is human . . . has been devised as a certain plaything of god, and that this is really the best thing about it. Every man and woman should spend life in this way, playing the noblest possible games, and thinking about them. . . . (803c)

The most serious thing is not in fact war; rather, Plato continued, "Each person should spend the greatest and best part of his life in peace. . . . One should live out one's days playing at certain games—sacrificing, singing, and dancing" (803e). Plato went on to conclude that we would get at most "small portions of truth" from this, but this glimpse at something fascinating in itself is worth not only our efforts, but also worth our being, our existing, when we need not have been at all.

Let me conclude this attempt to make an intellectual case for the validity of sports and to reflect on them in our lives as also ways to the highest things by returning to my initial observation that the nearest most of us get to contemplation is when we watch a good game. Here, in a way, we near what is best in ourselves, for we are spectators not for any selfish reason, not for anything we might get out of the game, money or exercise or glory, but just because the game is there and we lose ourselves in its playing, either as players or spectators. This not only should remind us that we are not sufficient unto ourselves, but that what is higher than we are, what is ultimately serious,

[2] See C. S. Lewis, *Perelandra* (New York, Macmillan, 1965); Johan Huzinga, *Homo Ludens: A Study of the Play Element in Culture* (Boston: Beacon, 1950).

is itself fascinating and joyful. Watching games, I suspect, teaches us about what was once called *homo ludens,* the being that plays. The sports writer, then, insofar as he too is caught up in this fascination of games, of players, referees, and fans, helps us bridge the seriousness of life and the seriousness of sports by helping show us that we too, watchers all, know about things that exist for their own sakes.

Seven Books on Sports and Serious Reflection

1. Johan Huzinga, *Homo Ludens: A Study of the Play Elements in Culture.*
2. Hugo Rahner, *Man at Play.*
3. Josef Pieper, *In Tune with the World: A Theory of Festivity.*
4. Paul Weiss, *Sport: A Philosophic Inquiry.*
5. Walter Kerr, *The Decline of Pleasure.*
6. James V. Schall, *Far Too Easily Pleased: A Theology of Play, Contemplation, and Festivity.*
7. Roger Caillois, *Man, Play, and Games.*

Chapter Nineteen

On the Difficulty of
Believing and Not Believing

If knowledge or learning and even sports can be a source of our attention in the pursuit of *what is,* we ought not to neglect faith itself as a factor that calls our attention to reality. But everyone recognizes that believing and not believing are subjects not so widely or so reasonably discussed among us. And there is much confusion about what it is in which we ought to believe or have faith, as it is sometimes put. Many substitutes for God exist among us. Not a few even have "faith" in these substitutes. And these are things worth talking about, even though we do not speak of them so much. I think, for example, of Samuel Johnson's conversations on original sin, and Flannery O'Connor's words on the costs of religion.

"I talked to him of original sin", Boswell related of Johnson on June 3, 1781,

> in consequence of the fall of man, and of the atonement made by our Saviour. After some conversation . . . , he, at my request, dictated to me as follows: "With respect to original sin, the inquiry is not necessary; for whatever is the cause of human corruption, men are evidently and confessedly so corrupt, that all the laws of heaven and earth are insufficient to restrain them from crime. . . .
>
> "Nothing could more testify the opposition between the nature of God and moral evil, or more amply display his justice, to men and angels . . . than that it was necessary for the highest and purest nature, even for the Divinity itself, to pacify the demands of vengeance, by a painful death; of which the

natural effect will be, that when justice is appeased, there is a proper place for the exercise of mercy. . . . "[1]

And Flannery O'Connor added, "What people don't realize is how much religion costs. They think that faith is a big electric blanket, when of course it is the cross. It is much harder to believe than not to believe."[2]

The principal locus of world reform remains self-reform, even though we cannot be certain, in any ultimate sense, that the world will ever in fact be "re-formed". We live in a curious era that, through a long, tortuous process, has taught itself to believe rather that human "selves" are improved only as a consequence of structural world reform. Nothing can be done until everything is done. Aristotle had indeed observed that man needs a sufficiency of material goods with which to practice virtue and to be happy. But, as Herbert Deane remarked, elaborating on Augustine, "as history draws to a close, the number of true Christians in the world will decline rather than increase. His words give us no support to the hope that the world will gradually be brought to belief in Christ and that earthly society can be transformed, step by step, into the Kingdom of God."[3]

The modern thinker is rather apt to hold that a sufficiently distributed material well-being is productive of human happiness and virtue. Man is good. Legal, economic, and institutional arrangements "make" him bad or evil. The rush to minimize personal responsibility has left us with few "persons", but with a mass of institutions charged with taking "care" of us. Chesterton, meanwhile, said that, from the Christian sense of the Fall, the comfortable environment was the most dangerous one, the

[1] Boswell, *Life of Samuel Johnson,* vol. 2, pp. 423–24.
[2] O'Connor, *The Habit of Being,* p. 354.
[3] Herbert Deane, *Political and Social Ideas of St. Augustine* (New York: Columbia University Press, 1956), p. 38.

one most likely to foster vice; virtue is largely found among the poor and the common.

Behind all of this lies the troubling question of what is wrong with the world in the first place. There is, likewise, a moral passion behind much of this discussion of what has gone wrong with the world, one that, too often, justifies the hatred of God for making this particular world and ourselves in it, a hatred purportedly legitimized on the basis that the poor suffer and the innocent are persecuted in it. God is thus "hated" because a plan of creation and redemption was followed that does not conform to our own much-debated priorities and principles of "justice". The charge against God is not, then, primarily that he does not "exist", but that he is not "good". (See Chapter 10.) Since, clearly, there are things that "ought not" to exist, but which, in fact, do exist, belief in God is undermined because God "ought" not to have placed us in such a world as this one. That is, in other words, a God could not have created precisely *this* world because in it we are not automatically good.

Clearly, at least some of the things that are wrong with men also have their causative origins within men themselves—people do *act,* the point of Aristotle's *Ethics.* If we deny this, we must reject our own proper existence in a world where we are evidently and directly responsible for what ought not to exist. We can do this theoretically only by reducing ourselves to behavioral automata. We can take three attitudes toward this alternative: (1) We can attempt to define and live in what is called "evil" as if it were good, as if evil were the result of merely an arbitrary religious bias with no roots in ourselves or in the being of things. (2) We can blame someone else for our predicament: God or other human persons or societies or groups. Or (3) we can seek to elevate our own disorder to some higher order in which what is wrong is rendered somehow potentially salvific, without denying at the same time its dire realities and evils. Christianity has thought of this latter theme under the shadow of the Cross.

The question naturally arises, then, about this "human condition", as it is called from Balzac to Hannah Arendt, in which men appear to be less than perfect, very prone to evil in many ways, however much they might aspire to do better. Is this human condition, shot through as it is with sin and finiteness, sufficient cause for disbelief? And do Christianity's spiritual ways of handling it really meet the issue? The first point to note, of course, is that Christianity has its own ideas about what each actual man and woman who exists is about. These ideas mean that Christianity must be careful not to jeopardize what it teaches, while not disapproving values or ideas that it might share with other philosophies or religions. Perhaps the first point to be made clear is that, in Christianity, what abides is the human person, the being considered the most fragile in the universe by the Greeks. But states and other societies, however significant, do not, ultimately, perdure. The conclusion from this must be carefully stated: The permanent being of each person for whom resurrection is a proper destiny can achieve its chosen goal—in grace and freedom—wherever in particular a person lives and acts in the world, no matter in what place, in what time, in what regime.

This position does not, to be sure, deny that some times and some places are more privileged than others—"many prophets have desired to see what you have seen and heard", as it says in the Gospels. On the other hand, this understanding of personal being and destiny as not identical with what we propose to ourselves prevents us from a kind of this-worldly utopianism. This latter would conceive the sacrifices of individuals to be justified exclusively in terms of some subsequent betterment for others down the ages, not for themselves. Often, it is conceived for some mere abstraction. Even though Christianity exhorts sacrifice of self, it does *not* believe in the annihilation of self. He who loses his life will save it.

In this sense, then, Christianity might even be called "individualist". That is, the conception of ultimate reality includes each concrete person, even though the status of that same person, good or bad, partly depends upon his own powers and choices. This sense of risk means that the world in which we live can be important, ultimately important for each person, even if his economic and political institutions are in fact absolutely corrupt. When Nero was in power, St. Paul wrote that we should be obedient to the emperor. There is no reason at all to suppose that the people who perished under a Nero, a Robespierre, a Hitler, or a Pol Pot are not in Augustine's City of God, whatever be the fate of those who sent them there.

We are anxious to find reasons for disbelief because we are afraid to admit that the truth has already been given to us and we have not recognized it. The root criticism of John Paul II in this regard is directly related to this point. He does *not* think Christianity, properly understood, is *not* true, that it is just another possible "view" of things. He does not think Christianity's main task is to accommodate itself to what the world believes as true or as possible. He is quite aware that the truth of Christianity is not often allowed to be clearly presented, even by Christians for Christians. Christianity is tolerable for contemporary humanism only so long as it is merely another of the myriads of confusing explanations of our lot. But it is "intolerable" if it claims to be the "truth". Christianity does not deny that many truths exist outside of itself, but it does insist that ultimate truth is in it, that all truth is compatible with it, indeed, a part of it. All truth is one.

A considerable effort is made, however, to label any attempt to identify and claim religious truth as potential "fascism" or "fanaticism". Flannery O'Connor put it well:

> One of the tendernesses of our age is to use the suffering of children to discredit the goodness of God, and once you have discredited his goodness, you are done with him. . . . In this popular piety, we mark our gain in sensibility and our loss in vision. If other ages felt less, they saw more, even though they saw with . . . faith. In the absence of this faith now, we are governed by tenderness. It is a tenderness which, long since cut off from the person of Christ, is wrapped in theory. When tenderness is detached from the source of tenderness, its logical outcome is terror.[4]

The greatest crimes, Aristotle said in the second book of *The Politics,* are not committed to keep us warm. The greatest crimes invariably have origins located in the refusal of reality, in doctrine.

Lloyd Cohen, moreover, noted how it is that even the greatest crimes can be reduced to necessity and, therefore, can be evaporated of any human responsibility. In his essay "Traditional and Modern Views of Crime and Punishment", Cohen wrote that the modern idea that crime has no personal cause is a rejection of our power to act, to be persons.

> By behaviorism we mean a belief that man is an object, a mechanism; he behaves according to law; he does not act. Hence, he is not responsible for his actions. . . . A crucial distinction between the traditional and modern views is associated with the use of the words "act" and "behave". If an agent is held to be responsible, it is said to act; on the other hand, if its movements are caused by some outside force, then the agent is

[4] Flannery O'Connor, *Mystery and Manners* (New York: Farrar, Straus, and Giroux, 1968), pp. 226–27.

not responsible, it is simply behaving in accord with the laws of causality as they apply to the universe in which it operates. . . .

The reason for the popularity of behaviorism among the more intellectual segment of mankind is that while on the non-reflective level of consciousness with which one usually views the world, one "recognizes" that man is not an object but a subject, on the reflective level of consciousness one cannot "comprehend" this. The faculty of intellect operating through the category of reason seeks for a responsible causal agent acting through the individual human being. The search ends in reason and cannot be found in the spatial-temporal world. The intellectual then concludes that the "recognizing" of a subject is a mistake, an illusion he must reject.[5]

We do not know ourselves except in knowing something else, as Aquinas put it. The intellectual ends up not merely doubting his faults, but doubting his very self—this in the name of escaping from personal responsibility. The Kantian tradition of simply positing this responsibility without certain roots in being does not save the day. It is difficult to believe if there is no one left to believe in but only mechanical responses that pass through our system.

Sometimes, it is said that believing is easy, and that only the intelligent are wise enough to disbelieve. This is mostly nonsense, of course. Not only is belief a gift, but it is a gift of intelligence. However heretical this might sound, believers think "better" because they are given the right questions to ask. Mortimer Adler even went so far, in his *How to Think About God,* as to suggest that no one has yet proved the existence of God but Adler himself, and he only recently, since all other "proofs" were rooted in faith.[6] If Adler is correct, it is an argument for

[5] Lloyd Cohen, "Traditional and Modern Views of Crime and Punishment", *Intercollegiate Review,* fall 1978, pp. 33–34.

[6] Mortimer Adler, *How to Think about God: A Guide for the Twentieth-Century Pagan* (New York: Macmillian, 1980).

Aquinas' notion in his "Treatise on Law" (I–II, 90–105) that most men, even all but one, needed revelation to know the truth of life and action.

Aristotle, probably the profoundest thinker of our lot, doubted, moreover, that we could be friends with God. In the Gospel of John, we read, however, "I no longer call you servants, but friends." Aristotle's First Mover had no friends, even though he moved by love and knowledge. He was too distant for friends. Christianity holds that God is Trinity. Plato seemed to suggest that if ever we are to know the Good, the Good must first tell us what he or it is like. In Christianity, grace is a gift of the inner life of God. Believing is not easy. Disbelief is rooted, ultimately, in these unacceptable answers, in Trinity, in grace, in divine friendship, in the Cross. Disbelief remains a choice, not an intelligence, or perhaps better, a choice of one intelligence over against another. Disbelief is tenderness without anyone to be tender about. It is compassion for the sake of compassion. It is sincerity about a cause without attending to the nature of the cause.

The modern world has divorced the virtues from persons, only to turn them around and use them, as abstractions, against persons. Abortion and euthanasia appear as "kindnesses" and compassion. Forced labor is economic development. Salvation has become a political term, while "exploitation" covers a multitude of sins, sins usually of our own making for which we refuse to be responsible. Christianity in recent times has, to the normal onlooker, deemphasized its "hard" doctrines. In many a university sermon, in many a parochial or plain sermon, it is difficult to detect that Rousseau did not write the Epistle to the Galatians. As a result, it is increasingly difficult for the young or even the old to know how to explain themselves in Christian terms to themselves, since the Christian "ideas" by which they might have their actions explained to them have been obscured.

In his Nobel lecture "The Economics of Being Poor", Theodore Schultz suggested that the main cause of poverty does not lie in lack of land or resources, but in a failure to understand "human capital", in a failure, that is, to understand what humans are and how they act.[7] The scourge of poverty, as it is called, is largely caused today by political and ideological understandings of man. The ultimate resource is the human brain, but it will not work correctly if it does not have the right ideas about God and man, about earth and sky.

Karl Menninger also remarked:

> Some clergymen prefer pastoral counseling of individuals to the pulpit function. But the latter is a greater opportunity to both heal and prevent. . . . There is much prevention to be done for large numbers of people who hunger and thirst after direction toward righteousness. Clergymen have a golden opportunity to prevent some of the accumulated misapprehensions, guilt, aggressive action, and other roots of later mental suffering.
>
> How? Preach! Tell it like it is. Say it from the pulpit. Cry it from the housetops.
>
> What shall we say?
>
> Cry comfort, cry repentance, cry hope. Because recognition of our part in the world transgression is our only remaining hope.[8]

Again, disbelief is both the result of the choice not to preach what Christianity is *and* the result of preaching what it is. How can it be both? Because, as Flannery O'Connor said, to believe is difficult; disbelief is easy. Some do not believe because they do not hear, because, as St. Paul said, there is

---

[7] Theodore Schultz, "The Economics of Being Poor", *The Journal of Political Economy,* no. 4 (1980): 639–51.

[8] Karl Menninger, *Whatever Became of Sin?* (New York: Hawthorne, 1973), 228.

no one to preach to them. But others hear very well. They do not want the salvation they hear preached. We are not prepared to believe that Christianity can be right when so comparatively few believe in it. On the other hand, we cannot believe in it unless it is preached to us as it is. We indeed may reject Christianity when we do know what it is. But as John Paul II said at Catholic University in Washington (October 7, 1979), Catholic intellectuals (or any other kind, for that matter) have no right to confuse us about what Christianity really teaches.

Yet when we reject Christianity, we must always do so for a lesser vision of the world. There is a sadness in denying resurrection, vision, the City of God, Trinity, the sadness that is aware that these are the most perfect answers to the deepest existential longings of our kind. The noble ideals of justice, tenderness, peace, sincerity are, detached from the Incarnation, indeed lethal, somehow productive of terror, as Flannery O'Connor remarked. The human condition is both our glory and our burden, the glory of what is not God, the burden of ourselves. Religion indeed "costs much", and we do not know it, do not want to pay the price.

And yet, as Samuel Johnson reminded us, it seems clear that our condition could not have been rectified except by a "painful death", from which we can learn mercy and leave aside the vengeance of justice. The difficulty in believing arises from the opposition of "God and moral evil", from the fact of the Cross, the cost that makes no sense except in terms of the mercy that flows from it, the mercy that enables us to be no longer servants but friends, friends of God, and thus friends with one another, without limit.

Sixteen Books on Belief and Disbelief

1. Henri de Lubac, *The Discovery of God.*
2. Jean-Marie Cardinal Lustiger, *Dare to Believe.*
3. George Huntston Williams, *The Mind of John Paul II: Origins of His Thought and Action.*
4. Jean Galot, *Theology of the Priesthood.*
5. Arnold Lunn, *Now I See.*
7. Eric Mascall, *Grace and Glory.*
8. Josef Pieper, *Problems of Modern Faith.*
9. Henri de Lubac, *The Christian Faith.*
10. Ronald Knox, *The Belief of Catholics.*
11. Kenneth Baker, *The Fundamentals of Catholicism.*
12. Ronald Lawler, *The Teachings of Christ.*
13. *The Church's Confession of Faith.*
14. Jean Galot, *Who Is Christ? A Theology of the Incarnation.*
15. Ignace Lepp, *Atheism in Our Time.*
16. C. S. Lewis, *The World's Last Night and Other Essays.*

Chapter Twenty

The Humanities and the "Basis of Excellence"

"[Samuel] Johnson's guiding perception", Walter Jackson Bate wrote, "is that 'the basis of excellence is truth'—the truth about what is, and the truth about the way we react".[1] The paradox of our era seems to be the reappearance of a thirst for universal excellence, but within a political system that sees all particular excellence as bias or injustice and an intellectual system that lacks any criterion for distinguishing truth in things human. "College professors share a skepticism about art and knowledge, the intellect and culture", Peter Shaw wrote in *Harper's*,

> not only with revisionist critics but with anti-intellectuals outside academe as well. In the end, nothing makes any sense; everything is relative, anyway; one man's opinion is as good as another's; moral distinctions are useless. They all reduce to power and desire—to my own opinion, the way I feel, what seems right to me.[2]

So it is with a certain ideological wariness that we approach the topic of excellence, particularly in the humanities. This, in turn, indicates that the very existence of what is not "the best" has come to imply that the condition of everyone less than "the best" is caused by so-called exploitation or injustice in society or even unfairness in the Divinity. No distinction or diversity in things can exist for which someone else, not ourselves, is not

[1] Walter Jackson Bate, *The Achievement of Samuel Johnson* (New York: Oxford, 1954), p. 200.
[2] Peter Shaw, "Degenerate Criticism", *Harper's* 259 (Oct. 1979): 93.

culpable. Thus, no radical distinction in things that arises from nature itself can be permitted outside human agency.

Someone gave me a postcard showing a dejected youth, arms on his knees, with the caption, "I was educated once, and it took me years to get over it." If we ask ourselves just why this remark is amusing, it is because behind it lies the suspicion that the real things that matter about life and reality do not come up in formal education, or, if they do, the educated answers do not correspond with lived experience, with other sources of wisdom. There can even be a conflict, then, between education and truth.

On August 7, 1921, C. S. Lewis wrote to his brother about staying in the King Arthur Hotel in Cornwall. With nothing else to do there, he roamed into the lounge, where he found quite a few uniformly bound books including a Persian epic poem and Aristotle's *Ethics*. This uniformity of binding somewhat perplexed Lewis until he realized that the books were part of a series of *The Hundred Best Books*. Lewis went on: "How I abominate such culture for the many, such tastes, ready-made, such standardization of the brain. To substitute for the infinite wanderings of the true reader through the bye-ways of the country he discovers, a carabanc tour. This whole place infuriates me."[3] Some unexpected touch of civilization, I think, hides in these annoyed remarks.

"The infinite wanderings of the true reader", as Lewis memorably put it, suggests that there ought to be a kind of cultural freedom that becomes the atmosphere in which we live, something that prevents the immediate and the urgent from so pressing on us that we have no leisure or time for reflection to discover what we did not suspect existed, no liberty to come upon the *what is* of Samuel Johnson and react to it because *it is.*

[3] C. S. Lewis, *The Letters of C. S. Lewis* (New York: Harper and Row, 1966), p. 70.

Lewis, I suppose, did not mean to suggest that we ought not to read the *Ethics* of Aristotle if some hapless professor assigns it to us, even if the professor himself does not believe a word of it, or if we happen to come upon it for the first time in some small hotel in Cornwall or even in a used bookstore in San Francisco. Rather, he meant that the wonder and attraction of what exists should not be conceived as a sort of duty that we must perform in lockstep, so that in fact we confront *what is* only in that sort of educational environment that takes us years to get over.

Idleness or indolence needs its defenders, no doubt, if we are to be *civilized,* a word whose very origins imply that the higher things are not directly political. Truth ought to be loved for its own sake, as the classical tradition held. A *Peanuts* series I once saw concerned Marcie, the proper intellectual, who always says "Sir". Marcie was taking Peppermint Patty, a sort of loveable but definitely flaky kid, to her first symphony. Marcie proceeded to inform Peppermint Patty that one does not snap one's fingers at the rhythm of the music. When asked, "Why not?" Marcie answered, "It's just not done"; to which Peppermint Patty sighed, "Weird!" Suddenly, however, the mood shifted. We observe Peppermint Patty sitting entranced, sort of confused: "That is the most beautiful music I have ever heard", she muttered to herself. Shyly, she reflected, "And all the time I thought classical music was boring. I owe Marcie an apology...." When she turned to Marcie, the intellectual, Marcie was sound asleep.[4] So that is, I suppose, the sum of it. We can sleep through the most beautiful music others have ever heard, while such music need not exist at all, or, since it does, we may either sleep through it or never encounter it in a condition where we need do anything else but listen to it simply because it is beautiful.

[4] *Peanuts,* United Features, Mar. 1, 1984.

How public policy relates to what we traditionally called "arts and letters", or sometimes simply "the humanities", is a subject of current interest and, indeed, controversy. The reason for this interest directly relates to the classical question of the status of truth in relation to the polity. At the same time, there seems to be a heightened sense of a loss of public standards, together with an almost irresistible drive to politicize all matter pertaining to the human condition—to the extent, almost, of allowing nothing else. The notion that truth and polity can come into conflict, of course, is both obvious and in need of explanation. The classical political philosophers, in fact, distinguished good or constitutional regimes from bad, that is, unconstitutional or illegal, regimes. Moreover, within the good and bad forms of regime there were degrees of excellence or degradation that could be accounted for, and the understanding of which constituted the test of practical prudence and feasibility in politics.

Speculative and practical truths, each with differing subject matters, were distinguished, then, into things that could not be otherwise and things that could be otherwise. Human actions in the particular were the primary examples of those things that could be otherwise, into which category politics especially fell. Indeed, the whole practical order, in which familial, economic, and political life occurred, was itself a good, but not the highest good, to which a person ought to devote himself as much as possible, as Aristotle said. The practical and the political, by being themselves, were ordered to *what is.* The free reaction to reality was, in essence, what constituted personal integrity and virtue when the human being accepted its order.

Political truth, to some degree, then, depended on speculative truth. The ends of the person were not objects of political change or choice. Aristotle expressed this by saying that politics does not make man to be man, but, taking him from nature, guides him to be good man. The very discipline of politics, to be complete, had to include descriptions of bad and less-perfect regimes, drawn from actual histories. Knowing evil in politics was not the same as doing evil, and the lesser evil in politics was often a reality of political choice even for the virtuous politician.

Two of the most attractive characters in philosophical literature, as I have mentioned earlier, are the young men Adeimantos and Glaucon (actually the names of Plato's own brothers) in *The Republic*. During the first book of *The Republic*, they impatiently listened to Socrates' debates with Polymarchus and especially Thrasymachus about the status of the worst regime, about ordinary concepts of justice, which began the argument. Finally, in book 2, Adeimantos and Glaucon have a chance to get Socrates a bit to the side to tell him quietly that they were not satisfied with the argument so far, because they wanted to hear justice praised for its own sake, not on account of some reward or punishment, what we "get" or do not "get" when we act virtuously or viciously. Then they proceeded to give the most profound arguments for *in*justice, even more fundamental than those of Thrasymachus in book 1. Yet, unlike Thrasymachus, they did not argue thus because they believed their own logic. Rather, they did not know what was wrong with their argument and wanted to hear the philosopher, Socrates, demonstrate its flaws to them. In other words, they loved the good without yet knowing it.

Socrates listened to these two young men with great admiration and even astonishment because they could state the case for injustice so well and yet suspect that it was not right. From this point, *The Republic* proceeded to that necessary, tightly reasoned argument all of us must go through in our hearts and minds if we would be truly educated, if we would learn what justice is, and, in learning this, learn more especially its limits, why it is of itself dangerous and inadequate. By the time we finish *The Republic* and can talk again of rewards and punishments to Adeimantos and Glaucon in book 10, because we have by then heard about justice and virtue for their own sake, we suspect that, like the rich young man in the Gospel, many will "go away sad" when they hear what is expected of them if they are truly to love justice: the giving up of family and property and all their own will in the interest of the polity, in which all order is seen in the good. The degree of the young men's "going away" from the best itself describes the various fates of the young men who choose regimes other than the best.

Several times in *The Republic,* the question arises about the location of this city-writ-large in which justice was to exist. Socrates would say only, cagily, that he was doubtful whether it could exist on earth or in reality. All that he did know about it was that, for it to exist at all anywhere, it had to exist in the mind according to the argument he had carefully presented. Without the active reproduction of this city in each person's mind, no education would be complete—or probably even be possible. This conclusion implied, further, as Socrates said in *The Apology,* that a philosopher ought to remain a private citizen, because in any *existing* state, even in the best, like Athens, a Socrates would always be killed.

This is why there was no sense for Socrates, in choosing his own punishment, to select anything other than free meals at the town hall. There was no point in selecting banishment to Thebes or Sparta because, if he were true to his vocation as a philosopher, the same things would happen to him as in Athens. Any public polity in any existing state, as represented and urged in *The Apology* by the poet, the craftsman, and the lawyer, with the majority of free voters concurring, would choose against truth whenever it came into conflict with the given political order. This conflict would corrupt youth, sons of the poet, craftsman, and lawyers. This recurring corruption meant nothing less than that no existing state could allow the philosopher to speak his truth if the said state wanted its given order to continue — except perhaps in two instances: namely, the democracy, wherein all truths are equally spoken and the philosopher can survive longer because no one can tell the difference between truth and error, and in the state being formed in speech in *The Republic*.

The conflict between truth and polity is perennial. To the relation of philosophy and politics, religion has added a further element: perhaps of strife, as Marsilius of Padua suggested, perhaps of completion and harmony, as Aquinas thought. This addition was, in Christianity, at least, the notion that some things did not belong to Caesar, which was likewise to say, perhaps more astonishingly from a religious point of view, that some things *did* belong to Caesar. Both Socrates and Christ, to recall again, were killed by the best states of their times, which leads us to suspect that truth may in fact be more insecure in democracies than even in tyrannies, where it is frankly recognized as dangerous. Solzhenitsyn would, I think, affirm that this latter position seems so, since those living in actual tyrannies know its untruth and are therefore spiritually freed of it, however little they might be able to act in a truly political fashion. Those citizens living in democracies, however, are actually tempted by the untruth of the worst regime and the argument for it when skillfully presented. Thus, democratic men appear willing to entertain the thought that the worst regime may be the best, to recall a theme from the first book of *The Republic*.

All this, furthermore, hinted at one of the great illusions in political philosophy, the one that holds that actual tyrannies will be easily recognized by a free people. The classics rather held that the recognition of tyranny itself required both freedom and virtue. This position is no doubt why the classics also argued that the normal preparation for tyranny was a democracy, in which all ideas indiscriminately were present and argued, with no criterion of resolution in *what is*. The immediate preparation for tyranny was a system that defined itself by the theoretic incapacity of mind to know any certain truth, so that tolerance was not just a political principle, but a metaphysical proposition. The same young men who, when virtuous, come to listen to Socrates, when dissolute, listen to the opposite of the philosopher-king, that is, to the one who has all the talents of the philosopher-king and none of his virtues, such as perhaps the Alcibiades described by Thucydides. Those who conform to the tyrannical order, however noble its constituted language, will be simply marginalized, like Socrates, as a private citizen or, better, "lopped off", as Aristotle observed of their most likely fate.

The classics generally thought that domestic (national) politics was the only area where freedom might exist as well as virtue. Necessity ruled international affairs, so, in certain circumstances, as Thucydides also remarked of Melos, human nature would necessarily and always act in exactly the same fashion: in ways thought immoral in domestic politics or by any absolute standards. The boundaries of the polity constituted, then, the existing limits of politics, of the morality of this or that political discourse or freedom. Yet the universal tradition, the contemplative order, persisted. Were not certain questions to be asked, to be opened, in every society? Ought not the gospel be likewise preached everywhere, even if politics would not allow it? Was there not a corpus of classic works that ought to be preserved in any polity, even, if necessary, underground or in secret writing, and was it not in the interest of a polity to foster such a tradition as part of its public order? Were the particularities of place, time, speech, habits, and culture, after all, such that the divergent polities simply saw things so differently that one polity was, by nature, a threat to the other, whatever the status of truth, which must, then, metaphysically be wholly relative?

In 1654, the sturdy Puritan Captain Edward Johnson wrote a book with the remarkable title *Wonder-Working Providence in Zion's Saviour in New England.* In this book, Johnson recounted something of the reasons for founding a certain Harvard College in the New World. He saw in this educational founding an act of Providence because "the foundations of learning" in England at that time were stopped up by politics. This should have meant, he thought, that these foundations would be preserved in the churches, but these alternative ecclesiastical streams were filled with "the stinking charnel of prelatial pride", so that the Lord turned aside from them. Satan, in fact, used this very situation to make people think that even learning itself was at fault and so to be shunned. Yet learning was in reality "the chief means for the conversion of [the Lord's] people and building them up in the holy faith". This early American description of the relation of faith, learning, and polity, with its effort to retain the tradition of reason and revelation in close cooperation with each other, still contained elements of the classical and Christian reflections on the various organs responsible in different ways for truth: polity, university, and church.[5]

In two notable addresses, "The Shattered Humanities" (November 20, 1982) and "The Public Life of the Humanities" (January 24, 1983), William Bennett, then chairman of the National Endowment for the Humanities, addressed himself to

[5] W. Trent and B. Well, eds., *Colonial Literature* (New York: Crowell, 1903), pp. 15–16.

the state of the classical tradition, to the question of the responsibility of the polity to arts and letters. Bennett argued that the humanities are disappearing from our view, both in polity and in academia (and probably also in the churches), but that the best way to save or revive them is not by direct governmental aid. Bennett found the reason for this decline of the humanities in the lack of the classical priorities, of the relation of contemplation to action, so that the humanities now appear in the public order as a series of irrelevant and discordant opinions, with no pertinence to anything at all significant or no principle of discrimination about what is important.

Bennett thus remarked:

> We can see the symptoms of the fragmentation of the humanities everywhere. Almost all requirements are gone. . . . We see the proliferation of unrelated, mediocre, and uninspired offerings "in the humanities", where any course is defended on the grounds that it might be "interesting", never on the grounds that what it will offer is true, or good, or noble.[6]

Bennett argued that the incorrect solution to this situation was that "the humanities can be applied on a case-by-case basis to resolve controversies and improve social conditions". Although this presupposition might create jobs under state auspices, it would, in fact, eventually corrupt both politics and the humanities.

William Bennett's view of the place of the classics and the

[6] William J. Bennett, "The Shattered Humanities", address to the 72nd Annual Convention of the National Council of Teachers of English, Washington, D.C., Nov. 20, 1982, p. 7. See also "The Public Life of the Humanities", address to the Annual Conference of the Conference of Academic Deans, Washington, D.C., Jan. 14, 1983; *To Reclaim a Legacy: A Report on the Humanities in Higher Education* (Washington: National Endowment for the Humanities, 1984).

humanities—their being not directly pertinent to ongoing solutions of domestic and international problems, however valuable for their own sakes—was criticized by Helene Moglen,
who argued rather that many "scholars and teachers of literary
studies . . . believe that neither texts nor students can be removed
from their social and historical contexts. . . . They regard all
criticism and teaching as political. . . . "[7] Behind this position
is the effort to legitimize the notion of ongoing or continual
learning—in schools, in the media, particularly the public
media, and in the universities—as a function of what is termed
community. This project would be supported by the public, for
public purposes, seeking to derive its norms and values not
from the traditions or religion or classics or even truth, but
from the "now" of local consensus and desire. Both of these
latter notions, locality and increased wisdom, can of course be de-
fended in the Aristotelian tradition, but the Aristotelian defense
itself presupposes the validity of the contemplative order.

Note carefully the philosophical presuppositions of this
so-called social approach. It presumes a "humanistic vision"
and a "communitarian spirit", which are said to counteract the
"dangers of alienation and isolation, of aggressive expansion
and the threat of world destruction; of racism, sexism, and
ageism; of inequity disguised as equal opportunity and individualism".[8] To the practiced ear, of course, these are clearly
utopian and apocalyptic claims. We are again, it seems, about
to build, in fact, not in speech, but on our own very turf, the
perfect "community", where we are "purged of the language
and spirit of competition", where we can substitute "the ideal
of community for the realities of individualism". Thus, the

---

[7] Helene Moglen, "Erosion in the Humanities: Blowing the Dust from
Our Eyes", *Profession* 83, Bulletin of the Modern Language Association, p. 3.
[8] Ibid., p. 6.

humanities are to become a network of public schoolings, "a learning society through institutions that would initiate, coordinate, nurture, and sustain cooperative activities that would be educational in the best and most comprehensive sense".[9]

The "good" words, it turns out, then, are clearly those like *cooperation, nurturing,* and *sustaining.* The "bad" words are *strife, competition, struggle, individual,* and *self-interest.* There is a conscious effort to substitute the community for the individual person, mildness for strife, with little sense of why strife or competition might be either useful or necessary in the whole of human experience. There is little attention to the alarming philosophical shift of attention from the individual as the center of action and choice to the community or collectivity as some sort of greater entity.

Thus, the philosophic root of this extraordinary view, which seeks to replace the classical idea of excellence and truth in the humanities, is worth much attention. In it, our teaching should be based on the views that

> all systems of belief derive from personal and cultural bias and . . . all systems of knowledge employ traditional assumptions that yield legitimizing theories and establish self-justifying structures. As interpreters, humanities come to value heterogeneity and prize ambiguity. Their disciplines prepare them to find richness in diversity and truth in contradiction.[10]

What seems particularly striking about this easily traced ideology is its bland assumption that all this enthusiasm is in the interest of the community, that it itself needs little critical examination. The traditional function of philosophy and letters, however, was to teach us how not to be immersed in the "now" of politics. "Truth" in this newer context lies in

[9] Ibid., p. 5.
[10] Ibid.

"contradiction", not in the argument that uses the valuable "principle of contradiction" to arrive at what is true. On the basis of local, cultural, and ideological premises, we are to erect deliberately what is, in effect, an unacknowledged ideological community using public policy, public institutions, and public power as its instruments.

What will happen to a society that accepts such ideas whose noble ends are not borne out by reality, by practice, by *what is?* Francis Canavan put the matter quite well:

> We may wish for a world free of crime, war, poverty, ignorance, disease, and death. To reduce these evils is a goal worth working for, but to expect their elimination is to hope for a return to the Garden of Eden. It should not escape our notice that the most massive tyrannies of our century have been established by men who intended to create an earthly paradise.
>
> Even without a crystal ball, one may venture certain predictions. We are not going to have a world peopled by altruists who are concerned as much or more with the welfare of others as with their own. A social, economic, and political order built upon the free and uncoerced cooperation of all citizens will not come into being, and no amount of change of social structures will bring it into being. Private property, however regulated for the common good, will continue to be necessary. So will police forces, courts, and jails.[11]

We have, I am beginning to suspect, become a people, many of whom are so impatient with this reality of the less-than-perfect polity, the context of all actual states, that we are unwilling or unable to live in the world *that is.*

The purpose of the humanities, in one sense, is to understand why this imperfect reality exists, so we will not be overly

[11] Francis Canavan, *The Catholic Eye,* Mar. 9, 1984, p. 2.

tempted to bring about in this world what is presented as a higher order. This utopian position, ultimately, requires a rejection of all theology or philosophy directed to this actual world and makes philosophy and religion—and the humanities in general—instruments for escape to a world of perfect peace and love, the Gnostic effort of the person to establish by himself *what is*. This perfectionism requires the rejection of all the institutions and realities of this world—principally, as Plato already saw, those of family, property, and the limited state. This position leads in turn to a radical disassociation from the world as it is. The only and constant result of this experience has been, since the French Revolution at least, the erecting of a greater and greater tyranny, but more and more one that we can no longer habitually recognize as such, since ideological constructs have replaced at the community level our visions of the often messy reality that constitutes itself outside our exalted hopes.

Let me conclude by going back to Adeimantos and Glaucon, the two young men Socrates praised because they understood the arguments for the worst regime so perfectly, yet were somehow unmoved by them. They wanted to hear justice praised for its own sake, during the course of which argument Socrates suggested that justice, the terrible virtue, cannot be understood except in the good, that is, in something that is more than justice, in something that can see the requirements of actual particularities in their manifold complexities. Augustine understood his Plato well at this point. Later, Thomas Aquinas put the problem quite simply when he observed in the prologue to the *Secunda Secundae* of the *Summa Theologiae: Sermones enim morales universales sunt minus utiles, eo quod actiones in particularibus sunt* ("Universal moral speech is less useful since actions are in the particular").

It was precisely this difficulty or context that this same Aquinas had earlier noted to be the second major reason why a revelation was "necessary" beyond reason, *propter incertitudinem humani judicii, praecipue de rebus contingentibus et particularibus* (I–II, 91, 4) ("Because of the uncertainty of human judgment, especially in particular and contingent things"). Thus, diverse human laws proceed from radically differing human judgments. This suggested a sort of abiding incompleteness in all human politics and ought to raise the question of the incompleteness of politics in any humanistic study.

Does this imply any public need for the humanities, then? Does it mean that the humanities can be indifferent to questions of polity, to questions of excellence and truth, so that just any study of what humans "do" or "want", the Machiavellian project, can be erected into a principle of action for the community, however divided or defined? It seems, rather, that the public good is most in danger when the voluntary visits to contemplation are neglected in favor of immediate communitarian action. Activists along these latter lines often seem to see no limits to politics or to this life. We almost need a version of something like the Peace Corps, which would propose, instead of projects in, say, Uganda or Peru or Nicaragua, rather a visit to one of those camps of *Darkness at Noon*. Or, much more often, we need visits to one of those monuments of the mind leading to truth and the good, so that the desires or the choices of the community will not lead merely to itself but will be enriched by that which belongs to the wealth of the great contemplative tradition of what is excellent and true, while seeing what human beings in fact do.

In the *Gorgias* of Plato, Callicles was finally reluctant to answer any more of Socrates' sharp questions. Socrates had to carry on the dialogue as a monologue:

Yet, if this is what we must do, I think all of us should vie with one another in the struggle to learn what is true in the matters under discussion, and what is false; for it is to be the common good of everyone of us that this should be made clear. So, then, I shall continue the discussion as seems best to me; but if anyone of you thinks that any statement of mine is contrary to the truth, he should take issue with me and refute it. For it is by no means from any real knowledge that I make my statements: it is rather a search in common with you, so that if my opponent's objection has any force, I shall be the first to admit it. This, however, is merely stated on the supposition that you wish to complete the argument; if not, let's say good-bye and go home.[12]

I suppose we can say with Plato, in the end, that we ought not pack up and go home to avoid seeing where arguments lead, no matter how benign or communitarian they might sound.

Finally, we can also repeat with Samuel Johnson that "the basis of excellence is truth", the truth of *what is,* and the truth of our proper reaction to it, in which we are delighted to discover that beautiful and true beings existed outside our making them so, or even outside our knowing that we might come across at least something of the truth of the excellence and beauty of what has been given to us. Civilization depends on our having at least some of our fellows who deny that truth and good are merely subjective interpretations of a system, or that what is right is merely what seems right to us. "The infinite wanderings of the true reader", who can still make contact with what has been handed on, with *what is,* remain our final defense against a view of the humanities that would reduce them simply to what we want or to mere metaphysical ambiguity.

Similar to Plato in the *Phaedrus,* then, we do want to be able to say that "yes, we were educated once and it is indeed taking

12 Plato, *Gorgias* (Indianapolis, Ind.: Library of the Liberal Arts, 1952), pp. 80–81.

our whole life to get over it, to cease being astonished at *what is.*" The "infinite wanderings of the mind" converge with "the most beautiful things we have ever heard". This is what the humanities, arts and letters, are about at their best, at that point where, to cite Johnson one last time, the basis of excellence becomes truth itself and we react to it in gratitude because *it is.*

Ten Books on the Humanities

1. Christopher Derrick, *Escape from Skepticism: Liberal Education as If the Truth Really Mattered.*
2. William Bennett, *To Reclaim a Legacy: A Report on the Humanities in Higher Education.*
3. Walter Jackson Bate, *The Achievement of Samuel Johnson.*
4. Christopher Dawson, *The Crisis of Western Education.*
5. John Senior, *The Restoration of Christian Culture.*
6. Russell Kirk, *Decadence and Renewal in the Higher Learning.*
7. Jacques Maritain, *The Education of Man: The Educational Philosophy of Jacques Maritain.*
8. T. S. Eliot, *Christianity and Culture.*
9. Allan Bloom, *The Closing of the American Mind.*
10. John Henry Newman, *The Idea of a University.*

Chapter Twenty-one

On Spiritual and Intellectual Life

According to the Greek philosophers, man's highest activity was contemplative, his search for knowledge of *what is,* of what cannot be otherwise, of what is not subject to our own power or will. This position was not to deny that practical activity and artistic productivity were not also proper to the kind of a being man possessed. The practical activities were, in fact, most proper, so much so that they seemed much closer and even more important to mankind. The great accusation made against the contemplative life has been, indeed, the one that charged it with deflecting man from his own "proper" good, his ethical or political good. This was already an objection that Aristotle mentioned at the end of his *Ethics,*

Nevertheless, man's very intellectual powers shaped in some sense his physical being. The activities of these powers are that for which all else, including man's physical capacities, were ordered. Knowing for its own sake what existed in its causes was that which caused the philosopher to set aside all else to seek what was the whole, what was the more important. Aristotle was right to maintain that our knowledge began in "wonder", not in need or pleasure. Even when cities killed philosophers such as Socrates, the philosophers had to remain true to their vocation.

Yet the intellectual life was strikingly subject to the vice Christians came to call pride. So charming, so compelling was the intellectual vocation that the philosopher was tempted to attribute to himself alone what he concluded in his reflections. The idea of "receptivity" for the highest things disturbed the philosopher. He was impatient with the notion that for all his admittedly valid knowledge of many things, he still had to "await" or "expect" what he did not know of *what is*. This requirement seemed to undermine the competency of philosophy itself. So much was this feeling of alienation predominant that the main line of modern philosophy from Descartes and Hobbes, through Kant, to Marx and Nietzsche has been a valiant, beguiling effort to remove explicitly any sign of receptivity from the "truth"-forming aspect of the human intellect. By narrowing his sights to what he himself made, the philosopher eliminated from his ken the *what is* of what he did not make or think or even dream.

Needless to say, the revelational tradition, which also claimed the truth that would set us free, did not limit openness toward the highest things to the philosophers. But, as Aquinas saw, most people, most of the time, would not have the leisure, the interests, or the capacities to acquire that limited knowledge of the highest things available in this life (I–II, 91, 4). In this sense, as Chesterton remarked, revelation was the most curiously "democratic" act in the history of mankind, since it made *what is* available to all in faith.[1] Nothing has served to chide the pride of the philosopher more than this idea that the humble have been exalted to openness to the highest things. This revelation to all is why ultimately the philosopher, the saint, and the common man all converge on the same truths.

Yet revelation, it is to be noted, like being itself, is not the result of or subject to the choice of the human will or the power of the human intellect, except its power to accept or reject it. The "receptivity" characteristic of philosophy is also characteristic of revelation. In fact, this similarity begins to make us wonder if the two are not somehow related. Both

[1] G. K. Chesterton, *St. Thomas Aquinas*, in *Collected Works of G. K. Chesterton*, vol. 2 (San Francisco: Ignatius Press, 1986), pp. 421–43.

revelation and philosophy are free only insofar as they are open to *what is*. The character of the highest things is determined outside our human capacities. Nevertheless, the philosopher does have a proper mind that does enable him, and ought to enable him, to reject, firmly and legitimately, what is false and contradictory, even in presumed revelation. The "receptivity" of being and revelation was not designed to destroy the proper functioning of other human powers, but rather to exalt them.

Nonetheless, the philosopher, who is a necessary figure in human society as such, by his own methods confronts, if he is alert and honest, a number of paradoxes that he cannot seem to resolve by himself. These paradoxes or ironies have to do with death, with friendship, with the primacy of person over society, with the final location of the Republic or the City of God. This relationship is why it is vitally important for the revelational tradition to insist upon genuine philosophy for those of its believers who pursue the intellectual life, why, as Leo Strauss noted, Christianity insisted that in even its seminaries, philosophy be taught to the clerics.[2] Revelation will be known as potentially "credible" only if at least some of our kind, the philosophers and the gentlemen, keep running into questions that seem insolvable in reason. What is characteristic of philosophy itself is both the little truth it does know together with the ease with which it gets lost in the myriad dead-end questions whose futility requires a whole lifetime to recognize. This futility too is worth knowing. But the health of the city even depends on the philosophers not venturing too far away from *what is*.

On August 22, 1957, Flannery O'Connor wrote a letter

---

[2] Leo Strauss, *Persecution and the Art of Writing* (Westport, Conn.: Greenwood Press, 1952), p. 19.

about her cousin's husband, a man who taught at Auburn University. The professor finally had come into the Church. Flannery O'Connor explained his conversion as follows: "We asked how he got interested and his answer was that the sermons were so horrible (when he had gone to Mass with his wife), he knew there must be something else there to make people come."[3] The mystery of conversion remains not merely a question of successful rhetoric.

The relation of intelligence and faith is, as I have suggested, a perplexing one. The philosopher seeks to know the whole by what powers he has been given in his being, which he does not himself cause to be. Yet the philosopher is not the whole, however much his intellect is open to all being, to *what is.* Already in St. Paul, we are familiar with the conflicts of the folly of wisdom and the unsettling challenges of faith. St. Paul did not hesitate to accuse the philosophers of irresponsibility and even moral fault if they did not see that God exists. And, to compound matters, the theologian who seeks to "know" with his own mind finds that most often the holy are the simple, not the philosophers. Sanctity and prestige of intellect are rarely coterminus, though, again, sometimes they are, as in the case of Aquinas himself.

Writing to the British poet laureate, John Betjeman, on January 4, 1947, Evelyn Waugh, a bit annoyed, emphasized:

> Intellectual doubt is the least of all the causes of infidelity. Pride, sloth, and cowardice all contribute more. I have not myself met the Catholics you speak of who are subject to assaults of doubt. I am sure they exist because there are Catholics of every kind. There is certainly a stage in the mystical life (of which I know nothing) when many saints have had to wrestle with doubt for years. But your doubts seem to me

---

[3] O'Connor, *The Habit of Being,* p. 347.

much more *terre à terre.* They are the eruptions of a thoroughly
bad intellectual constitution.[4]

Whatever the validity of Waugh's sharp judgment of Betjeman,
there can be little doubt that spiritual life and intellectual life
have some basic connection, even though, probably, doubt, as
Waugh often intimated, arises for reasons other than intellectual ones. The "something more than the intellectual" of our
average parochial or plain sermon surely does not arise solely
from the human talents of the clergy.

No doubt too, as the philosopher Eric Voegelin noted, one
of the most curious phenomena of cultures based on Christianity
is the ease with which especially intellectuals fall into ideology.
We live in such an era, no doubt, in which the number of dons
and clerics who subscribe to the leading ideologies of our time
is very large, so large, in fact, that it requires, as Voegelin
understood, some explanation.[5] This explanation can only
be found in the faith itself, which, indeed, seeks intelligence,
but which gives so much more because it is rooted in God's
intelligence, not in our own. The effort to substitute an "activist"
ideology for the faith, which we did not make, is, of course,
rooted in the very project of modern intelligence as an autonomous reality, which systematically accepts nothing it did not
cause to be or make.

In a remarkable essay, "Ideology and Aquinas", Joseph Owens
wrote that "ideology has regularly considered the bearing on
practical activity to be essential to it. Thought is meant for
action. With Aquinas, in direct contrast, action in its entirety is
meant for intellectual contemplation."[6] And, of course, the

[4] Evelyn Waugh, *The Letters of Evelyn Waugh* (New York: Penguin,
1982), p. 244.

[5] Eric Voegelin, *Science, Politics, and Gnosticism* (Chicago: Regnery-
Gateway, 1964), pp. 83–114.

[6] Joseph Owens, "Ideology and Aquinas", in *Thomistic Papers I,* ed.
Victor B. Brezik (Houston, Tex.: Center for Thomistic Studies, 1984), p. 142.

whole spiritual side of social and political life will be radically different, if it is thought to be something, ideally, imposed on man from a pure form from inside himself rather than learned in freedom, friendship, and contemplation about what man is, with the knowledge that man did not cause himself.

The radicalization of Christian spiritual life into ideological politics and activism is absolutely to be expected, once we understand that, previously, this spiritual life has been reduced to purely artistic intellectual categories, misapplied to politics, and deprived of the contemplation of being. John Senior was quite correct when he implied that the very first thing that we must do to save the social order is to reestablish the primacy of contemplation.

> The greatest contribution to the restoration of order in all human society would be the founding in every city, town, and rural region, of communities of contemplative religious committed to the life of consecrated silence. . . . [7]

Our philosophical tradition works, as it were, from the lowest to the highest, while our revelational tradition does the opposite. When the two approaches become confused, both aspects of reality suffer.

Thomas Aquinas made the point, which Eric Voegelin elaborated on, in this way:

> God carries human reason through to its natural perfection by its native light, and to its supernatural perfection by the theological virtues. Although the supernatural is more sublime than the natural, it is less securely established in us. Natural perfection is our own full endowment, whereas grace is, as it were, not quite grasped, for we imperfectly know God and love him (I–II, 68, 2).

[7] John Senior, *The Restoration of Christian Culture* (San Francisco: Ignatius Press, 1983), p. 198.

And yet this latter condition, our imperfectly knowing the highest things, can be maddening if we insist on a very narrow definition of philosophy, which would allow it to be open only to what the human intellect is itself responsible for causing to be.

Since politics, in particular, then, is the highest of the practical, but not the speculative, sciences, as Aristotle taught, it is in a way more peculiarly *human* than metaphysics, which is closer to the divine. In this context, there is, in the human spirit, an abiding temptation, already suspected by Aristotle at the beginning of the *Metaphysics* and the end of the *Ethics,* to devote our whole being to the "truth" of politics, itself made over in the image of art. But in the lack of any contemplative awareness of the prior givenness of human ends, what will be left, and this in the name of a spurious "freedom", will be the nearest ideology, complete in itself because it has no origin other than the human intellect itself, now deliberately cut off from *what is.*

In a book he wrote in 1968, *La crise actuelle de l'intelligence,* Jean Daniélou concluded:

> Intelligence is not something that can be exercised in I do not know what sort of gratuitous manner. Intelligence has consequences and weighs on the destiny of humanity. That destiny is not only determined by material conditions, but it is also oriented by great spiritual inspirations.[8]

The condition of our mind changes the conditions of matter, not vice versa. Our material conditions, especially the fact that we can change them, themselves depend on the philosophical view of the world we have derived from our understanding about what the world is.

[8] Jean Daniélou, *La crise actuelle de l'intelligence* (Paris: Fleche, 1968), p. 59.

In this regard, it is of some importance to note how Aquinas looked upon the priority that ought to be derived from our conditions as believers. " 'Now faith comes from hearing'; truths are proposed for belief as things heard of, not seen; in that condition do we assent to them. Faith is engaged first of all and mainly with First Truth, secondly with created truths, and last of all with the direction of our human needs" (II–II, 8, 6). Needless to say, this latter priority has recently been reversed in much of the Christian Church, so that the essential contribution of faith, even to the public order, is itself obscured. By teaching first of human needs, however much they are not to be neglected, Christians confuse those searching for something that practical life cannot give. Further, the relation of the being of man to his activities is misunderstood when it appears that what man is, is also a product of man himself, something quite the opposite of both faith and reason.

Only in this background of the primacy of *what is,* particularly the given being of man himself, his orientation to what he does not make, can what he can and does make take on the dimensions of spirit whereby man's material needs can be met. George Gilder has put it well:

> Resources are not natural; they are created by the art and artifices of man.... The crucial capital of the system is always metaphysical: the ideas and creativity of men who find uses and evoke values from what were previously dismissed as dross, dirt, vapor.... Why is it that as real human possibilities expand almost boundlessly, our intellectuals feel only new pangs of claustrophobia? The contemporary intellectual, denying God, is in a trap, and he projects his entrapment onto the world. But the world is not entrapped; man is not finite; the human mind is not bound in material brain. Like most of the hype and hysterics of modern intellectuals, the

energy crisis is most essentially a religious disorder, a failure of
faith.[9]

This reflection is the proper setting for considering all "material"
problems. Disorder in the spiritual life can lead to disorder in
the intellectual life, and this latter almost certainly will lead to
disorder in the material conditions of man. The finiteness of
man is open to the abundance of the cosmos, but only if man
does not replace this same cosmos with himself.

Revelation has suggested that the philosopher to be a philosopher needs to be open to *all* being, even the being that
arises outside of human making and control. One sort of
modern philosopher has reveled in "doomsday". He tells us
that we are violating the order of the world because we are
increasing and multiplying, because we use all the other things
on the face of the earth for our own good. And yet it is this
very pessimism about the true resources of this earth, those
ultimately rooted in the human brain and the human hand,
that causes us to neglect what we can do. Poverty in the world
has, consequently, become the last and only justification for
anything. As a result, the sense of wonder and abundance,
which is what is actually characteristic of this creation, is
denied to those who might profit by it most: namely, the
poor.

But when we look at this latter conclusion, true as it is, we
suddenly become aware that the ancient confrontation of reason and revelation is appearing in a new form, and we are
unprepared for it. The preservation of being as the ultimate
source of our reality remains the necessary contribution of the
contemplative religious person. Yet in the tradition of Aquinas,
the contemplative life in revelation is addressed to the specula-

[9] George Gilder, "The Explorer", *Yale Literary Magazine* 150, No. 1
(1982): 33–34.

tive life from reason. The saint and the philosopher are not, in essence, in opposition. Nonetheless, it was the politician, the poet, and the craftsman in *The Apology* who killed Socrates, as it was the Roman governor and specific Jewish officials who killed Christ. That is, those devoted to the truth and those obligated by the public order came into conflict. It was Pilate, after all, who said, "I find no guilt in him." We do, evidently, as St. Paul said, what we would not.

But, in conclusion, I am concerned here more with the relation of the spiritual and the intellectual life. We must not doubt that it is the same human being who rises to the contemplation of *what is,* who acts in the world, and who is the one to whom the highest things are revealed. The most interesting thing about revelation is not that it is "above" reason, but that it is addressed to reason, that reason has, if it be authentic, already arrived at certain problems for which it can find by its own resources no really adequate solutions. In this sense, revelation is presented as an "option" for us to consider rationally, one option among many that also could be considered if we had a lifetime of leisure.

Chesterton said of Aquinas that,

> as compared with many other saints, and many other philosophers, he was avid in his acceptance of Things; in his hunger and thirst for Things. It was his special spiritual thesis that there really are things; and not only the Thing; that the Many existed as well as the One.[10]

We need not think that the saint and the philosopher must be the same person. Usually, they are not. On the other hand, sometimes they are. This makes us wonder whether all truth is one.

Not everybody needs to be an intellectual. Not everybody

[10] Chesterton, *St. Thomas Aquinas,* p. 505.

is a saint. Yet we must acknowledge that it is dangerous for ourselves, for the public order, when there are no philosophers. We suspect it is even more perilous for there to be no saints. When we wonder why, the answer returns to "receptivity", to the realization that the highest things, which we rightfully seek because of what they are, are not for us to "make" or concoct. Aquinas wrote:

> Nature is a prelude to grace. It is the abuse of science and philosophy which provokes statements against faith. These mistakes can be confuted by showing how impossible or unconvincing they are. Remember this, that as the truths of faith cannot be demonstratively proved, so the denial of them sometimes cannot be demonstratively disproved, though any lack of cogency can be exposed (Exposition, *de Trinitate*, 2, 3).

The philosopher, thus, remains tactically necessary for the faith and existentially necessary because of what we are, the being that, by nature, contemplates *what is*. But the philosopher reaches impasses in his own order, precisely because he is a finite being, not God.

The spiritual life is not the life of the philosopher, but it is not against the life of the philosopher. The spiritual life is that life to which something is directed, something not of human making yet addressed to human intellect and life. That which is directed to us is the life and intelligence of the First Being, now seen as containing all those aspects of being denied to it in the classics, not out of hatred for it, but out of respect. The modern era at its roots has rejected a God larger than itself. In this, it has narrowed its vision. The liberty of the sons of God is that *what is* is larger than what we are. This openness we possess to all being is our grace and our blessing, what we have accepted because we receive, not make, our own being. When wonder is addressed by grace, we are. This is the spiritual life given to intelligent beings.

Fourteen Books on the Intellectual and Spiritual Life

1. G. K. Chesterton, *St. Thomas Aquinas.*
2. Josef Pieper, *The Silence of St. Thomas.*
3. Ralph McInerny, *St. Thomas Aquinas.*
4. Gilbert Meilaender, *A Taste for the Other: The Social and Ethical Thought of C. S. Lewis.*
5. Herbert Butterfield, *Christianity and History.*
6. C. S. Lewis, *The Abolition of Man.*
7. Walter Kaspar, *Faith and the Future.*
8. Ronald Knox, *Enthusiasm.*
9. Nicholas Berdyaev, *The Destiny of Man.*
10. Etienne Gilson, *God and Philosophy.*
11. Christopher Derrick, *The Rule of Peace.*
12. Jacques Maritain, *The Peasant of the Garonne.*
13. Henri de Lubac, *The Splendor of the Church.*
14. Hans Urs von Balthasar, *The Glory of the Lord.*

Conclusion

Education, philosophy, science, politics, history, revelation—these are the themes that I have considered here in various ways. I have often talked of Plato and Aristotle, of Augustine and Aquinas, of Chesterton, Pieper, and C. S. Lewis. I have done this to underscore their importance. And I have repeated favorite book titles worth emphasizing in differing contexts. I wanted to suggest that anyone with some diligence and some good fortune can find his way to the highest things even if such higher level concerns are not formally or systematically treated in the schools, even if they are in fact denied there or by our own friends or culture. Indeed, I would suspect that there is a certain basic loneliness in our relationships to the highest things. I am not a skeptic here, but we should not expect too much from our formal educational institutions in this regard.

Throughout these pages, I have talked of "another sort of learning". I have talked about why we should read, what we should read, books we should keep. In a sense, we can tell a lot about anyone by looking at what books, if any, he reads, at what books are on his shelves. I do not intend to be concerned here with the "practical" things in the normal sense of that term. The normal events of life, too, cause us to wonder. Sooner or later, we each must come to wonder about the things that ultimately count, count for our place within *what is.* For these purposes, we cannot exclude the questions of faith or even politics. Neither can we neglect those whom our tradition tells us are the great teachers. Of these, there are not so many. This is an advantage, in a way. But there is much competition for our attention. We are being drawn to many often conflicting things, many things that have something attractive about them or else we would not be drawn to them. Yet we have the same restless hearts that Augustine had, and this causes us to wonder.

At first sight, it will seem that I am mostly interested here in books to be read. I have always found books to be helpful, yet they must be good books. So there are books mentioned here that I have found of importance. But beyond books there are always good people, people who may or may not be "educated" in the normal sense of the term. Life can teach much. As I have often intimated, all of reality exists in every life, in every culture and time, in some radically basic sense. This fact alone should be enough to prevent us from ever placing too much credibility on academic or formal knowledge. And yet at least some people need to pay attention to this side of our lives and civilization. Here is where a book such as this, I think, can be of some assistance. No one can read or think for us. We need to face the challenge of error and evil, even in our very lives. But we also need to hear the other side, as it were, the case to be made for sanity, for reality, for our limited yet transcendent nature, the one found in each of us.

So these reflections are intended to challenge us, to cause us to wonder about the validity of what it is we are formally taught. I do not think that our higher educational institutions encourage in us a serious consideration of the power of the highest things. I have noticed too many intelligent and sensitive young men and women who darkly suspect this lack, especially in the best schools, I would say, because the best schools often do not realize that they are missing the most important things. Thus, there is a sort of "recruitment" aspect to these reflections, one that tends to call us beyond the formal structures and established forms of our schools.

Whether we pass to more elevated topics, however, will depend on what further avenues of thought and reflection we are willing to follow. I know that I myself have been "called" to such higher things by many of the writers and books to which I have directed the curious reader in these pages. That is to say, I am confident that this account is something more than just another course or another list of someone's favorite books, though these books are often my favorite works on which to begin reflection.

In conclusion, then, let me return to my somewhat unorthodox subtitle, to the idea that we need to "complete our knowing" even if we are busily engaged in a university but not really confronting the higher things. Our leisure time is our most precious time, as Aristotle had already intimated. I do not mean to downgrade ordinary concerns, because these are necessary and our meeting of *what is* takes place within our very lives, in our ordinary affairs, not in some abstract beyond. On the other hand, we can easily be confused.

The higher experiences of friendship, death, love, truth, and beauty leave us unsettled even when we experience them at their highest. This book is about the mystery of our capacity to find real good and love and delight in our lives, yet at the same time, we recognize that we are not complete. This is what lies behind these reflections on "another sort of learning". Our highest "earned" academic degree, whether it be a high school diploma or two doctorates of philosophy, will not guarantee that we really confront the *what is* that is given to us wherever we exist. The recruitment for this latter search is what this book is about.

Indeed, this seeking is what life is about, this life that we are given, and we begin our search from our own insufficiency. But we are not alone, and this is testified to by the many men and women who have gone before us, those who did not live in our own time or in our own place. Sometimes we can find our way because others have found theirs, because they realized that the higher things were worth pursuit, as Aristotle told us and our religious tradition has often repeated to us.

Bibliography

The following bibliography contains the books mentioned in the text. It also includes other books that I think might be helpful and insightful for anyone looking further for writers who have somehow seen some aspect of *what is.* This list is far from complete; it is intended to open up avenues that would otherwise be neglected or overlooked or simply not known. Thus, this list includes titles in science, history, theology, philosophy, and politics, some novels, some biographies. Behind this effort to uncover what is available, even if some works are difficult to come by, is an endeavor to make sense of reality, of *what is.* Aristotle's sense of wonder remains the guiding mood and principle behind what I have listed here.

Adam, Karl. *The Spirit of Catholicism.* Garden City, N.Y.: Doubleday Image, 1954.

Adler, Mortimer. *The Difference of Man and the Difference It Makes.* New York: Holt, 1967.

_____. *How to Read a Book.* New York: Simon and Schuster, 1940.

_____. *How to Think About God: A Guide for the Twentieth-Century Pagan.* New York: Macmillan, 1980.

_____. *Ten Philosophical Mistakes.* New York: Macmillan, 1985.

Albright, William Foxwell. *From the Stone Age to Christianity.* Garden City, N.Y.: Doubleday Anchor, 1957.

Allers, Rudolf. *The Philosophical Works of Rudolf Allers.* Edited by Jesse Mann. Washington, D.C.: Georgetown University Press, 1965.

_____. *The Psychology of Character.* New York: Sheed and Ward, 1930.

Alvis, John, and Thomas G. West, eds. *Shakespeare as a Political Thinker.* Durham, N.C.: Carolina Academic Press, 1981.

Anderson, Carl, and William Gribbin. *The Wealth of Families.* Washington, D.C.: The American Family Institute, 1982.

Anderson, James F. *The Metaphysics of St. Thomas Aquinas.* Chicago: Regnery, 1953.

Aquinas, Thomas. *An Aquinas Reader.* Edited by Mary T. Clark. Garden City, N.Y.: Doubleday Image, 1972.

_____. *Introduction to St. Thomas Aquinas.* Edited by Anton C. Pegis. New York: Modern Library College Editions, 1948.

_____. *St. Thomas Aquinas.* Edited and translated by Thomas Gilby. New York: Oxford, 1955; Durham, N.C.: Labyrinth, 1982.

Arendt, Hannah. *Between Past and Future.* New York: Viking, 1973.

_____. *The Human Condition.* Garden City, N.Y.: Doubleday Anchor, 1959.

_____. *The Life of the Mind.* 2 vols. San Diego: Harcourt, 1978.

_____. *On Revolution.* New York: Viking, 1973.

_____. *The Origins of Totalitarianism.* New York: Meridian, 1958.

Aristotle. *The Basic Works of Aristotle.* Edited by Richard McKeon. New York: Random House, 1941. (Paperback editions of individual works of Aristotle, such as *The Ethics* or *The Politics,* are easily available.)

Arkes, Hadley. *First Things: An Inquiry into the First Principles of Morals and Justice.* Princeton, N.J.: Princeton University Press, 1986.

_____. *The Philosopher in the City.* Princeton, N.J.: Princeton University Press, 1981.

Auclair, Marcelle. *Teresa of Avila.* Garden City, N.Y.: Doubleday Image, 1959.

Auer, Johann. *Faith in Christ and the Worship of Christ.* San Francisco: Ignatius Press, 1986.

Augustine. *The Basic Works of St. Augustine.* 2 vols. Edited by Whitney J. Oates. New York: Random House, 1948. (Editions of individual works of Augustine, particularly *The Confessions,* are easily available.)

Austen, Jane. *Pride and Prejudice* New York: Washington Square, 1968.

Baker, Kenneth. *The Fundamentals of Catholicism.* 3 vols. San Francisco: Ignatius Press, 1982.

Baring, Maurice. *Lost Lectures.* New York: Knopf, 1932.

Barzun, Jacques. *The House of Intellect.* New York: Harper and Row, 1959.

Bate, Walter Jackson. *The Achievement of Samuel Johnson.* New York: Oxford, 1961.

Bauer, P. T. *Reality and Rhetoric: Studies in the Economics of Development.* Cambridge, Mass.: Harvard University Press, 1984.

Becker, Carl L. *The Heavenly City of the Eighteenth-Century Philosophers.* New Haven, Conn.: Yale University Press, 1932.

Beckermann, Wilfred. *Two Cheers for the Affluent Society: A Spirited Defense of Economic Growth.* New York: St. Martin's, 1975.

Belli, Humberto. *Breaking Faith.* Westchester, Ill.: Crossway, 1985.

Belloc, Hilaire. *Cranmer: Archbishop of Canterbury.* Philadelphia: Lippincott, 1931. (For a complete list of Belloc's works, see Speaight.)

––––––. *The Cruise of the "Nona".* London: Constable, 1925.

––––––. *The Crusade.* London: Cassell, 1937.

––––––. *The Four Men.* London: Oxford, 1984.

––––––. *On Nothing.* London: Methuen, 1908.

––––––. *The Path to Rome.* [1902.] Garden City, N.Y.: Doubleday Image, 1956.

––––––. *Selected Essays of Hilaire Belloc.* Edited by J. B. Morton. London: Methuen, 1948.

––––––. *The Servile State.* Bloomington, Ind.: Liberty Fund, 1981.

––––––. *Survivals and New Arrivals.* London: Sheed and Ward, 1929.

––––––. *The Verse of Hilaire Belloc.* London: Nonsuch, 1954.

Bennett, William J. *To Reclaim a Legacy: A Report on the Humanities in Higher Education.* Washington, D.C.: National Endowment for the Humanities, 1984.

Berdayev, Nicholas. *The Destiny of Man.* New York: Harper Torchbooks, 1960.

Berger, Peter. *The Capitalist Revolution: Fifty Propositions about Prosperity, Equality, and Liberty.* New York: Basic Books, 1986.

––––––. *The Noise of Solemn Assemblies.* Garden City, N.Y.: Doubleday Anchor, 1961.

Berman, Harold J. *Law and Revolution: The Formation of the Western Legal Tradition.* Cambridge, Mass.: Harvard University Press, 1983.

Bishirjian, Richard J. *The Nature of Public Philosophy.* Lanham, Md.: University Press of America, 1982.

Blamires, Harry. *The Christian Mind: How Should a Christian Think?* Ann Arbor, Mich.: Servant, 1978.

Bloom, Allan. *The Closing of the American Mind.* New York: Simon and Schuster, 1987.

———. and Harry Jaffa. *Shakespeare's Politics.* Chicago: University of Chicago Press, 1964.

Bochenski, J. M. *Philosophy: An Introduction.* New York: Harper Torchbooks, 1972.

Boswell, James. *The Life of Samuel Johnson.* 2 vols. London: Oxford, 1931.

Bourke, Vernon J. *Will in Western Thought.* New York: Sheed and Ward, 1964.

Bouyer, Louis. *Woman in the Church.* San Francisco: Ignatius Press, 1979.

Brennan, William. *Medical Holocausts.* New York: Nordland, 1980.

Brezik, Victor B., ed. *One Hundred Years of Thomism.* Houston, Tex.: Center for Thomistic Studies, 1981.

———. *Thomistic Papers.* Houston, Tex.: Center for Thomistic Studies, 1984.

Brinton, Crane. *The Shaping of Modern Thought.* Englewood Cliffs, N.J.: Prentice-Hall, 1963.

Brown, Peter. *Augustine of Hippo.* Berkeley: University of California Press, 1979.

Buckley, Cornelius. *Your Word, O Lord: Meditations for College Students and Anyone Else.* San Francisco: Ignatius Press, 1987.

Burke, Edmund. *Reflections on the Revolution in France.* Chicago: Gateway, 1955.

Burtt, E. A. *The Metaphysical Foundations of Modern Science.* Garden City, N.Y.: Doubleday Anchor, 1954.

Butterfield, Herbert. *Christianity and History.* London: Collins, 1957.

———. *Herbert Butterfield: Writings on Christianity and History.* Edited by C. T. McIntire. New York: Oxford, 1979.

———. *The Origins of Modern Science.* New York: Collier, 1962.

Cage, John. *Silence.* Cambridge, Mass.: MIT Press, 1970.

———. *A Year from Monday.* Middletown, Conn.: Wesleyan University Press, 1969.

Caillois, Roger. *Man, Play, and Games.* New York: Free Press, 1961.

Cameron, J. M. *On the Idea of a University.* Toronto: University of Toronto Press, 1978.

Canavan, Francis. *Freedom of Expression: Purpose as Limit.* Durham, N.C.: Carolina Academic Press, 1984.

Cantor, Paul. *Shakespeare's Rome: Republic and Empire.* Ithaca, N.Y.: Cornell University Press, 1976.

Cassirer, Ernst. *An Essay on Man.* Garden City, N.Y.: Doubleday Anchor, 1944.

_____. *The Myth of the State.* New Haven, Conn.: Yale University Press, 1946.

Charles, Rodger. *The Social Teaching of Vatican II.* San Francisco: Ignatius Press, 1985.

Chautard, Dom Jean-Baptist. *The Soul of the Apostolate.* Trappist, Ky.: Gethsemani, 1946.

Chesterton, G. K. *All Things Considered.* New York: Sheed and Ward, 1956.

_____. *As I Was Saying: A Chesterton Anthology.* Edited by Robert Knille. Grand Rapids, Mich.: Eerdmans, 1985.

_____. *The Autobiography of G. K. Chesterton.* New York: Sheed and Ward, 1936.

_____. *The Catholic Church and Conversion.* New York: Macmillan, 1926.

_____. *Charles Dickens.* New York: Schocken, 1965.

_____. *A Chesterton Anthology.* Edited by P. J. Kavanagh. San Francisco: Ignatius Press, 1985.

_____. *Collected Works of G. K. Chesterton.* San Francisco: Ignatius Press, 1985–87. vol. 1: *Heretics, Orthodoxy,* and *The Blatchford Controversies;* vol. 2: *St. Francis of Assisi, The Everlasting Man,* and *St. Thomas Aquinas;* vol. 4: *What's Wrong with the World, The Superstition of Divorce, Eugenics and other Evils,* etc.; vol. 5: *The Outline of Sanity, The End of the Armistice, Utopia of Usurers, The Appetite of Tyranny,* etc.; vol. 27: *Illustrated London News,* 1905–07; vol. 28: *Illustrated London News,* 1908–1910; vol. 29: *Illustrated London News,* 1911–1913. (All of Chesterton's works projected to be republished in this series.)

_____. *The Defendant.* London: Dent, 1901.

_____. *The Man Who Was Thursday.* New York: Dodd, Mead, 1952.

_____. *The Quotable Chesterton.* Edited by George Marlin, et al. San Francisco: Ignatius Press, 1986.

_____. *The Thing.* New York: Sheed and Ward, 1957.

_____. *The Uses of Diversity.* New York: Dodd, Mead, 1921.

_____. *The Well and the Shallows.* New York: Sheed and Ward, 1935.

_____. *What I Saw in America.* New York: Sheed and Ward, 1942.

_____. *What's Wrong with the World?* New York: Sheed and Ward, 1910.

Cicero, Marcus Tullius. *On the Good Life.* New York: Penguin, 1979.

_____. *Selected Works.* Translated by Michael Grant. New York: Penguin, 1967.

Clark, Mary T. *Augustine: Philosopher of Freedom:* A Study in Comparative Philosophy. New York: Desclée, 1958.

Cochrane, Charles Norris. *Christianity and Classical Culture.* New York: Oxford, 1977.

Copleston, Frederick. *Aquinas.* Harmondsworth: Penguin, 1955.

_____. *A History of Philosophy.* 9 vols. Garden City, N.Y.: Doubleday Image, 1962.

Cranston, Maurice. *What Are Human Rights?* New York: Taplinger, 1973.

Cropsey, Joseph. *Political Philosophy and the Issues of Politics.* Chicago: University of Chicago Press, 1977.

Cullmann, Oscar. *The State in the New Testament.* New York: Scribner's, 1956.

Daniélou, Jean. *The Advent of Salvation.* New York: Paulist, 1962.

_____. *The Salvation of the Nations.* New York: Sheed and Ward, 1950.

D'Arcy, Martin C. *The Mind and Heart of Love.* New York: Meridian, 1967.

_____. *St. Augustine.* New York: Meridian, 1957.

Dawson, Christopher. *Beyond Politics.* London: Sheed and Ward, 1939.

_____. *Christianity and the New Age.* Manchester, N.H.: Sophia Institute Press, 1985.

_____. *The Crisis of Western Education.* Garden City, N.Y.: Doubleday Image, 1965.

———. *The Dynamics of World History.* LaSalle, Ill.: Sherwood Sugden, 1980.

———. *Enquiries into Religion and Culture.* New York: Sheed and Ward, 1933.

———. *The Gods of Revolution.* New York: Minerva, 1975.

———. *The Historical Reality of Christian Culture.* New York: Harper Torchbooks, 1960.

———. *The Judgment of the Nations.* New York: Sheed and Ward, 1942.

———. *The Making of Europe.* New York: Meridian, 1965.

———. *The Movement of World Revolution.* New York: Sheed and Ward, 1959.

———. *Progress and Religion.* New York: Sheed and Ward, 1938.

———. *Religion and Culture.* London: Sheed and Ward, 1948.

———. *Religion and the Rise of Western Culture.* Garden City, N.Y.: Doubleday Image, 1958.

Deane, Herbert. *Political and Social Ideas of St. Augustine.* New York: Columbia University Press, 1956.

Deeken, Alfons. *Growing Old and How to Cope with It.* San Francisco: Ignatius Press, 1986.

de Lubac, Henri. *A Brief Catechesis on Nature and Grace.* San Francisco: Ignatius Press, 1984.

———. *The Christian Faith.* San Francisco: Ignatius Press, 1986.

———. *The Discovery of God.* Chicago: Regnery, 1967.

———. *The Drama of Atheist Humanism.* New York: World, 1963.

———. *The Mystery of the Supernatural.* New York: Herder and Herder, 1965.

———. *The Splendor of the Church.* San Francisco: Ignatius Press, 1986.

Dennehy, Raymond. *Reason and Dignity.* Lanham, Md.: University Press of America, 1981.

d'Entreves, Alexander Passerin. *The Natural Law: An Historical Survey.* New York: Harper Torchbooks, 1965.

Derrick, Christopher. *Church Authority and Intellectual Freedom.* San Francisco: Ignatius Press, 1981.

———. *C. S. Lewis and the Church of Rome.* San Francisco: Ignatius Press, 1981.

_____. *Escape from Skepticism: Liberal Education as If the Truth Really Mattered.* LaSalle, Ill.: Sherwood Sugden, 1977.

_____. *Joy Without a Cause.* LaSalle, Ill.: Sherwood Sugden, 1979.

_____. *The Rule of Peace.* Still River, Mass.: St. Bede, 1980.

_____. *Sex and Sacredness.* San Francisco: Ignatius Press, 1982.

_____. *Too Many People? A Problem in Values.* San Francisco: Ignatius Press, 1985.

de Sales, Francis. *Introduction to the Devout Life.* New York: Doubleday Image, 1955.

Dessain, C. S. *Newman's Spiritual Themes.* Dublin: Veritas, 1977.

De Vaux, Roland. *Ancient Israel.* 2 vols. New York: McGraw-Hill, 1965.

De Wulf, Maurice. *Philosophy and Civilization in the Middle Ages.* New York: Dover, 1953.

D'Souza, Dinesh. *The Catholic Classics.* Huntington, Ind.: Our Sunday Visitor Press, 1986.

Eliade, Mircea. *Cosmos and History.* New York: Harper Torchbooks, 1959.

_____. *The Sacred and the Profane.* San Diego: Harcourt, 1959.

Eliot, T. S. *Christianity and Culture.* New York: Harvest, 1968.

Ellul, Jacques. *The Betrayal of the West.* New York: Seabury, 1978.

_____. *The Political Illusion.* New York: Vintage, 1967.

Fairlie, Henry. *The Seven Deadly Sins Today.* Notre Dame, Ind.: University of Notre Dame Press, 1979.

Fickett, Harold, and Douglas R. Gilbert. *Flannery O'Connor: Images of Grace.* Grand Rapids, Mich.: Eerdmans, 1986.

Finnis, John. *Natural Law and Natural Right.* New York: Oxford, 1980.

Fortin, Ernest. *Political Idealism and Christianity in the Thought of St. Augustine.* Villanova, Penn.: Villanova University Press, 1972.

Frossard, Andre, and Pope John Paul II. *Be Not Afraid.* New York: St. Martin's Press, 1984.

Galot, Jean. *Theology of the Priesthood.* San Francisco: Ignatius Press, 1984.

_____. *Who Is Christ? A Theology of the Incarnation.* Chicago: Franciscan Herald Press, 1981.

German Bishops' Conference. *The Church's Confession of Faith.* San Francisco: Ignatius Press, 1987.

Germino, Dante. *Political Philosophy and the Open Society.* Baton Rouge: Louisiana State University Press, 1982.

Gilby, Thomas. *Between Community and Society.* London: Longmans, 1953.

――――. *Principality and Polity: Aquinas and the Rise of State Theory in the West.* London: Longmans, 1958.

Gilder, George. *Men and Marriage.* New York: Pelican, 1986.

――――. *Wealth and Poverty.* New York: Basic Books, 1981.

Gilson, Etienne. *A Gilson Reader.* Edited by Anton C. Pegis. Garden City, N.Y.: Doubleday Image, 1957.

――――. *God and Philosophy.* New Haven, Conn.: Yale University Press, 1941.

――――. *History of Christian Philosophy in the Middle Ages.* New York: Random House, 1955.

――――. *Painting and Reality.* New York: Pantheon, 1957.

――――. *Reason and Revelation in the Middle Ages.* New York: Scribner's, 1966.

――――. *Thomist Realism and the Critique of Knowledge.* San Francisco: Ignatius Press, 1986.

――――. *The Unity of Philosophical Experience.* New York: Scribner's, 1937.

Giordani, Ignio. *The Social Message of Jesus.* Boston: St. Paul Editions, 1977.

Guardini, Romano. *The Conversion of St. Augustine.* Chicago: Regnery, 1960.

――――. *The End of the Modern World.* New York: Sheed and Ward, 1956.

Guitton, Jean. *Great Heresies and Church Councils.* New York: Harper's, 1965.

――――. *Man in Time.* Notre Dame, Ind.: University of Notre Dame Press, 1966.

――――. *Student's Guide to the Intellectual Life.* Notre Dame, Ind.: University of Notre Dame Press, 1964.

Hales, E. E. Y. *The Catholic Church in the Modern World.* Garden City, N.Y.: Doubleday Image, 1960.

———. *Revolution and Papacy.* Notre Dame, Ind.: University of Notre Dame Press, 1966.

Hallowell, John. *Main Currents in Modern Political Thought.* New York: Holt, 1950.

Harrington, Michael. *The Vast Majority.* New York: Simon and Schuster, 1977.

Harrison, Lawrence. *Underdevelopment Is a State of Mind.* Lanham, Md.: University Press of America, 1985.

Havard, William C. *The Recovery of Political Theory.* Baton Rouge: Louisiana State University Press, 1984.

Hawkins, D. J. B. *Being and Becoming.* New York: Sheed and Ward, 1954.

Hazard, Paul. *The European Mind.* New York: World, 1963.

———. *European Thought in the Eighteenth Century.* New York: Meridian, 1963.

Heer, Friedrich. *The Intellectual History of Europe.* London: Weidenfeld and Nicolson, 1953.

Highet, Gilbert. *The Art of Teaching.* New York: Knopf, 1950.

———. *Poets in a Landscape.* London: Hamish Hamilton, 1960.

Himmelfarb, Gertrude. *The Idea of Poverty.* New York: Knopf, 1984.

———. *Lord Acton: A Study in Conscience and Politics.* Chicago: University of Chicago Press, 1952.

———. *Marriage and Morals in Victorian England.* New York: Knopf, 1986.

Hitchcock, James. *Catholicism and Modernity.* Boston: Seabury, 1978.

———. *Years of Crisis: Collected Essays 1970–1983.* San Francisco: Ignatius Press, 1985.

Horgan, Paul. *Maurice Baring Reconsidered.* New York: Farrar, Straus, and Giroux, 1970.

Hughes, Emmet John. *The Church and the Liberal Society.* Notre Dame, Ind.: University of Notre Dame Press, 1961.

Huzinga, Johan. *Homo Ludens: A Study of the Play Element in Culture.* Boston: Beacon, 1950.

Hyde, Henry. *For Every Idle Silence.* Ann Arbor, Mich.: Servant, 1985.

Isaac, Rael Jean, and Eric Isaac. *The Coercive Utopians.* Chicago: Regnery-Gateway, 1983.

Jaeger, Werner. *Aristotle: Fundamentals of the History of His Development.* Translated by R. Robinson. New York: Oxford, 1948.

Jaffa, Harry V. *The Conditions of Freedom: Essays in Political Philosophy.* Baltimore: Johns Hopkins University Press, 1975.

_____. *Thomism and Aristotelianism.* Westport, Conn.: Greenwood, 1952.

Jaki, Stanley L. *And on This Rock: The Witness of One Land and Two Covenants.* Notre Dame, Ind.: Ave Maria Press, 1978.

_____. *Brain, Mind, and Computers.* South Bend, Ind.: Gateway, 1969.

_____. *Chance or Reality, and Other Essays.* Lanham, Md.: University Press of America, 1986.

_____. *Chesterton: A Seer of Science.* Urbana: University of Illinois Press, 1986.

_____. *Cosmos and Creator.* Edinburgh: Scottish Academic Press, 1980.

_____. *The Origin of Science and the Science of Its Origins.* South Bend, Ind.: Regnery, 1978.

_____. *The Road of Science and the Ways to God.* Chicago: University of Chicago Press, 1978.

_____. *Uneasy Genius: The Life and Work of Pierre Duhem.* Boston: Nijhoff, 1984.

Jerrold, Douglas. *The Lie about the West.* New York: Sheed and Ward, 1954.

John Paul I. *Illustrissimi.* Boston: Little, Brown, 1978.

John Paul II. *The Acting Person.* Boston: D. Reidel, 1979.

_____. *Faith according to St. John of the Cross.* San Francisco: Ignatius Press, 1982.

_____. *Fruitful and Responsible Love.* New York: Seabury, 1979.

_____. *Sacred in All Its Forms: John Paul II on Human Life.* Boston: St. Paul Editions, 1984.

_____. *Toward a Philosophy of Praxis.* Edited by A. Bloch and G. Czuczka. New York: Crossroad, 1981.

_____. *The Whole Truth about Man: John Paul II to University Students and Faculties.* Boston: St. Paul Editions, 1981.

Johnson, Leonard. *A History of Israel.* New York: Sheed and Ward, 1964.

Johnson, Paul. *A History of Christianity.* New York: Atheneum, 1976.

_____. *A History of the Jews.* New York: Harper and Row, 1987.

_____. *Modern Times: The World from the Twenties to the Eighties.* New York: Harper Colophon, 1983.

_____. *Pope John Paul II and the Catholic Restoration.* New York: St. Martin's, 1981.

Journet, Charles. *The Meaning of Grace.* New York: Paulist, 1962.

Kaspar, Walter. *The Christian Faith.* New York: Paulist, 1980.

_____. *Faith and the Future.* New York: Crossroad, 1984.

_____. *Jesus the Christ.* New York: Paulist, 1976.

Kass, Leon. *Toward a More Natural Science: Biology and Human Affairs.* New York: Free Press, 1985.

Kelly, George. *The Battle for the American Church.* New York: Doubleday, 1979.

Kempis, Thomas à. *The Imitation of Christ.* Many translations; the most recent was edited by Joseph Tysenda, S.J. Wilmington, Del.: Michael Glazier, 1984.

Kerr, Walter. *The Decline of Pleasure.* New York: Simon and Schuster, 1962.

_____. *Letters from Hilaire Belloc.* Selected and edited by Robert Speaight. New York: Macmillan Co., 1958.

Kippley, John, and Sheila *The Art of Natural Family Planning.* Cincinnati: Couple-to-Couple League, 1985.

Kirk, Russell. *The Conservative Mind.* Chicago: Regnery, 1953.

_____. *Decadence and Renewal in the Higher Learning.* South Bend, Ind.: Gateway, 1978.

_____. *Enemies of the Permanent Things: Observations of Abnormity in Literature and Politics.* LaSalle, Ill.: Sherwood Sugden, 1984.

_____. *Reclaiming a Patrimony.* Washington: Heritage Foundation, 1982.

_____. *The Roots of American Order.* LaSalle, Ill.: Open Court, 1974.

Kirkpatrick, Jeane. *Dictatorships and Double Standards.* New York: Simon and Schuster, 1982.

Kirkpatrick, William Kirk. *Psychological Seduction*. San Francisco: Ignatius Press, 1984.

Klubertanz, George, P. *An Introduction to the Philosophy of Being*. St. Louis: Modern Schoolman, 1952.

Knowles, David. *The Evolution of Medieval Thought*. New York: Vintage, 1962.

Knox, Ronald. *The Belief of Catholics*. Garden City, N.Y.: Doubleday Image, 1958.

_____. *Enthusiasm*. Westminster, Md.: Christian Classics, 1983.

_____. *The Occasional Sermons of Ronald A. Knox*. New York: Sheed and Ward, 1960.

_____. *The Pastoral Sermons of Ronald A. Knox*. New York: Sheed and Ward, 1960.

_____. *A Spiritual Aeneid*. New York: Sheed and Ward, 1958.

Krapiec, Mieczyslaw Albert. *I–Man: An Outline of Philosophical Anthropology*. Trans. Marie Lescoe, Andrew Woznicki, Theresa Sandok et al. New Britain, Conn: Mariel, 1983.

Kreeft, Peter. *Making Sense Out of Suffering*. Ann Arbor, Mich.: Servant, 1986.

Kristol, Irving. *Two Cheers for Capitalism*. New York: Basic Books, 1978.

Lawler, Philip. *Coughing in Ink: The Demise of Academic Ideals*. Lanham, Md.: University Press of America, 1983.

Lawler, Ronald, et al. *The Teachings of Christ*. Huntington, Ind.: Our Sunday Visitor Press, 1976.

Leary, John P. *Don't Tell Me You're Not Confused (A Critical Look at College)*. San Francisco: New College Press, 1979.

Lepp, Ignace. *Atheism in Our Time*. New York: Macmillan, 1963.

Lewis, C. S. *The Abolition of Man*. New York: Macmillan, 1944.

_____. *An Anthology of C. S. Lewis: A Mind Awake*. Edited by Clyde S. Kilby. San Diego: Harcourt-Harvest, 1968.

_____. *Christian Reflections*. Grand Rapids, Mich.: Eerdmans, 1967.

_____. *The Chronicles of Narnia*. New York: Collier, 1971.

_____. *Four Loves*. New York: Harcourt, Brace, 1983.

_____. *George MacDonald: An Anthology*. New York: Macmillan, 1974.

_____. *The Great Divorce*. New York: Macmillan, 1978.

———. *Miracles.* New York: Macmillan, 1978.

———. *Mere Christianity.* London: Fontana, 1961.

———. *Out of the Silent Planet.* New York: Avon, 1949.

———. *Perelandra.* New York: Macmillan, 1965.

———. *Present Concerns: Ethical Essays.* London: Collins, 1986.

———. *The Problem of Pain.* New York: Macmillan, 1978.

———. *Reflections on the Psalms.* San Diego: Harcourt, 1958.

———. *The Screwtape Letters.* New York: Macmillan, 1977.

———. *Surprised by Joy: The Shape of My Early Life.* New York: Harvest, 1955.

———. *That Hideous Strength.* New York: Collier, 1962.

———. *Till We Have Faces.* Grand Rapids, Mich.: Eerdmans, 1956.

———. *The Weight of Glory and Other Essays.* New York: Macmillan, 1980.

———. *The World's Last Night and Other Essays.* New York: Harvest, 1959.

Lord, Carens. *Education and Culture in the Political Thought of Aristotle.* Ithaca, N.Y.: Cornell University Press, 1982.

Lovat, Laura. *Maurice Baring: A Postscript.* London: Hollis, 1947.

Lunn, Arnold. *Now I See.* New York: Sheed and Ward, 1938.

Lustiger, Jean-Marie Cardinal. *Dare to Believe.* New York: Crossroad, 1986.

McCarthy, John, P. *Hilaire Belloc: Edwardian Radical.* Indianapolis, Ind.: Liberty Press, 1978.

McCoy, Charles N. R. *The Structure of Political Thought.* New York: McGraw-Hill, 1963.

McInerny, Ralph. *St. Thomas Aquinas.* Notre Dame, Ind.: University of Notre Dame Press, 1977.

———. *Thomism in an Age of Renewal.* Notre Dame, Ind.: University of Notre Dame Press, 1966.

MacIntyre, Alasdair. *After Virtue.* Notre Dame, Ind.: University of Notre Dame Press, 1981.

McKenzie, John L. *Dictionary of the Bible.* New York: Macmillan, 1965.

———. *Vital Concepts of the Bible.* Denville, N.J.: Dimension, 1969.

Marcel, Gabriel. *Creative Fidelity.* New York: Farrar, Straus, and Giroux, 1964.

_____. *Homo Viator: An Introduction to a Metaphysics of Hope.* New York: Harper Torchbooks, 1962.

_____. *The Mystery of Being.* Vol. 1: "Reflection and Mystery". Vol. 2, "Faith and Reality". Chicago: Regnery, 1960.

Maritain, Jacques. *Approaches to God.* New York: Collier, 1963.

_____. *Art and Scholasticism.* Notre Dame, Ind.: University of Notre Dame Press, 1974.

_____. *Christianity and Democracy and The Rights of Man and Natural Law.* San Francisco: Ignatius Press, 1986.

_____. *Creative Intuition in Art and Poetry:* Andrew Mellon Lectures in the Fine Arts, no. 1. Princeton, N.J.: Princeton University Press, 1952.

_____. *The Education of Man: The Educational Philosophy of Jacques Maritain.* Edited by Donald and Idella Gallagher. Garden City, N.Y.: Doubleday, 1962.

_____. *Existence and the Existent.* Garden City, N.Y.: Doubleday Image, 1957.

_____. *The Grace and Humanity of Jesus.* New York: Herder and Herder, 1969.

_____. *Man and the State.* Chicago: University of Chicago Press, 1951.

_____. *The Peasant of the Garonne.* New York: Holt, 1968.

_____. *Prayer and Intelligence.* London: Sheed and Ward, 1929.

_____. *A Preface to Metaphysics.* New York: Mentor, 1962.

_____. *Reflections on America.* New York: Scribner's, 1958.

_____. *St. Thomas Aquinas.* New York: Meridian, 1958.

_____. *Scholasticism and Politics.* Garden City, N.Y.: Doubleday Image, 1960.

_____. *Social and Political Philosophy of Jacques Maritain.* Edited by Joseph W. Evans and Leo R. Ward. Notre Dame, Ind.: University of Notre Dame Press, 1976.

Mascall, Eric. *Christian Theology and Natural Science.* London: Longmans, 1936.

_____. *The Christian Universe.* London: Darton, Longman, and Todd, 1966.

_____. *Grace and Glory.* Denville, N.J.: Dimension, 1961.

_____. *He Who Is.* Hamden, Conn.: Archon, 1970.

_____. *The Openness of Being.* London: Darton, Longman, and Todd, 1971.

_____. *The Secularization of Christianity.* London: Darton, Longman, and Todd, 1965.

_____. *Theology and the Future.* New York: Morehouse-Barlow, 1968.

_____. *Theology and the Gospel of Christ.* London: SPCK, 1977.

Maurer, Armand A. *About Beauty: A Thomistic Interpretation.* Houston, Tex.: Center for Thomistic Studies, 1983.

Meilaender, Gilbert C. *Friendship: A Study in Theological Ethics.* Notre Dame, Ind.: University of Notre Dame Press, 1981.

_____. *A Taste for the Other: The Social and Ethical Thought of C. S. Lewis.* Grand Rapids, Mich.: Eerdmans, 1978.

_____. *The Theory and Practice of Virtue.* Notre Dame, Ind.: University of Notre Dame Press, 1984.

Menninger, Karl. *Whatever Became of Sin?* New York: Hawthorne, 1973.

Merton, Thomas. *No Man Is an Island.* Garden City, N.Y.: Doubleday Image, 1967.

Messner, Johannes. *Ethics and Facts.* St. Louis: Herder, 1952.

_____. *Social Ethics: The Natural Law in the Western World.* St. Louis: Herder, 1965.

Midgley, E. B. F. *The Natural Law and the Theory of International Relations.* London: Elek, 1975.

Miller, Walter M. *A Canticle for Leibowitz.* New York: Bantam, 1959.

Molnar, Thomas. *Politics and the State.* Chicago: Franciscan Herald Press, 1980.

Montgomery, Marion. *Reflective Journey toward Order: Essays on Dante, Wordsworth, Eliot, and Others.* Athens: University of Georgia Press, 1978.

_____. *Why Flannery O'Connor Stayed Home.* LaSalle, Ill.: Sherwood Sugden, 1981.

_____. *Why Hawthorne Was Melancholy.* LaSalle, Ill.: Sherwood Sugden, 1984.

————. *Why Poe Drank Liquor.* LaSalle, Ill.: Sherwood Sugden, 1983.

Moore, Thomas Verner. *The Life of Man with God.* Garden City, N.Y.: Doubleday Image, 1962.

Morton, J. B. *Through the Lands of the Bible.* New York: Dodd, Mead, 1959.

Muggeridge, Anne Roche. *Desolation in the City: Revolution in the Catholic Church.* New York: Harper and Row, 1986.

Muggeridge, Malcolm. *Chronicles of Wasted Time: The Infernal Grove.* 2 vols. New York: Morrow, 1974.

————. *The End of Christendom.* Grand Rapids, Mich.: Eerdmans, 1980.

————. *Jesus Rediscovered.* London: Collins, 1969.

Murray, John Courtney. *We Hold These Truths.* Garden City, N.Y.: Doubleday Image, 1984.

Navone, John. *A Theology of Failure.* New York: Paulist, 1974.

————, and Thomas Cooper. *Tellers of the Word.* New York: Le Jacq, 1981.

Newman, John Henry. *The Essential Newman.* Edited by Vincent Blehl. New York: Mentor, 1963.

————. *The Idea of a University.* Garden City, N.Y.: Doubleday Image, 1959.

Nisbet, Robert A. *History of the Idea of Progress.* New York: Basic Books, 1980.

————. *The Quest for Community.* New York: Oxford, 1969.

Norman, E. O. *Christianity and the World Order.* New York: Oxford, 1979.

Novak, Michael. *Freedom with Justice: Catholic Social Thought and Liberal Institutions.* San Francisco: Harper and Row, 1984.

————. *The Spirit of Democratic Capitalism.* New York: Simon and Schuster, 1982.

————. *Will It Liberate? Questions about Liberation Theology.* New York: Paulist, 1986.

Nozick, Robert. *Anarchy, State, and Utopia.* New York: Basic Books, 1974.

O'Connor, Flannery. *The Complete Stories.* New York: Farrar, Straus, and Giroux, 1972.

_____. *The Habit of Being: The Letters of Flannery O'Connor.* Edited by Sally Fitzgerald. New York: Farrar, Straus, and Giroux, 1979.

_____. *Mystery and Manners.* New York: Farrar, Straus, and Giroux, 1968.

O'Connor, John J. *In Defense of Life.* Boston: St. Paul Editions, 1981.

Owens, Joseph. *An Elementary Christian Metaphysics.* Houston, Tex.: Center for Thomistic Studies, 1985.

Pegis, Anton C. *At the Origins of the Thomistic Notion of Man.* New York: Macmillan, 1963.

Pelikan, Jaroslav. *Jesus through the Centuries: His Place in the History of Culture.* New Haven, Conn.: Yale University Press, 1985.

Percy, Walker. *Conversations with Walker Percy.* Edited by Lewis A. Lawson and Victor A. Kramer. Jackson: University Press of Mississippi, 1985.

_____. *Lost in the Cosmos: The Last Self-Help Book.* New York: Farrar, Straus, and Giroux, 1983.

Pieper, Josef. *Death and Immortality.* New York: Herder and Herder, 1969.

_____. *The End of Time: Meditations on the Philosophy of History.* New York: Pantheon, 1954.

_____. *Enthusiasm and the Divine Madness: On the Platonic Dialogue "Phaedrus".* San Diego, Harcourt, 1964.

_____. *The Four Cardinal Virtues* (Prudence, Justice, Fortitude, and Temperance). Notre Dame, Ind.: University of Notre Dame Press, 1966.

_____. *A Guide to Thomas Aquinas.* New York: Mentor, 1964.

_____. *Happiness and Contemplation.* New York: Pantheon, 1958.

_____. *Hope and History.* New York: Herder and Herder, 1969.

_____. *In Tune with the World: A Theory of Festivity.* Chicago: Franciscan Herald Press, 1973.

_____. *Leisure: The Basis of Culture.* New York: Mentor, 1963.

_____. *No One Could Have Known: An Autobiography: The Early Years, 1904–1945.* San Francisco: Ignatius Press, 1987.

_____. *On Hope.* San Francisco: Ignatius Press, 1986.

_____. *Problems of Modern Faith.* Chicago: Franciscan Herald Press, 1985.

_____. *Reality and the Good.* Chicago: Regnery, 1967.

_____. *Scholasticism.* New York: McGraw-Hill, 1964.

_____. *The Silence of St. Thomas.* Chicago: Gateway, 1957.

_____. *What Catholics Believe: A Primer of the Catholic Faith.* New York: Pantheon, 1951.

Plato. *The Laws.* Edited with an interpretative essay by Thomas Pangle. New York: Basic Books, 1980.

_____. *The Republic.* Edited with an interpretative essay by Allan Bloom. New York: Basic Books, 1968.

Plutarch. *The Lives of the Noble Greeks and Romans.* New York: Modern Library, n.d.

Pocock, J. G. A. *Politics, Language, and Time.* New York: Atheneum, 1973.

Rahner, Hugo. *Man at Play.* New York: Herder and Herder, 1967.

Ratzinger, Joseph, Cardinal. *Daughter Zion: Meditations on the Church's Marian Beliefs.* San Francisco: Ignatius Press, 1984.

_____. *Feast of Faith: Approaches to a Theology of the Liturgy.* San Francisco: Ignatius Press, 1986.

_____. *Principles of Catholic Theology.* San Francisco: Ignatius Press, 1987.

_____. *The Ratzinger Report: Interview with Vittorio Messori.* San Francisco: Ignatius Press, 1985.

_____, et al. *Principles of Christian Morality.* San Francisco: Ignatius Press, 1986.

Rawls, John. *A Theory of Justice.* Cambridge, Mass.: Harvard University Press, 1971.

Regan, Richard J. *The Moral Dimensions of Politics.* New York: Oxford, 1986.

Revel, Jean-François. *How Democracies Perish.* New York: Doubleday, 1984.

Ricci, David M. *The Tragedy of Political Science.* New Haven, Conn.: Yale University Press, 1984.

Rommen, Henrich C. *The Natural Law.* St. Louis: Herder, 1947.

_____. *The State in Catholic Thought.* St. Louis: Herder, 1945.

Russell, Jeffrey Burton. *Lucifer: The Devil in the Middle Ages.* Ithaca, N.Y.: Cornell University Press, 1984.

Rutler, George W. *Beyond Modernity.* San Francisco: Ignatius Press, 1987.

St. John-Stevas, Norman. *The Right to Life.* New York: Holt, 1963.

Sayers, Dorothy. *The Mind of the Maker.* New York: Meridian, 1956.

_____. *The Whimsical Christian.* New York: Macmillan, 1978.

Schall, James V. *Christianity and Life.* San Francisco: Ignatius Press, 1981.

_____. *Christianity and Politics.* Boston: St. Paul Editions, 1981.

_____. *The Church, the State, and Society in the Thought of John Paul II.* Chicago: Franciscan Herald Press, 1982.

_____. *The Distinctiveness of Christianity.* San Francisco: Ignatius Press, 1982.

_____. *Far Too Easily Pleased: A Theology of Play, Contemplation, and Festivity.* Los Angeles: Benziger-Macmillan, 1976.

_____. *Human Dignity and Human Numbers.* Staten Island, N.Y.: Alba House, 1971.

_____. *Liberation Theology.* San Francisco: Ignatius Press, 1982.

_____. *Play On: From Games to Celebrations.* Philadelphia: Fortress Press, 1971.

_____. *The Politics of Heaven and Hell: Christian Themes from Classical, Medieval, and Modern Political Philosophy* (Lantham, Md.: University Press of America, 1974).

_____. *The Praise of "Sons of Bitches": On the Worship of God by Fallen Men.* Slough, Eng.: St. Paul Publications, 1978.

_____. *Reason, Revelation, and the Foundations of Political Philosophy.* Baton Rouge: Louisiana State University Press, 1987.

_____. *Redeeming the Time.* New York: Sheed and Ward, 1968.

_____. *The Sixth Paul.* Canfield, Ohio: Alba, 1977.

_____. *Welcome Number 4,000,000,000.* Canfield, Ohio: Alba, 1977.

_____. *Unexpected Meditations Late in the XXth Century.* Chicago: Franciscan Herald Press, 1985.

Schlier, Heinrich. *The Relevance of the New Testament.* New York: Herder and Herder, 1968.

Schrems, John. *The Principles of Politics.* Englewood Cliffs, N.J.: Prentice-Hall, 1986.

Schumacher, E. F. *Good Work.* New York: Harper's, 1979.

_____. *A Guide for the Perplexed.* New York: Harper Colophon, 1977.

Scott, Nathan A. *The Broken Center: Studies in the Theological Horizon of Modern Literature.* New Haven, Conn.: Yale University Press, 1966.

Senior, John. *The Death of Christian Culture.* New Rochelle, N.Y.: Arlington House, 1978.

_____. *The Restoration of Christian Culture.* San Francisco: Ignatius Press, 1983.

Sertillanges, A. G. *The Intellectual Life.* Translated by Mary Ryan. Westminster, Md.: Christian Classics, 1980.

Shafarevich, Igor. *The Socialist Phenomenon.* New York: Harper and Row, 1980.

Sheed, Frank J. *God and the Human Condition.* New York: Sheed and Ward, 1966.

_____. *Theology and Sanity.* New York: Sheed and Ward, 1946.

_____. *To Know Jesus Christ.* New York: Sheed and Ward, 1962.

Simon, Julian L. *The Ultimate Resource.* Princeton, N.J.: Princeton University Press, 1981.

Simon, Yves. *The Philosophy of Democratic Government.* Chicago: University of Chicago Press, 1977.

_____. *The Tradition of Natural Law.* New York: Fordham University Press, 1965.

Siri, Joseph Cardinal. *Gethsemane: Reflections on the Contemporary Theological Movement.* Chicago: Franciscan Herald, 1981.

Sobran, Joseph. *Single Issues: Essays on Crucial Social Questions.* New York: Human Life Press, 1982.

Solzhenitsyn, Aleksandr. *Solzhenitsyn at Harvard.* Edited by Ronald Berman. Washington, D.C.: Ethics and Public Policy Center, 1980.

Sontag, Frederick. *God, Why Did You Do That?* Philadelphia: Westminster, 1970.

Speaight, Robert. *The Life of Hilaire Belloc.* New York: Farrar, Straus, and Giroux, 1957.

Stanlis, Peter. *Edmund Burke and the Natural Law.* Shreveport, La.: Huntington House, 1986.

Strauss, Leo. *City and Man*. Chicago: University of Chicago Press, 1964.

_____. *Liberalism: Ancient and Modern*. New York: Basic Books, 1968.

_____. *Natural Right and History*. Chicago: University of Chicago Press, 1953.

_____. *Persecution and the Art of Writing*. New York: Free Press, 1952.

_____. *Studies in Platonic Political Philosophy*. Edited by Thomas Pangle. Chicago: University of Chicago Press, 1983.

_____. *Thoughts on Machiavelli*. Chicago: University of Chicago Press, 1958.

_____. *What Is Political Philosophy?* New York: Free Press, 1959.

Talmon, J. L. *The Origins of Totalitarian Democracy*. New York: Praeger, 1960.

Thérèse of Lisieux. *The Autobiography of St. Thérèse of Lisieux*. Edited by John Beevers. Garden City, N.Y.: Doubleday Image, 1960.

Thibon, Gustav. *What Ails Mankind?* New York: Sheed and Ward, 1947.

Thompson, James J., Jr. *Christian Classics Revisited*. San Francisco: Ignatius Press, 1983.

_____. *Fleeing the Whore of Babylon: A Modern Conversion Story*. Westminster, Md.: Christian Classics, 1985.

Tinder, Glenn. *Against Fate: An Essay on Personal Dignity*. Notre Dame, Ind.: University of Notre Dame Press, 1981.

_____. *Community: Reflections on a Tragic Ideal*. Baton Rouge: Louisiana State University Press, 1980.

_____. *Political Thinking: The Perennial Questions*. Boston: Little, Brown, 1974.

Tolkien, J. R. R. *The Hobbit*. New York: Ballantine, 1965.

_____. *The Letters of J. R. R. Tolkien*. Edited by Humphrey Carpenter. Boston: Houghton Mifflin, 1981.

_____. *The Lord of the Rings*. New York: Ace, n.d.

_____. *The Silmarillion*. London: George Allen, 1977.

_____. *The Tolkien Reader*. New York: Ballantine, 1966.

Tresmontant, Claude. *A Study of Hebrew Thought*. New York: Desclee, 1959.

Undset, Sigrid. *Kristin Lavransdatter.* New York: Knopf, 1940.

———. *St. Catherine of Siena.* New York: Sheed and Ward, 1954.

van der Leeuw, Gerardus. *Sacred and Profane Beauty.* Nashville: Abingdon, 1963.

Vann, Gerald. *The Heart of Man.* Garden City, N.Y.: Doubleday Image, 1960.

van Steenberghen, Ferdinand. *Ontology.* New York: Wagner, 1970.

Veatch, Henry. B. *Aristotle: A Contemporary Appreciation.* Bloomington: Indiana University Press, 1974.

———. *For an Ontology of Morals.* Evanston, Ill.: Northwestern University Press, 1971.

———. *Human Rights: Fact or Fancy?* Baton Rouge: Louisiana State University Press, 1985.

———. *Rational Man: A Modern Interpretation of Aristotelian Ethics.* Bloomington: Indiana University Press, 1966.

———. *Two Logics.* Evanston, Ill.: Northwestern University Press, 1969.

Vitz, Paul C. *Psychology as Religion: The Cult of Self-Worship.* Grand Rapids, Mich.: Eerdmans, 1977.

Voegelin, Eric. *Conversations with Eric Voegelin.* Edited by R. Eric O'Connor. Montreal: Thomas More Institute, 1980.

———. *From Enlightenment to Revolution.* Edited by John Hallowell. Durham, N.C.: Duke University Press, 1975.

———. *The New Science of Politics.* Chicago: University of Chicago Press, 1952.

———. *Order and History.* 4 vols. Baton Rouge: Louisiana State University Press, 1974.

———. *Science, Politics, and Gnosticism.* Chicago: Regnery-Gateway, 1968.

Voillaume, Rene. *The Christian Vocation.* Denville, N.J.: Dimension, 1973.

von Balthasar, Hans Urs. *Convergences: To the Source of Christian Mystery.* San Francisco: Ignatius Press, 1983.

———. *Does Jesus Know Us?* San Francisco: Ignatius Press, 1980.

———. *The Glory of the Lord.* 3 vols. San Francisco: Ignatius Press, 1984.

———. *The God Question and Modern Man.* New York: Seabury, 1967.

———. *New Elucidations.* San Francisco: Ignatius Press, 1986.

———. *The Office of Peter and the Structure of the Church.* San Francisco: Ignatius Press, 1986.

———. *Prayer.* San Francisco: Ignatius Press, 1986.

———. *A Short Primer for Unsettled Laymen.* San Francisco: Ignatius Press, 1985.

von Hildebrand, Dietrich. *Marriage: The Mystery of Faithful Love.* Manchester, N.H.: Sophia Institute Press, 1984.

———. *Transformation in Christ.* Garden City, N.Y.: Doubleday Image, 1963.

Von le Fort, Gertrude. *Eternal Woman.* Los Angeles: Bruce, 1954.

Waugh, Evelyn. *The Letters of Evelyn Waugh.* Edited by Mark Amory. New York: Penguin, 1982.

Weisheipl, James A. *Friar Thomas D'Aquino: His Life, Thoughts, and Works.* Washington, D.C.: Catholic University Press, 1983.

Weiss, Paul. *Sport: A Philosophic Inquiry.* Carbondale: Southern Illinois University Press, 1969.

Wild, John. *Plato's Modern Enemies and the Theory of Natural Law.* Chicago: University of Chicago Press, 1950.

Wilder, Thornton. *The Eigth Day.* New York: Avon, 1976.

Wilhelmsen, Frederick D. *Christianity and Political Philosophy.* Athens: University of Georgia Press, 1978.

———. *Hilaire Belloc: No Alienated Man.* New York: Sheed and Ward, 1954.

———. *Man's Knowledge of Reality.* Englewood Cliffs, N.J.: Prentice-Hall, 1954.

———. *The Metaphysics of Love.* New York: Sheed and Ward, 1962.

Williams, Charles. *The Figure of Beatrice: A Study in Dante.* New York: Farrar, Straus and Cudahy, 1961.

Williams, George H. *The Mind of John Paul II: Origins of His Thought and Action.* New York: Harper and Row, 1981.

Williams, W. E. *A Book of English Essays.* London, Penguin, 1981.

Wilson, A. N. *Hilaire Belloc: A Biography.* New York: Atheneum, 1984.

———. *How Can We Know? An Essay on the Christian Faith.* New York: Atheneum, 1985.

Wilson, Ellen. *An Even Dozen.* New York: Human Life Press, 1981.

Wippel, John F. *Metaphysical Themes in Thomas Aquinas.* Washington, D.C.: Catholic University Press, 1984.

Woznicki, Andrew. *A Christian Humanism: Karol Wojtyla's Existential Personalism.* New Britain, Conn.: Mariel, 1980.

Zaehner, R. C. *The City within the Heart.* London: Unwin, 1980.

Acknowledgements

For permission to use materials previously published, the author wishes to thank the following journals: *The Guardian,* a student journal at Georgetown University, for Chapter 1; *The YCC Word,* for Chapter 2; *The Hoya Review,* the student newspaper at Georgetown University for Chapters 3, 4, and 5; *The Classical Bulletin* for Chapter 6; *Teaching Political Science,* for Chapter 7; *Modern Age,* for Chapter 8; *Homiletic and Pastoral Review,* for Chapters 9, 12, and 13; *Claremont Review of Books,* for Chapter 10; *Freedom-at-Issue,* for Chapter 11 (reprinted from Sept.–Oct., 1984 issue with the permission of Freedom House); *Faith and Reason,* for Chapter 14; *University Bookman,* for Chapter 15; *Spiritual Life,* for Chapter 16; *Vital Speeches,* for Chapter 17; and *Center Journal,* for Chapter 20.